CHINA IN THE GERMAN ENL.

Edited by Bettina Brandt and Daniel Leonhard Purdy

Over the course of the eighteenth century, European intellectuals shifted from admiring China as a utopian place of wonder to despising it as a backwards and despotic state. That transformation had little to do with changes in China itself, and everything to do with Enlightenment conceptions of political identity and Europe's own burgeoning global power.

China in the German Enlightenment considers the place of German philosophy, particularly the work of Leibniz, Goethe, Herder, and Hegel, in this development. Beginning with the first English translation of Walter Demel's classic essay "How the Chinese Became Yellow," the collection's essays examine the connections between eighteenth-century philosophy, German Orientalism, and the origins of modern race theory.

(German and European Studies)

BETTINA BRANDT is a teaching professor of German and Jewish Studies at Penn State University.

DANIEL LEONHARD PURDY is a professor of German Studies at Penn State University.

GERMAN AND EUROPEAN STUDIES

General Editor: Jennifer L. Jenkins

China in the German Enlightenment

Edited by

BETTINA BRANDT and
DANIEL LEONHARD PURDY

UNIVERSITY OF TORONTO PRESS
Toronto Buffalo London

Reprinted in paperback 2022

ISBN 978-1-4426-4845-6 (cloth)   ISBN 978-1-4426-1700-1 (EPUB)
ISBN 978-1-4875-4555-0 (paper)   ISBN 978-1-4426-1699-8 (PDF)

German and European Studies

Publication cataloguing information is available from Library and Archives
Canada.

We wish to acknowledge the land on which the University of Toronto Press
operates. This land is the traditional territory of the Wendat, the Anish-
naabeg, the Haudenosaunee, the Métis, and the Mississaugas of the Credit
First Nation.

University of Toronto Press acknowledges the financial support of the
Government of Canada, the Canada Council for the Arts, and the Ontario
Arts Council, an agency of the Government of Ontario, for its publishing
activities.

Canada Council Conseil des Arts
for the Arts   du Canada

ONTARIO ARTS COUNCIL
CONSEIL DES ARTS DE L'ONTARIO
an Ontario government agency
un organisme du gouvernement de l'Ontario

Funded by the   Financé par le
Government   gouvernement
of Canada   du Canada

Canadä

For Vera

Contents

Acknowledgments

A small republic of letters brought these essays together. In many ways, we replicated the interdisciplinary, transcultural networks we analyse. Our volume grew out from a conference held at Pennsylvania State University on 24–25 February 2012, entitled "Reading China during the Enlightenment." Our initial gathering was made possible by generous support from the German Academic Exchange Program (DAAD), the Penn State Max Kade Research Institute, and the Penn State Asian Studies Department. Additional funding was provided by the Department of Germanic and Slavic Languages and Literatures, as well as by the Global Studies program. We wish particularly to thank Eric Hayot for his stout support of our venture. Without the aid of our colleagues we would not have been able to pull off this German-Chinese collaboration. Heartfelt thanks also go to Gregg Roeber, On-cho Ng, Ronnie Hsia, Richard Page, and Sandy Stelts.

We were able to complete our editorial and translation work related to this edited volume during the fall of 2014 while residing in Heidelberg, Germany, under the generous support of the Karl Jaspers Centre for Advanced Transcultural Studies. We would like to thank Gita Dharampal-Frick, Barbara Mittler, Axel Michaels, and the members of the Heidelberg Cluster of Excellence: Asia and Europe in a Global Context for providing an intense and congenial scholarly environment.

Finally, we would like to thank our editor, Richard Ratzlaff, at the University of Toronto Press, for being enthusiastic about and supporting this project from the beginning, as well as Kate Baltais for her assiduous copy-editing.

Introduction

DANIEL LEONHARD PURDY AND BETTINA BRANDT

Few Germans travelled to China in the early modern period, yet in Berlin, Hanover, and Göttingen lively discussions were taking place about Chinese philosophy, system of government, and arts. The reception of China in northern Europe during the seventeenth and eighteenth centuries was guided less by direct experience than by a secondary one: through reading and gazing at the images and texts brought back by Europeans to represent the Middle Kingdom.

Europe's philosophical engagement with Chinese culture began with the memoirs published by the Jesuits about their work to bring Christianity to the Middle Kingdom. Intellectual histories cite not only the importance of the Jesuit translations of Chinese works but, just as relevantly, the Jesuits' willingness to assimilate into the society of the mandarin elite, that is, to accommodate their own teaching to Chinese traditions as a pedagogical strategy for conversion. Michele Ruggieri (1543–1607), founder of the Jesuit China mission, wrote religious works and poetry in Chinese, for instance, while courting the scholarly company of the mandarins. Expanding upon the success of his predecessor, Matteo Ricci (1552–1610) continued in this tradition while dropping any unintended references to Buddhism. Studying early Confucian texts Ricci and his followers sought to demonstrate that these were compatible with Christian teaching since Confucian teaching served as a natural theology that through rational thought, not unlike Plato and Aristotle, had come to understand the existence of a single God and had formulated ethical teachings remarkably similar to Christianity. These Jesuits stressed sameness between the Chinese and Europeans over time; however, as the Enlightenment increasingly differentiated knowledge into specific disciplines, intensified the classification of data within them, and insisted on defining national character, the earlier Jesuit efforts at establishing identifications between China and Europe were undermined.

The essays in this collection, *China in the German Enlightenment*, trace the shifting and multilayered views of China as constructed by European enlightened readers of Asian travel accounts without subscribing to a simple linear development. They demonstrate how over a period of 150 years European intellectuals switched from admiring China as a utopian place of wonder to treating China disdainfully as a despotic state and argue that German philosophy from Gottfried Leibniz to Georg Wilhelm Friedrich Hegel participated in this dramatic reversal. Finally, these essays make clear that the shifting status of Chinese thought in Europe had little to do with China itself but everything to do with the Enlightenment's new constructions of political self-identity, as well as with Europe's expanding economic, military, and media channels between the two regions.

Since the Second World War scholarship on the reception of Chinese culture in early modern Germany has been grounded in Donald Lach's massive, lifelong study, *Asia in the Making of Europe*.[1] The importance of German scholarship in evaluating and circulating Jesuit treatises is shown by the fact that Lach begins his sweeping history in the 1940s with a series of articles and his University of Chicago dissertation, *Contributions of China to German Civilization 1648–1740*.[2] Virtually all subsequent scholars rely on Lach to trace out the European distribution of the first three centuries of travel narratives, missionary reports, histories, and translations about China. In the 1980s David Mungello extends Lach's history by concentrating specifically on the elite Jesuit treatises written . in Latin during the seventeenth century. He also devotes three chapters to Leibniz's correspondence with Jesuit missionaries, as well as the ill-fated efforts of Andreas Müller and Christian Mentzel in Berlin to find a simple European code for understanding Chinese writing. Both Lach and Mungello recognize that even though they were far removed from the mercantile (Lisbon, Antwerp, Amsterdam) and ecclesiastical (Paris, Rome) centres of the China trade, German Enlightenment scholars relied on scholarly publications to formulate their own second- and third-hand interpretations of Chinese culture. Scholarship on the Jesuit writings continues in ever-greater detail to this day, though recent work focuses particularly on how representations of China circulated within Europe.

China in the German Enlightenment recounts the initial wonder and awe that German thinkers felt for the peaceful order of Chinese society and for Confucianism in particular.

Leibniz's correspondence with Jesuits travelling to China, and his visions of China as an ideal society ruled by an emperor trained in Confucian ethics reflected a larger European initial amazement at Chinese civilization. This respect for Confucianism helped shape Enlightenment political theories about justice and personal ethics. Indeed, Leibniz's enthusiasm was so great that without irony he reversed the entire purpose of the Jesuit mission by arguing that the Chinese ought to send missionaries to Europe to teach political philosophy and the administration of peace as a form of cultural exchange.

Leibniz serves both as a major European philosophical figure endorsing Confucianism and as the anonymous member of the early modern Republic of Letters, constantly reading, revising, and recirculating texts on Chinese thought – a nodal point in the media network of early modern China Studies and a foundational thinker for the rationalist appropriation of Confucianism. Donald Lach translated Leibniz's *Novissima Sinica* into English.[3] David Mungello begins his long scholarly career on the Jesuits in China with a work on Leibniz and Confucianism.[4] For more recent scholars, Leibniz embodies the intersection of Enlightenment metaphysics and the Jesuit exegesis of Confucian thought. The Jesuit policy of accommodation embodies a subtle, sympathetic approach to negotiating difference, and Leibniz's enthusiasm for the Jesuits' presentation of China has become the reference point for scholars who value the Enlightenment's reception of China.

Yet rationalists did not by any means all follow the Jesuit line. Jonathan Israel argues, for instance, that Radical Enlightenment thinkers interpreted Confucianism *against* Jesuit intentions as representing a demonstration of the universality of rational thought and the falsity of all religion.[5] Chinese philosophy, then, was understood as an example of an admirable moral system that did not require belief in God. Thus, radicals of all sorts, from anti-clerical rationalists to Spinozists to Socinians and Universalists, could align themselves with Confucianism as confirmation that societies and individuals could be just without recourse to scripture or revelation.[6]

In his controversial 1724 "Lecture on the Moral Teaching of the Chinese" Christian Wolff (1679–1754) followed in the footsteps of Ricci and Leibniz when he announced his intention to find the secret and hidden foundational truths ("geheime und verborgene Grundwahrheiten") of Confucianism. Wolff finds support for his approach to Confucian texts in the traditional claim by the Chinese philosopher himself that he was not espousing a truth so much as restoring an ancient truth that had been lost. This Confucian manoeuvre within the tradition of the Chinese literati opened the door for outsiders such as Wolff to place Confucianism itself in a longer philosophical genealogy that hierarchizes Western and Asian thought. Pursuing a project similar to the long-standing Christianization of Greek philosophy by claiming that both share an understanding of the same principles, Wolff left open the possibility of uncovering a truth unknown even to the Chinese. This gesture laid the ground for the later Orientalist claim to understand the Orient better than its inhabitants themselves.

The historical narrative often moves on to Charles de Montesquieu's critical turn against the Chinese imperial system. Montesquieu describes the Asian monarch as being above the law, driven by moods and whim as opposed to rational reflection. This despot brooks no opposition: he deploys an administrative elite, which unlike an aristocracy is subject to removal at any time. Subjects are reduced to an almost slavelike condition, and private property is not recognized. Finally, despotic systems are unconcerned with economic growth or progress as they are locked in an eternal present of short-term exploitation.

The fashionable spread of chinoiserie across European courts from the mid-seventeenth century onward did little to alter this increasingly close association between the Confucian maxims of the literati and absolute political control.[7] This downward narrative becomes more complicated in the second half of the eighteenth century as ethnographic theories model themselves on Carl Linnaeus's natural classification, where Immanuel Kant posits the first organization of race based on skin colour. Hegel's dismissive account of China's absence in the historical unfolding of "Geist" reiterates attributes already described by Montesquieu.

With the rise of anti-monarchical critiques in Germany, a more hostile view of Chinese society steadily emerged: the missionary accounts of China were now assessed more critically. For later Enlightenment writers, such as Johann Gottfried Herder, the consumption of luxury goods from China at European courts suggested that China was a society of stiff formality enforced by rules and ceremony rather than a land of free thinkers, capable of following their own paths. The anthropological and racial theories by Christoph Meiners, Immanuel Kant, and others further darkened the German image of China.

By the end of the eighteenth century, German intellectuals were faced with an ocean of travel literature. Rather than relying on a handful of first-person travelogues, as Leibniz and Wolff had done, critics now began to interpret and critique the conflicting descriptions of China to synthesize them into *universal histories* that placed China within a global narrative of the development of civilization.

Whereas Leibniz views China and Europe as the two highest societies in human advancement, philosophers from Montesquieu to Hegel, by contrast, place China at the start of a historical succession that ultimately led to a global European dominance. Implicit within these historical narratives is a correspondence between Chinese society and the European ancien régime, so that Hegel could readily critique China as if it were equivalent to the baroque court. In the aftermath of the French Revolution, the close connection between consuming Chinese luxuries and the European aristocracy became a liability.

Despite the apparent arch to its history, the reception of China in Europe did not proceed in a simple linear manner. Instead, as the essays in our volume show, the history is marked by a constant critical reassessment of all previous reporting on China. The late eighteenth century, in other words, did not *know* significantly more about China than the late seventeenth century did, but it was far less persuaded by missionary representations of China as an ideally moral society run by a wise emperor and meritorious Confucian mandarins. From the start of the first Jesuit mission, China had served as a fabulous ideal about which competing European intellectuals contended. The negative turn against China really amounted to a shift in how European intellectuals accommodated alterity.

The current German interest in postcolonial topics clearly reflects the influence of anglophone investigations of the British Empire, in particular Edward Said's *Orientalism*. The interdisciplinary nature of German Studies, including the emerging field of German-Asian Studies, has encouraged cross-disciplinary borrowing.[8] However, the impact of Edward Said's *Orientalism* was not immediate within German Studies. Intellectual historians have been quite resistant to this new theoretical critique of the Enlightenment, while critically inclined historians have been more concerned with uncovering precursors to Nazi racism and the Holocaust than with the long lead-up to modern colonialism. As a result, scholars have framed their critical investigations more often in terms of racism rather than in terms of Orientalism. This concern continues in contemporary investigations of colonialism during the Wilhelmine period, as scholars debate whether colonial wars – often involving the destruction of Native peoples – could be connected causally or otherwise with the Nazi genocide.[9] In her recent study of Herder,

Sonia Sikka, for instance, is careful to weigh Herder's rejection of race theory in relation to Nazi efforts to appropriate his anthropology of *Völker* (Nations).[10] The question of how German representations of Asia contributed to the development of modern racism seems a more pressing, more specifically German problem.

Not until the 1990s was Said's thesis adapted to German-language representations of Asia.[11] Initially, German scholars seemed to presume that Said's arguments were not immediately relevant to German historical sources, particularly not to the period before the Kaiserreich established colonies in Africa, Asia, and the Pacific.[12] But such presumptions were immediately challenged by scholars such as Swiss historian Urs Bitterli and put to the test again more recently by Susanne Zantop in her *Colonial Fantasies*.[13] As investigations of German colonial culture expanded in works such as Nina Berman's *Orientalismus, Kolonialismus und Moderne: Zum Bild des Orients in der deutschsprachigen Kultur um 1900* (Orientalism, Colonialism, and Modernity: On the Image of the Orient in the German-Speaking Culture around 1900) and Todd Kontje's *German Orientalism*, the German exclusion from European colonial discourses became less and less plausible.[14]

In her overview of German research into Orientalism, Andrea Polaschegg points out that studies on the fictional and poetic representation of China have always been a minor tradition in German Studies.[15] However, until Edward Said's *Orientalism* these investigations were usually confined to a single author and a particular geographical context – Goethe and Persia, Hesse and India, and so forth.[16] While nineteenth-century readers may have been perplexed by Goethe's interest in Hafez, today the *West-östliche Divan* stands as a canonical text in Germany's intercultural Germanistik, especially when German politicians are addressing Muslim audiences.[17] The secondary literature on Goethe's relation to Islam, Persia, and the Arab world is also extensive, even if much remains to be written about the *Divan*'s individual poems.[18]

The first intellectual histories focused on the Jesuits' translations into Latin of canonical Chinese texts and their philosophical reception in Europe. Jürgen Osterhammel, in his immense *Die Entzauberung Asiens: Europa und die asiatischen Reiche im 18. Jahrhundert* (The Demystification of Asia: Europe and the Asian Empires in the Eighteenth Century),[19] takes up the task of showing the history of how the scholarly and economic networks running between northern Europe and China were intertwined. Published in 1998, *Die Entzauberung Asiens* is the most comprehensive history of eighteenth-century German economic and scholarly engagement with China. Osterhammel concentrates particularly on the increased ethnographic reporting made available as the British and Dutch East India trading companies expanded to show how German, French, English, and Scottish Enlightenments developed their sophisticated, even-handed responses to Chinese civilization. Osterhammel traces the many mediating connections that made scholarly and economic interest in China interdependent.

As Andrea Polaschegg notes, German discussion of Edward Said's *Orientalism* generally does not connect with the larger English-language commentary and critique of this work.[20] Osterhammel's methodological discussion in *Die Entzauberung Asiens* is in many ways a case in point. In it we can see a simultaneous resistance and acceptance of Said's *Orientalism* thesis. Osterhammel shows how German writers were fully integrated within the larger European discussions about China, which in the eighteenth century were dominated by French and English sources. Osterhammel makes a political statement as he opens the book by acknowledging Europe's arrogant belief in its superiority over other parts of the world, its confidence in controlling world markets, and its sense of inherent superiority over other peoples. Having made this admission, he wishes to establish a clear distance between these fatal flaws in foreign policy and the Enlightenment by suggesting that Europe's aggrandizing tendencies have their origin first in the nineteenth century.

Osterhammel is quite right in warning against anachronistic interpretations that project nineteenth-century colonial ideologies and practices onto the early modern period; however, we should also be wary of the tendency in eighteenth-century German Studies to insist that their particular period is blissfully immune from the later evils of modernity. Thus, for example, John Noyes argues forcefully against the presumption that Germans were unaware of colonial oppression. He cites Herder as the most outspoken critic, but then also calls attention to Goethe as a reluctant colonial critic.[21] Noyes shows how Goethe's long-standing fascination with the mobility of his characters and their ability to escape the enclosure of European institutions presumes the availability of colonial space. Whereas some eighteenth-century writers, such as Goethe and Jane Austen, were famously averse to ideological statements, professional political thinkers, such as the Göttingen professor A.H.L. Heeren, foregrounded how important colonies were to the European state system. Surveying the European political order in 1809, Heeren warns the historian not to underestimate the importance of colonies:

> That [the historian] needs to include the colonies, their development, and their influence on Europe is clearly called for now. They belong to

the European system of states; the levers of world trade are connected to them, and their completely immeasurable influence on politics; how limited would the [historian's] perspective remain without their inclusion.

(Daß er aber auch die Colonien, ihre Fortbildung, und ihren Einfluß auf Europa selber mit hineinziehen mußte, liegt am Tage. Sie gehören dem Staatensystem von Europa an; an sie knüpfte sich der Gang des Welthandels, und sein ganzer unermeßlicher Einfluß auf die Politik; wie beschränkt würde also ohne sie die Ansicht geblieben seyn!)[22]

Because Heeren is writing at a moment when he believes that the sovereign state has been destroyed, he imagines that he can provide a comprehensive account of how it once worked. In referring to the importance of colonies, he clearly was thinking of all European states and their colonies, yet he would have also been more conscious than scholars in the twenty-first century of the eighteenth-century German overseas projects such as the sporadic attempts by Brandenburg-Prussia, from before the Great Elector to Friedrich II, to enter the slave market in order to finance an East India trading company and the Halle Pietists' effort to compete with the Jesuits in Asia by establishing a mission in Tranquebar, India.[23] These failed enterprises are hardly remembered today given the immensity of the later British Empire, but in the eighteenth century they were still plausible, if underfunded start-up ventures.[24]

More recent discussions of Enlightenment engagements with Asia seek to overcome the opposition between discourse analysis and close reading, and this troubles Osterhammel. Historians such as Ulrich Johannes Schneider have in the meanwhile shown how useful Foucault's archaeological theories are for understanding the organization of eighteenth-century libraries and collections dedicated to China.[25] Srinivas Aravamudan cobbles the two terms together in his 2012 book, *Enlightenment Orientalism*, where he acknowledges the absence of colonial empires while still wanting to extend the insights that discourse analysis provide in tracing the will to power inherent in characterizations of Asia. Aravamudan's definition of Enlightenment Orientalism as "a fictional mode for dreaming with the Orient – dreaming with it by constructing and translating fictions about it, pluralizing views of it, inventing it, by reimagining it, unsettling its meaning, brooding over it ... a Western style for translating, anatomizing, and desiring the Orient" answers many of Osterhammel's concerns about uncritically pushing Said's model into the early modern period.[26] Both scholars insist that any investigation must concentrate on individual texts, and they thus avoid generalizations that characterize the eighteenth century as a transition from the Sinophilia of Leibniz to the Sinophobia of Hegel.

The epistemological implications of Edward Said's argument have been elaborated upon within the German context through the application of media theory. Birgit Tautz's important book, *Reading and Seeing Ethnic Differences in the Enlightenment from China to Africa*, traces the epistemic shift from the Republic of Letters reliance on texts as direct reproductions of reality to a reliance on personal visual immediacy.[27] She provides a theoretically informed media history to show how the elaboration of an aesthetic subjectivity alters European perceptions of difference, so that the switch from textuality to visuality defines the emergence of race theory in Enlightenment ethnography. Tautz transforms Friedrich Kittler's brief remarks on baroque literature into a postcolonial history of German Enlightenment's engagements with difference and its invention of ethnicity. In terms of media theoretical approaches, Ulrich Johannes Schneider's research presents a more direct application of Foucault's archaeology of knowledge to the Enlightenment's reception of China.[28]

Investigating how modes of reading and interpretive frameworks shifted in the eighteenth century is important to the historian, because even though the late Enlightenment possessed a wealth of written reports about China, these travelogues now were being read in a new critical light. Even before the Society's suppression, Jesuit accommodationist reports were being viewed sceptically by a variety of European reading communities, and the empirical descriptions of the new travelogues were increasingly seen as contradictory and inconclusive. How the accumulated information about China was being processed during the Enlightenment is one of the fundamental questions our volume seeks to address.

China in the German Enlightenment follows three critical and self-reflective modes of addressing differences between German and Chinese culture: (1) The Jesuit project to blend Confucianism, Christianity, and ancient philosophy remains a remarkable undertaking, even more so in light of the postcolonial critiques of European expansionism. The essays here join the already extensive scholarship on the Enlightenment adaptation of Jesuit accommodation. (2) The debate over the contribution of German philosophy in formulating modern race theory begins in the late Enlightenment and includes its defining thinkers as both advocates for and critics of race as a legitimate category for organizing knowledge of human beings. Our volume shows how the history of race theory in German philosophy is still being written today. (3) The essays in *China in the German Enlightenment* show that contemporary German Studies has incorporated postcolonial theory to such an extent that scholars are now able to employ its analytical tools and lines of interrogation without having to repeat the old question: how German is it?

Our essays call and respond to each other's interpretations. Each one engages with the canonical figures of German intellectual history, even as they draw lesser-known writers on China into the discussion. As one reads across this volume, many of the same primary sources are interpreted from different vantage points, suggesting that German discussions of China drew from many of the same sources, even as their critical approaches shifted dramatically across the eighteenth century.

Walter Demel's "How the Chinese Became Yellow: A Contribution to the Early History of Race Theories," represents a comprehensive account of the emergence of race theory in the late eighteenth century as an apparatus in the new science of anthropology. Published in German in 1992, this seminal essay has previously not been available in English, yet it has served as the basis for important recent studies of race, including Michael Keevak's *No Longer White: The Nineteenth-Century Invention of Yellowness*, and, even more recently, Sabine Doran's *The Culture of Yellow, or the Visual Politics of Late Modernity*.[29] Two essays by Immanuel Kant – "On the Different Human Races" and "Determination of the Concept of a Human Race" – are often cited as the first race theories based on skin colour. Demel's essay situates this Kantian moment within the very long history preceding racial stereotyping.[30] Demonstrating the many different sources of racial characterization, Demel makes clear that the racial depiction of Asians as yellow must be understood in relation to global conflicts between Europeans and others. Distinctions of blood and purity, deployed in Europe during the drive to expel Islam from the Iberian Peninsula, were elaborated in the Americas as traders and plantation owners tried to legitimate the brutality of the Atlantic slave trade. Race theory as applied to Asia cannot, in other words, be understood without investigating the history of European representations of sub-Saharan Africans. Demel connects the discourse around slavery with late Enlightenment German thought, an association that still suffers under the double burden of being both controversial and ignored. He bases his argument not just on the terms

Europeans used to describe the Chinese but on their own comparisons between Asian and European inhabitants. Territories were populated by people of many different shadings. No one category summarized their qualities, rather Demel stresses the multiplicity of distinctions used to describe peoples and territories. His history of racism has a specifically German component once the narrative arrives in the eighteenth century, serving as an antecedent to the current debates over to what extent Immanuel Kant "invented" the category of modern skin-based racism.[31]

Robert Bernasconi's essay in this volume exposes a similar philosophical adding on to ethnography, namely, that Hegel augmented the terms used in travel writing with distinctly racist stereotypes. Demel's broad historical survey provides a crucial framework for the current debates on race in German philosophy because a great deal of the scholarly debate over how racist language was used in the Enlightenment requires close readings comparing the implications of different formulations. Demel's survey allows us to recognize not only how for centuries world travellers were writing within different frames of reference; his long history also makes clear how discourses on alterity shifted in the late eighteenth century as everyday descriptors were transformed into philosophical categories that defined newly emerging sciences, like anthropology. Demel highlights the enormous difference between priests and merchants recounting their experiences abroad and a philosopher mobilizing a hundred such tales to formulate a universal distinction within mankind.

Franklin Perkins, in his essay, "Leibniz on the Existence of Philosophy in China," provides a cornerstone for the collection by raising the question of why Confucian thought was initially considered philosophical by European intellectuals only to be disregarded in the late eighteenth century. The same argument that first was presented to celebrate Chinese thought was later invoked to devalue it, namely, that Confucianism was skilled in practical ethics, whereas European philosophy excelled in theoretical reflection. This devaluation went hand in hand with a shift that occurred over the course of the Enlightenment in which a conception of philosophy as a way of life was gradually replaced with a conception of philosophy as a "systematic science." Perkins explains how the place of Chinese thought altered with this shift in defining philosophy as an academic discipline. Ultimately Perkins calls for a thorough re-evaluation of the philosophical discourse to include Chinese traditions. His argument also shares with Demel and

Bernasconi a focus on the eighteenth-century introduction of racial categories to separate and hierarchize cultures. Like Bernasconi, Perkins sees Hegel's *Lectures on the History of Philosophy* as a point when this racial hierarchy found expression within European philosophical discourse. Perkins recognizes that the ancient understanding of philosophy as examining how one leads a good life was also supplanted in the larger shift towards defining philosophy in terms of abstract concepts and systems.

Michael Carhart's essay, "Leibniz between Paris, Grand Tartary, and the Far East: Gerbillon's Intercepted Letter," shows that the philosopher's interest in China grew out of his obligations as a courtier to uncover and write the dynastic history of the Hanoverian Elector. His investigations into the origins of the Saxons led Leibniz to Central Asia as the birthplace of European languages and peoples. Leibniz concentrated on the history of languages and their similarities with the aim of demonstrating the Asian origins of northern Europeans. His famous correspondence with Jesuit missionaries in India and China grew out of this linguistic investigation as well. Carhart traces the complex itineraries of correspondence between Jesuit missionaries in China and European intellectuals. By laying out the tremendous geographical and political barriers to communication, Carhart makes the reader feel just how difficult it was for Leibniz to gather the material for his *Novissima Sinica*. By providing a micro-history of one letter and detailing the torturous route this particular missionary's letter took from China to Europe, Carhart elucidates the competing interests in European engagement with Asia. In the process he confirms the characterization made by network theorists, such as John Law and Bruno Latour, about the instability and fragility of early modern overseas routes. Although most modern scholars marvel at the Jesuits' prodigious publications from their China mission, Leibniz worried that they were not publishing enough. Ultimately, Leibniz's zealous drive to communicate reflects the utopian character of the Republic of Letters, and its idealized suspension of distance.

Carl Niekerk's essay, "The Problem of China: Asia and Enlightenment Anthropology (Buffon, de Pauw, Blumenbach, Herder)," situates Herder's account of China in his *Ideen* (1787) within the larger Enlightenment discussion of anthropology and human lineages. Specifically Niekerk shows how Herder moves between De Pauw's and the Abbé Raynal's surveys of China in the *Histoire philosophique des deux Indes*. Herder's position, in other words, emerges as a third-order response to the vast travel writing on China: he responds to earlier commentaries while incorporating the latest first-hand travel reports. Niekerk's contribution thus shows that the reception of China did not follow a simple two-step process of eyewitness accounts followed by critical and synthetic commentaries. Rather, the process of reviewing China entailed a constant reassessment of anthropology, or the study of mankind, as a whole. Niekerk quotes Blumenbach stating that he collects anthropological accounts with a political purpose in mind: defending the rights of humanity. Finally, Herder's account of China and his debates with De Pauw and Raynal, are likewise attempts to define the moral character of humanity. Like Jeffrey Librett's contribution to this volume, Niekerk points to the underlying comparison German thinkers made between Chinese and Jewish society, in scriptural terms – that is, in both the writing and the canonical religious texts.

In "Localizing China: Of Knowledge, Genres, and German Literary Historiography," Birgit Tautz questions the common scholarly assumption that Western thought shifted from Sinophilia to Sinophobia by focusing on minor genres that stood outside the grand narrative of history. Examining how writing about China circulated in the Enlightenment at the local level, Tautz urges a move away from canonical figures such as Johann Wolfgang Goethe to consider how writing in different genres produces hierarchies of knowledge. By focusing on local publications (tea poems and articles in regional journals, but also encyclopedias), she traces the channels of distribution that ran far beyond the grand controversies of Jesuit missionaries and rationalist philosophers. Finally, she uses the example of Goethe's late, mostly posthumous poems on China to show that all intellectuals were caught up in these local lines of communication. Goethe adapts English commentaries and translations of Chinese poems into his own words, thereby extending a chain of intertextual transformations wherein Chinese language texts become expressions of both a specific cultural identity and a universal mode of knowledge that then became known as *Weltliteratur* or *world literature*.

Tautz joins David Porter in arguing that the historical emphasis on modernity and progress when comparing Europe with China entails an "instrumental amnesia": a calculated forgetting that pushes aside earlier moments of parity and admiration. Enlightenment encyclopedia entries are particularly useful in tracing the many forgotten sources and opinions that made up early modern writing on China. Like baroque compilations, eighteenth-century encyclopedias incorporated diverse sources to bundle together multilayered representations. Personal tea poems, on the other hand, are a highly subjective alternative to the public knowledge of the encyclopedia. In the end, Tautz makes clear that the image of China penetrated into the most varied and intimate eighteenth-century German discourses, many of these far removed from the cosmological conflicts of the philosophical canon.

In "Eradicating the Orientalists: Goethe's *Chinesisch-deutsche Jahres- und Tageszeiten*," John Noyes also engages with a question that Birgit Tautz raises: to what extent can Goethe's late cycle, *Chinesisch-deutsche Jahres- und Tageszeiten*, be considered a historical and literary engagement with China? Noyes shows that the poems' Chinese themes enable the forces of nature to be reconciled with the creative production of the mind – a central question in all of Goethe's lyrical poems. To understand Goethe's lyrical adaptation of Chinese forms, Noyes points to the lesson he learned from Herder on how to conceptualize a general humanity in foreign poetry while still recognizing its differences. Noyes then traces Goethe's Oriental engagement from even before he began to write the *West-östliche Divan*. For example, Goethe's heretical interpretation of a debate between the Jesuit missionary Matteo Ricci and a Buddhist monk in Nanjing shows how Goethe imagined a shared understanding of nature that joined Buddhism with Spinoza and German Idealism.

In "China on Parade: Hegel's Manipulation of His Sources and His Change of Mind," Robert Bernasconi reviews the travel reports Hegel selected as the basis for his five lectures on China between 1822 and 1831 in order to examine specifically how the Berlin thinker deviates from these representations. Like Walter Demel in "How the Chinese Became Yellow," and Birgit Tautz's essay in this volume, Bernasconi does not treat racist characterizations of China in isolation, but rather understands them within a larger ideology that uses hostile stereotyping of black Africans as its fundamental standard. Although many scholars have cited Hegel's negative stereotypes, Bernasconi's argument is far more detailed, for he shows how Hegel's position shifted each time he taught his course on the philosophy of world history. Not only does Bernasconi demonstrate that Hegel's negative stereotyping goes beyond that in his principle sources, but he also explains how Hegel's typecasting exceeds the requirements of his philosophical position. Hegel's judgments also underwent a development, from his wonder at the Chinese Empire in 1822 to his later degradation of it.

In the most modernist contribution to our collection, Jeffrey Librett, in "Neo-Romantic Modernism and Daoism: Martin Buber on the

Teaching as Fulfilment," extends Franklin Perkins's call to take Chinese thought seriously as a philosophical project by exploring the late neo-Romantic reception of Daoist thought. As Martin Buber argues, German thinkers' later "discovery" of Daoism cast a new light on the Enlightenment's fascination with Confucianism. Librett shows how the reception of Chinese thought lasted well beyond the arc running from Leibniz's enthusiasm for Confucianism to Hegel's dismissal of it. Indeed, the historical character of the Enlightenment's engagement with Confucianism is revealed by Germans' later interest in Daoism, a point sinologist Wolfgang Bauer makes in his history of the "other" China – the Buddhism and Daoism left out from the Jesuit presentation of Chinese thought to early modern Europe. Buber argues against the Jesuit accommodation of Confucianism that Chinese teaching should not be understood simply as an imperfect version of Christian doctrine. Furthermore, Librett's essay reminds us that the Christian engagement with Chinese teachings is always framed by its debate with Judaism at the origin of church history. The Jesuit debates with Buddhist monks that John Noyes describes in his essay had a long pre-history in the disputations between Christians and Jews in antiquity and in the Middle Ages. By insisting that China's religions were "great teachings" that needed to be understood in their own terms as "ways of life," Buber was also re-establishing a place for Judaism in German thought.

Our chapters examine the still pressing question of how Europe during the Enlightenment could switch from admiring China to disparaging its culture. Our answers do not focus on colonial politics or industrial progress – instead we burrow into the organization of knowledge about China. In the early modern period, transcultural relations both within Europe and from China to Germany were not yet caught up in nationalism. The essays in this volume demonstrate that information about China circulated across territorial borders, and that media channels ran far beyond the capital cities and ports of the largest trading partners. German thinkers thus saw themselves within a large network of intellectual and material exchange to which they contributed their own utopian aspirations and critical schemas. Only slowly were the earliest courtly and religious attempts to discover parity between the two domains replaced by an insistence on the existence of separate unique identities for all parties. The theological presumption that Christians and Confucians shared an original moral teaching was supplanted, at the end of the eighteenth century, by a universal and yet narrow concept of humanity.

The Enlightenment's ideal of progress, its celebration of material, scientific, technological, and political progress, left eighteenth-century German intellectuals in the awkward position of having to question their own advanced state. The fear that they, too, might belong to "the Orient" plagued Central Europeans well into the twentieth century. Only through their cultural claim to literary and philosophical accomplishment could German thinkers insist that they were not. Their increasingly abstract concepts of Enlightenment produced an ever sharper differentiation between Europe and the Orient. As many of the essays in this volume show, the eighteenth century's elaboration of race theories and its increasingly asymmetrical views on Asia had serious implications in the twentieth century that applied to Jews and Africans as much as to the Chinese and Japanese.

NOTES

1 Donald F. Lach, *Asia in the Making of Europe* (Chicago: University of Chicago Press, 1965–1993), 9 vols. The last four volumes were co-authored with Edwin J. Van Kley.
2 Donald F. Lach, *Contributions of China to German Civilization, 1648–1740*, Ph.D. dissertation, University of Chicago, June 1941.
3 *The Preface to Leibniz' Novissima Sinica*, translated by Donald F. Lach (Honolulu: University of Hawaii Press, 1957). For a new German translation that purports to correct some of Lach's translation of the Latin into English, see Georg Wilhelm Leibniz, *Das Neueste von China (1697): Novissima Sinica, mit ergänzende Dokumenten*, translated by Heinz Günther Nesselrath and Hermann Reinbothe (Cologne: Deutsche China Gesellschaft, 1979).
4 David Mungello, *Leibniz and Confucianism: The Search for Accord* (Honolulu: University Press of Hawaii, 1977).
5 Jonathan I. Israel, *Radical Enlightenment: Philosophy and the Making of Modernity, 1650–1750* (Oxford: Oxford University Press, 2001), 588. See in particular Israel's chapter on "Spinoza, Confucius, and Classical Chinese Philosophy," in *Enlightenment Contested: Philosophy, Modernity, and the Emancipation of Man 1670–1752* (Oxford: Oxford University Press, 2006), 640–62.
6 William Poole, "Heterodoxy and Sinology: Isaac Vossius, Robert Hooke, and the Early Royal Society's Use of Sinology," in *Intellectual Consequences of Religious Heterodoxy, 1600–1750*, eds. Sarah Mortimer and John Robertson (Leiden: Brill, 2012), 135–53.

7 Willy Richard Berger, *China-Bild und China-Mode im Europa der Aufklärung* (Cologne: Böhlau, 1990); Günther Berger, *Chinoiserien in Österreich-Ungarn* (Frankfurt: Peter Lang, 1995); Johannes Franz Hallinger, *Das Ende der Chinoiserie* (Munich: Scaneg, 1996); David Porter, *The Chinese Taste in Eighteenth-Century England* (Cambridge: Cambridge University Press, 2010); Eugenia Zuroski Jenkins, *A Taste for China: English Subjectivity and the Prehistory of Orientalism* (Oxford: Oxford University Press, 2013).

8 Russell Berman, "Colonialism, and No End: The Other Continuity Theses," in *German Colonialism: Race, the Holocaust, and Postwar Germany*, eds. Volker Langbehn and Mohammad Salama (New York: Columbia University Press, 2011), 168.

9 Volker Langbehn and Mohammad Salama, eds., "Introduction: Reconfiguring German Colonialism," in *German Colonialism: Race, the Holocaust, and Postwar Germany* (New York: Columbia University Press, 2011), ix–xxiv. A notable exception is Isabel V. Hull, *Absolute Destruction: Military Culture and the Practices of War in Imperial Germany* (Ithaca: Cornell University Press, 2005).

10 Sonia Sikka, *Herder on Humanity and Cultural Difference: Enlightened Relativism* (Cambridge: Cambridge University Press, 2013), 126–59.

11 Hendrick Birus, "Goethes imaginativer Orientalismus," *Jahrbuch des freien deutschen Hochstifts*, 1992, 107–28.

12 Said addresses the relationship between German Orientalists and colonialism briefly in his introduction to *Orientalism*, 19. For recent histories that critically engage Said, see Sabine Mangold, *Eine "weltbürgerliche Wissenschaft" – Die deutsche Orientalistik im 19. Jahrhundert* (Stuttgart: Franz Steiner, 2004), and Suzanne L. Marchand, *German Orientalism in the Age of Empire* (Cambridge: Cambridge University Press, 2009).

13 Urs Bitterli, *Die "Wilden" und die "Zivilisierten": Grundzüge einer Geistes- und Kulturgeschichte der europäisch-überseeischen Begegnung* (Munich: Beck, 1975); Susanne Zantop, *Colonial Fantasies: Conquest, Family, and Nation in Precolonial Germany, 1770–1870* (Durham: Duke University Press, 1997). Although Zantop examines early modern German involvement in American expeditions, the broad psychoanalytic terms of her argument provide an avenue for connecting pre-colonial German writers with Said's Orientalism thesis.

14 Nina Berman, *Orientalismus, Kolonialismus und Moderne: Zum Bild des Orients in der deutschsprachigen Kultur um 1900* (Stuttgart: Metzler, 1997); Todd Kontje, *German Orientalisms* (Ann Arbor: University of Michigan Press, 2004).

15 Andrea Polaschegg, *Der andere Orientalismus: Regeln deutsch-morgenländischer Imagination im 19. Jahrhundert* (Berlin: de Gruyter, 2005), 3–4.

16 Adrian Hsia has written extensively connecting individual works to China, e.g, *Chinesia: The European Construction of China in the Literature of the 17th and 18th Centuries* (Tübingen: Max Niemeyer, 1998).

17 The most recent critical editions of the *West-östliche Divan* can be found in J.W. Goethe, *Sämtliche Werke, Briefe, Tagebücher und Gespräche*, edited by Hendrik Birus (Frankfurt: Deutscher Klassiker Verlag, 1994), vol. 3, and J.W. Goethe, *Sämtliche Werke*, edited by Karl Richter, Katharina Mommsen, and Peter Ludwig (Munich: Carl Hanser, 1998), vol. 11. For a sophisticated early interpretation of Goethe in intercultural German Studies, see Fawzi Boubin, "Goethes Theorie der Alterität und die Idee der Weltliteratur: Ein Beitrag zur neueren Kulturdebatte," in *Gegenwart als kulturelles Erbe: Ein Beitrag der Germanistik zur Kulturwissenschaft deutschspachiger Länder* (Munich: Iudicum Verlag, 1985), 269–302.

18 Katharina Mommsen, *Goethe und die arabische Welt* (Frankfurt: Insel, 1988); Gerhart von Graevenitz, *Das Ornament des Blicks: Über die Grundlagen des neuzeitlichen Sehens, die Poetik der Arabeske und Goethes "West-östlichen Divan"* (Stuttgart: Metzler, 1994); Andrea Polaschegg, "'Diese geistig technischen Bemühungen ...' zum Verhältnis von Gestalt und Sinnversprechen der Schrift: Goethes arabische Schreibübungen und E.T.A. Hoffmanns *Der goldene Topf*," in *Schrift: Kulturtechnik zwischen Auge, Hand und Maschine*, eds. Gernot Grube, Werner Kogge, and Sybille Krämer (Munich: Fink, 2005), 279–304.

19 Jürgen Osterhammel, *Die Entzauberung Asiens: Europa und die asiatischen Reiche im 18. Jahrhundert* (Munich: Beck, 1998).

20 See her short history of Orientalism research in German: Polaschegg, *Der andere Orientalismus*, 10–38.

21 John Noyes, "Goethe on Cosmopolitanism and Colonialism: *Bildung* and the Dialectic of Critical Mobility," *Eighteenth-Century Studies* 39.4 (2006): 443–62.

22 A.H.L. Heeren, *Handbuch der Geschichte des Europäischen Staatensystems und seiner Colonien* (Göttingen: Röwer, 1809), vii.

23 Gita Dharampal-Frick, *Indien im Spiegel deutscher Quellen der Frühen Neuzeit [1500–1750]: Studien zu einer interkulturellen Konstellation* (Tübingen: Niemeyer, 1994); Daniel Jeyaraj, "Mission Reports from South India and Their Impact on the Western Mind: The Tranquebar Mission of the Eighteenth Century," in *Converting Colonialism: Visions and Realities in Mission History, 1706–1914*, ed. Dana L. Robert (Grand Rapids, MI: William B. Eerdmans, 2008), 21–42. Hanco Jürgens, "On the Crossroads: Pietist, Orthodox and Enlightened Views on Mission in the Eighteenth Century," in *Halle and the Beginnings of Protestant Christianity in India*, vol. 1, eds. Andreas Gross, Y.

Vincent Kumaradoss, and Heike Liebau (Halle: Verlag der Franckeschen Stiftungen, 2006), 7–36; Anthony Gregg Roeber, *Hopes for Better Spouses: Protestant Marriage and Church Renewal in Early Modern Europe, India, and North America* (Grand Rapids, MI: William B. Eerdmans, 2013).

24 Noyes also cites the Brandenburg-Prussia ventures in "Goethe on Cosmopolitanism and Colonialism," 443. The most complete history on Brandenburg-Prussia's slave trade and the East India companies was written in support of nineteenth-century colonialization: see Richard Schück, *Brandenburg-Preußens Kolonial-Politik unter dem Großen Kurfursten und seinen Nachfolgern* (Leipzig: Grunow, 1889). See also Ulrich van der Heyden, *Roter Adler an Afrikas Küste: Die Brandenburgisch-preußische Kolonie Großfriedrichsburg in Westafrika* (Berlin: Selignow, 2001).

25 Ulrich Johannes Schneider, "Ordnung als Schema und als Operation, 'Die Bibliothek Herzog Augusts,'" *Foucault und die Künste* (Frankfurt: Suhrkamp, 2004), 315–38

26 Srinivas Aravamudan, *Enlightenment Orientalism: Resisting the Rise of the Novel* (Chicago: University of Chicago Press, 2012), 8.

27 Birgit Tautz, *Reading and Seeing Ethnic Differences in the Enlightenment from China to Africa* (New York: Palgrave Macmilllan, 2007).

28 Schneider, "Ordnung als Schema und als Operation," 315–38.

29 Michael Keevak, *No Longer White: The Nineteenth-Century Invention of Yellowness* (Princeton: Princeton University Press, 2011), 3; Sabine Doran, *The Culture of Yellow, or the Visual Politics of Late Modernity* (New York: Bloomsbury, 2013).

30 Demel criticizes Keevak's history for not reaching back far enough into the early modern period to consider texts describing the Chinese as the same as European. Walter Demel, "Review of Michael Keevak's *Becoming Yellow*," *East Asian Science, Technology, and Medicine* 34 (2012): 231–3.

31 Robert Bernasconi, ed., *Race: Blackwell Readings in Continental Philosophy* (Malden, MA: Blackwell, 2001); Sara Eigen and Mark Larrimore, eds., *The German Invention of Race* (Albany: State University of New York Press, 2006).

1 How the Chinese Became Yellow: A Contribution to the Early History of Race Theories[1]

WALTER DEMEL

"Di nostra qualità" – Testimonials by European Travellers from the Early Sixteenth Century to the End of the Eighteenth Century

"Di nostra qualità," the Chinese are "of our quality." So wrote Andrea Corsali, an Italian in Portuguese service, to the Florentine Duke Giuliano de' Medici in the year 1515. Following the collapse of the medieval connection between Europe and East Asia, this was the first printed statement of its time about the recently rediscovered most populous people of the earth.[2] Several years later, having spoken with returning sailors, the Imperial Privy Secretary Transsylvanus substantiated Corsali's observation that the Portuguese had discovered the Chinese to be "a white-skinned people with an advanced society" "similar to our Germans."[3]

Transsylvanus would not remain the only commentator to believe that he had recognized a particular external similarity between Chinese and Germans. In the first monograph about the Chinese Empire, published in 1569, the Portuguese missionary Gaspar da Cruz determined that, with the exception of the inhabitants on the coast and in the mountains, Chinese females were "very white and graceful women." He also went so far as to make the remarkable assertion that the western border of China reached all the way to Germany, which he presumed to be at the River Don.[4] Accordingly, the first compilers of reports about China describe the north Chinese as white, even to some extent, blond, or even reddish-blond like the Germans. Only the Cantonese were considered to be "brown" or "golden brown" – "like the Berbers," claimed the Spaniard González de Mendoza in 1585, and "like the Spanish," according to the French Jesuit Du Jarric.[5]

At the same time, the first correspondents praised beyond all measure the intellect, the industriousness, and the politeness of the Chinese. They went on in the highest terms about their wealth and political order as well, particularly in Europe itself, where for certain writers China embodied the ideal state of the fairytale Orient.[6]

Critical comments uttered by individual clerics were, of course, not unusual either, especially not when they were dissatisfied with their success as missionaries. In one such case, the "ugliness" of the Chinese, of grown men in particular, is mentioned. The small eyes, flat faces and noses, and the sparse beards did not conform to the beauty ideal of contemporary European visitors.[7] And one critical missionary, the Spaniard Pantoja, maintained that the Chinese were white, but not as white as Europeans.[8] These statements, however, contradict numerous other eyewitnesses in the seventeenth century, such as the Jesuit Superior Alvarez Semedo or Joan Nieuhof, who accompanied the Dutch Embassy to the Peking court in 1655–57. Both expressly mention that the Chinese are as white as the Europeans, with the exception, of course, of the Cantonese.[9] Admittedly, travellers who had only visited Guangdong Province gained a different impression from those who had seen the northern parts of China as well. William Dampier, for example, who in 1687 was cast up on the shore there, spoke of the Chinese population as having an "ashy complexion."[10] Other shades of colour including black were mentioned. Francis Bacon had already referred to the skin of the Chinese as "olive-colored."[11] Any references to a yellowish skin colour, therefore, must be understood in this context, as with an initially unpublished report of an Upper Austrian traveller in the first half of the seventeenth century and in the exposition of a Dutch cleric in the first half of the eighteenth century.[12] These examples, however, remained exceptions. Nevertheless, the reports about the Cantonese having a complexion that as a rule was referred to as "brown" caused the author of the standard eighteenth-century scholarly work on China, the Jesuit Du Halde, to warn his readers in 1735 against drawing the wrong conclusions: "The complexion of their faces is not as described by those who have seen only the Chinese on the coast in the southern provinces. The great heat in these provinces ... gives the craftsmen and the people of the country a dark-olive skin; but in the other provinces they are naturally as white as in Europe."[13]

As a matter of fact, most European eyewitnesses from whom we have printed reports presumed, up until the end of the eighteenth century, that the Chinese, with the exception of the Cantonese, were white.[14]

This was still the scholarly consensus in 1772, when the Paris *Diction-naire universel* described the Chinese as being white-skinned with a pleasant physiognomy.[15]

The inevitable variation in skin colour in the vast Middle Kingdom seemed to Europeans in general completely natural, familiar to them from their own continent with its various shadings of skin colour. The French compiler Du Jarric opined to that end that Chinese children were beautiful, as many of them were as white as the children in Europe, with the understanding that in Canton their skin was like those of the Spanish, whereas in Peking it seemed more like that of the Italian or French children, for he perceived some Spanish to be rather "brownish."[16] The Dutch traveller to India, Jan van Linschoten, saw it no differently.[17]

Although Europeans generally probably considered themselves to be relatively "white," there was no talk of a "white race" among any of the commentators mentioned here. Even at the start of the nineteenth century such an idea had not become commonly accepted, as confirmed by a list apparently drawn up from contemporary documents of the members of Napoleon's Sénat Conservateur. The list contains descriptions of numerous members of this board concerning their body size, hair colour, etc., and, in the case of 104 Senators, the colour of their faces is listed as well. Only two of them are described as "white" (blanc), the most common description mentioned, reported in thirty-five of the cases, is "brown" (brun), immediately followed by "clair" (33 cases). In addition, "basané" (nine times), "ordinaire" (eight times), "brun-clair" (six times), "pale" (five times), "coloré" – in other words, "coloured" (four times) – as well as, finally, in two cases, "blond" are named.[18] If anything, the French at that time would have considered themselves as a "lightly browned race." Yet in the general consciousness such a view seems to have been as unlikely as the existence of a "white" or even "yellow race." Other qualities that would later be called "racial characteristics" were also not generally recognized. In the seventeenth century, Michael Baudier, for example, found an explanation for the flat noses of the Chinese by arguing that they made a point of impressing their children's noses, so that foreigners would be immediately recognizable, thereby allowing the Chinese to defend themselves against their corrupting influence – a protective measure that seemed sensible to Baudier in light of the overall concern to maintain the purity of morals.[19]

Let us recapitulate: not a single traveller from the sixteenth century to the eighteenth century hit upon the idea that the Chinese might have belonged to a "yellow race."[20] That members of other East Asian peoples, in particular "Tartars," would have to be "white" or rather "whiter" than the average Chinese person was a common suggestion.[21] The most widespread explanatory model for the different skin colours was based on the climate theory inherited from antiquity:[22] The Chinese "are completely white," reported Pastor Peter Osbeck, who was inducted into the Swedish Academy of Sciences on account of his trip to China, "the only exceptions are those who are in the sun much of the time and therefore become brown from it."[23] This provided an easy explanation for many authors in the seventeenth century for why a Cantonese farmer was inevitably darker than a Peking mandarin.[24] A yellow taint could thus be perceived as a transitional colour: Jürgen Andersen, a sailor from Schleswig, maintained that Chinese people in the twentieth latitude had dark-brown faces, further north they were yellow, and in the cold north they were "as white as Europeans."[25]

The Formulation of Racial Categories and the Beginnings of Racial Discrimination

Until around 1800 the concept of "race" – whose etymology remains controversial – signified "generation" or "lineage," often in the sense of a "noble descent."[26] As the previous examples have shown, it was common in the sixteenth and evidently still in the seventeenth century to distinguish between white, black, and a wide range of interspersed brown tones.[27] Such a brownish skin, which many Europeans, particularly in countries around the Mediterranean, would have attributed to themselves, initially was of little significance for the value of a person. Nevertheless, members of the "black" race – in the sense of hereditary descent – were increasingly discriminated against since the late Middle Ages.[28] Three factors seem to have played a role: (1) the already existing prejudice against black skin colour; (2) the consequences of slavery; and (3) the ideal of "blood purity" as it was cultivated in the Iberian states.

In the Middle Ages the prejudice against the colour black was connected to the belief that "black" – according to the *Oxford English Dictionary* – was associated with "deeply stained with dirt; soiled, dirty, foul" and in the early modern period with "having dark or deadly purposes, malignant; pertaining to or involving death, deadly," and so forth.[29] Perhaps because of the influence of the Manichean light-darkness duality, the devil has since the early Middle Ages been characterized as the dark opponent to the blinding light surrounding the

Christian God. Earnestness and sadness, as well as mourning, have been associated since the sixteenth century with the colour black. A black list of negatively connotated terms gives us a sense of how deeply the adverse associations with the colour black have penetrated the vocabulary of Europeans: Black Friday, black magic, black sheep, black Peter, a blackened reputation, and not just in German: *dénigrer, noirceur* (in the sense of evil), *negra suerte, negromante*, blackleg, blackmail.[30]

The Christian biblical tradition was not completely uninvolved in painting the colour black black. One explanation that originated at the University of Leiden for the inferiority of the term "Neger" – from the Latin *niger*, as a derogatory word in English, "Nigger," and that quickly spread, was the biblical story of Noah's curse. Earlier already Isidore of Seville had declared Europe as the realm of Noah's son Jafet (Japheth), whom he considered to be the progenitor of Europeans. Accordingly, the Semites, that is, Asians, were descended from Sem and from Ham (Cham), the Hamites, which included the Africans. But Noah had cursed Ham, or more specifically his son Canaan, and asked God if he could find room for Jafet, who was supposed to live in Sem's tents. Canaan, however, should not remain God's servant – which became a justification for enslaving black Africans.[31]

The Christian teaching of discrimination, however, based on genealogy had its built-in limitations. Negroes and Native Americans were, after all, descendants from Adam as well, therefore authentic human beings with a soul, capable of receiving salvation.[32] Set against this doctrine was a teaching that was considered heretical by all confessions in the seventeenth century, namely, the "Pre-Adamites" – beings created before Adam, who were supposed to represent the progenitors of the coloured races. However, this polygenetic hypothesis did not find much approval until about 1800. Initially more successful was the "mark of Cain" doctrine, whereby God punished Cain for the murder of Abel with a black skin and that his descendants – the Negroes – were required to bear the mark of this sin into the present.[33] This doctrine allowed for a formulation of an interpretation loyal to the scriptures while simultaneously avoiding the problems produced by the climate theory, which, in its pure form, could not explain why there were blacks in Africa but not in the tropical regions of the Americas, and why Negro slaves, even after living for generations in northern latitudes, had not turned white.[34]

One thing is certain: that the widespread slavery that existed in the Mediterranean already in the fifteenth century contributed substantially to the emergence of racist, or perhaps better, pre-racist, prejudices.[35] In a feudally structured society it was simply impossible to treat people with a particular skin colour for centuries as slaves, without viewing their external appearance as a sign of inborn inferiority. If earlier prejudices against blacks had led the slave trade to be concentrated on the "black continent,"[36] slavery itself produced a disdain for all Negroids.[37]

European xenophobia and ethnocentrism did not stop at the discrimination against all "blacks," either. During the late Middle Ages the religious campaign against every form of heterodoxy and – in a secondary capacity – the social confrontation with economically influential Jews on the Iberian Peninsula provoked the first "racist" concept: the idea of "blood purity." For the earlier mentioned reasons, nobody in the late Middle Ages who, up until a certain generation back in time, had had a Jewish or Moorish ancestor, could hold public office or be accepted in the feudal corporation. This created a population group that was constantly discriminated against and threatened by the Inquisition, the so-called New Christians, or "Conversos." Baptism alone – whether voluntary or forced – did not alleviate the diminished legal status of this group. Out of religious discrimination there emerged a hereditary one.

Arguments based on descent were, of course, regularly invoked in early modern Europe: the Goth myth in Spain, the legend of the Franks in France, the general justification for the aristocracy's existence based on the assumption of the special quality of their semen, or rather blood[38] – one need only think of "blue blood" – introduced such lines of thought into the social-political discussion. However, this reasoning was used mostly to justify the favoured position of a specific minority. In Spain and Portugal the obsessive search for traces of hereditary "impurity" led directly to the exclusion of an entire section of the population during the fifteenth and sixteenth centuries. Seen from an ethnological perspective this obsession was entirely senseless, as the following anecdote shows. Upon a recommendation from the Inquisition, King Joseph of Portugal contemplated requiring everyone without pure blood to wear a white hat. The next day, his enlightened Minister Pombal arrived with three white hats – one for the king, one for himself, and one for the Grand Inquisitor: "Si non è vero, è ben trovato!"[39]

Even though Pombal eventually eliminated the legal discrimination against so-called impotent or infected races – which in addition to Jews, Moors, and New Christians soon would include blacks and Native Americans, the social discrimination against people of colour in the

colonies was unrestrained. The linguistic similarities of Spanish "mar-
rano," or Portuguese "marrã," that is, pig, swinish, dirty, also meaning
Jewish forced converts, with "marron" (Brazilian, "marrom"), meaning
"brown," might also partially account for their disdainful treatment. In
any case, *mestizo*, or mixed breeds, were rarely considered fit, even for
the military, and seldom reached positions of leadership. People with
darker skin colour were also increasingly discriminated against in the
church as well. In 1517, at the insistence of the Portuguese king, Pope
Leo X still appointed, though with some reluctance, a Congolese prince
educated in Lisbon as a titular bishop. A little over a hundred years
later, when the next non-European was designated a bishop, though of
course only *in partibus infidelium* (in the lands of the unbelievers), this
light-skinned and highly educated, pious Brahman was obscenely and
offensively called a "nigger with a naked ass" by the honourable Jesuit
patriarch of Ethiopia.[40]

Given such racist prejudices the development of a Native priesthood
in other parts of the world proceeded very slowly, in India as well as
in East Africa and the Americas.[41] Even the monastic orders – above
all the Society of Jesus – enacted regulations, already in the sixteenth
century, whereby they refused entry to members of races designated
as unsuitable.[42] At the instigation of the provincial superior Valignano,
Japanese and Chinese, who were after all considered "white," were initially excluded from this edict, even though Valignano himself complained that the Portuguese made a habit of disqualifying these highly
cultivated people as "niggers."[43] There were still Chinese members of
the monastic orders in the seventeenth century, and one of them, the
Dominican Gregorio Lopez (his new name) was also anointed bishop.
He, too, did of course have to fight against prejudices, apparent even in
the praise from a brother monk, who lauded him for his "self-control,
sense of justice and purity, a rare virtue among the Chinese, who are
avaricious by nature." Thus, even in China the development of an
Indigenous priesthood proceeded but slowly.[44]

The idea of "blood purity" that dominated the Iberian Peninsula was
merely one of the first systematic formulations of pre-racist thinking.
According to Charles Ralph Boxer, one of the most outstanding scholars
of the history of European expansion, the feeling of racial superiority
among the Dutch and the English was even more distinct than among
the Spanish and the Portuguese. The Dutch, for example, already introduced numerous restrictions on marriages between members of the
Dutch East India Company (VOC) and coloureds in 1617. However,

with the possible exception of some Japanese and Chinese Buddhists, an Asian woman who married a European lost all respect from her own society, to the extent that the VOC, which was generally uninterested in missionary work, required the woman's conversion to Calvinism.[45]

Prejudices on the European side seem to have formed particularly in places, and at times, when European colonists were in repeated conflicts with Natives. Thus, the settlers of New England had a firm concept of a "Native American" throughout the seventeenth century but not of a "red skin." Following the bloody conflicts with Indigenous tribes, however, terms such as "dark-skinned pagans" came into use.[46] More important still: according to Immanuel Geiss, "around 1680 a self-understanding began circulating among white settlers in the North American English colonies that contrasted the new concept of 'white' against native Americans and forcibly imported (black) slaves."[47] Up until then cultural and religious differences had been key in classifying people around the world, while external features generally played only a secondary role.[48] The inclusion of skin colour as an essential criterion in explaining conflicts marked the first step towards attributing paramount importance to racial viewpoints. The second decisive step did not occur in the colonies but in Europe.

The Beginnings of Race Theories[49]

Around the same time, in the year 1684, a Frenchman, François Bernier, published his *Nouvelle division de la terre*. The widely travelled doctor had visited Persia and India, where he had served as the personal physician of the Great Mogul for a long time, and where he had written his two-volume treatise. Bernier came to recognize the suffering of the people behind the Oriental splendour of the princes and concluded that life back at home, in Paris, was surely still the best, even though he conceded that he had not seen Japan or China yet. Incidentally, towards the end of his life, he became a great admirer of Confucian social morality.[50]

This man, who was critical of but by no means biased against other peoples, came upon the idea, based on his travel experiences, to no longer divide the world into continents, as geographers had been doing for centuries, but rather according to races. Bernier noted that an experienced traveller could often recognize the ethnicity of a person based on external features and that, furthermore, there were primarily four or five human types or races, whose differences were so obvious that they could reasonably serve as a new means of dividing the world.[51]

In the first race, Bernier paired Europeans – with the exception of some Muscovites – with the inhabitants of the north African coast, as well as with those living in the Asian parts of the Ottoman Empire, Persians, Indians, and a large part of South East Asia (including, e.g., Borneo). Although he considered Egyptians and Indians, for example, as "very black or more likely burned brown," he attributed this only to the consequences of the strong sun. Whoever does not set himself out in the sun is no darker than many a Spaniard. While most Indians did have a different facial structure and tended towards a yellow colour, this did not suffice to classify them as a separate race. Otherwise one would have had to do the same for various European peoples as well.

The second race, which is confined to the remainder of Africa, is characterized by black shining skin along with woolly hair. The distribution of the third race stretches across the remainder of South East Asia, as well as East and large portions of Central Asia. Its members are all "truly white," yet possess broad shoulders as a rule, a flat face and nose, and slit eyes. Bernier considered the fourth race to be Laplanders, whereas he cautiously included American Indians with the first race, despite their supposedly olive skin colour and different facial structure, and without addressing the question of their isolated development on their own continent. However, he drew accurate distinctions about the external appearance of Native Cape dwellers and other black Africans.[52] In addition, Bernier also perceived significant differences within the races and found feminine beauty everywhere in the world – admittedly with regional differences.[53]

In other words, the Frenchman undertook his racial divisions based exclusively on the external appearances of the earth's humans without attributing many judgments about them. Skin colour was just one important but by no means the decisive criterion in the process.[54] Some decades later, the Swedish naturalist Linnaeus had a revolutionary impact when he systematically integrated humans into the animal kingdom – whereby he grouped sloth initially with humans. Unlike Bernier, when Linnaeus divided humans up, he followed the traditional geographical continents; *Homo Europaeus albescens – Homo Americanus rubescens – Homo Asiaticus fuscus – Homo Africanus niger* were the terms he used in the third edition of his *Systema Naturae* published in 1740.[55] It is noteworthy that Linnaeus considered the brownish-skinned Native Americans to be "reddish," overlooking the fact that the red colour, which numerous travel reports mentioned, was due solely to the oils or dyes that many tribes used to rub on their skin.[56] In the thirteenth edition of his work (1767), Native Americans eventually even appeared as *rufus* "red," or "fox red." At the same time, at least since the ninth edition (1756), Europeans moved from being *albescens*, of "tending towards whiteness," or "whitish" to becoming *albus*, "white." Asians underwent a more crass transformation. In the third edition, they were still labelled as *fuscus* = dark, dark brown, blackish gold, blackish. They then transformed, like chameleons, into *luridus*, a pale yellow, or simply "yellow." Only their eyes remained *fusci*![57]

How did this astounding transformation come about? Linnaeus does not address the issue. It would certainly not be out of the question that the account published by the French natural historian Buffon in 1749 played a role. Buffon traced the variations of human races back to climate, which, in his understanding, would have had its most obvious impact on skin colour, but also on form and size as well as on the temperament of the different peoples. In addition he could cite other defining influences such as nutrition, customs, or ways of life, and their supposed uniformity, with which he justified the more or less brown skin colour – but not the black of people in the tropical zones – of the many different Native Americans.

Buffon did not presume, as many authors before him had, that human skin colour darkened continuously from the polar regions to the tropics, from a colourless paleness or red to a deep black.[58] The many wild peoples of the north (Lapps, north Tartars, and Eskimos) which he lumped together and labelled as one race, and whose skin colour he described as ranging from brown, or even dark olive to deep black were also distinct by their, in his view, abysmal hideousness, which is why he referred to them all as deformed monstrosities. The somewhat more civilized Tartar race seemed to him a little more beautiful with a slightly lighter skin colour. Buffon doubted that the Chinese were actually a race distinct from the Tartars. Only fundamental difference in character and in morals supported, in his mind, such a distinction. He reinforced this view by citing the reports of various travellers who attributed the different shadings of skin colour among the Chinese – from brown to white – primarily to the prevailing climate. The following explanation is typical for Buffon's conception: the Japanese are so similar to the Chinese that one could speak of them as a single race, they are only more yellow, or browner than them, simply because they live in a more southern climate. Still further south in Indochina, the members of this race, according to Buffon, became increasingly darker, yet despite similar skin colour they are different, in his view, from Malays, who are more closely related to Indians.

Reflecting these differentiations, Buffon discovered as a rule in his observations a parallel between dark skin colour and a corresponding stupidity, or, a lack of civilization. The most beautiful, whitest, and well-formed people, he found naturally in the moderate longitudes, especially in northern India, north Iran, Turkey, and above all in Europe, where the southern Europeans seemed backward compared with the rest of the population. Among the Spanish, "little children are born very white & are very beautiful, but as they get older, their skin colour changes in surprising ways, the air makes them yellow, the sun burns them, and it is easy to recognize a Spaniard from among all the other European nations." Among the Negroes this process goes one or two steps further: "their children are born white, or rather red, like those of other men, but two or three days after they are born, the colour changes, they appear to be a darkish yellow that, little by little, becomes browner, & and on the seventh or eighth day they are all black. One knows that on the second or third day all children have a kind of jaundice; this jaundice has but a temporary effect on white children, and does not leave a mark on their skin; in the case of the Negroes, on the other hand, the jaundice gives the skin an indelible colour that gets blacker and blacker over time."[59]

Implicitly Buffon presumed that skin colour, along with climate, as well as culture and civilization, was organized according to a hierarchy – white, yellow, brown, and black. In the process, "coloured" skin shades were generally an expression of biological degeneration, which went hand in hand with cultural backwardness. Migrations, whether voluntary or forced, also initially did little to alter these circumstances, for Buffon suspected, that that skin colour adapted to its climatic environment only very slowly.[60] Skin colour was, in his eyes, already relatively fixed by descent, though admittedly not in such a manner that every race could be assigned a single, unambiguous colour.

Inspired by Buffon, countless authors worked on developing a race theory over the next decades. There were considerable contradictions, nevertheless, in assessing the various skin colours of individual peoples and the divisions that were extrapolated from them subsequently.[61] Alongside writers who – following the accounts of countless travel writers – distinguished between the light complexion of the northern and the darker complexion of the southern Chinese, there were those who, remarkably, ascribed a more or less uniform skin colour to all

Chinese, or even all Asians for that matter. They just could not agree on the particular skin colour.

The first writer, who discovered a "yellow race" in the context of an overarching race theory, was neither a travel writer like Bernier nor the administrator of a vast curiosity cabinet like Buffon, but rather the German philosopher Immanuel Kant. In his 1775 lecture, "On the Different Races of Humans" (Von den verschiedenen Racen der Menschen), he proved himself, following Buffon, to be a convinced monogeneticist and offered the first clear definition: among the considerable variations of living beings belonging to the same species, he considered those to be a race that remained constant over generations, even after being dislocated into a foreign part of the world, and that produced real hybrids when mixed with other variations of the same species.

Kant believed to have been able to distinguish four such races: (1) whites, which included Europeans, Moors, Arabs, Persians, Turkish-Tartars, and other Asiatic peoples; (2) Negroes, found only in Africa and New Guinea; (3) the Hunnish race, which included various central Asian people, such as the Eleuthes, or Kalmyks; and (4) the Hindostan race living in India. Of all the remaining peoples, such as the inhabitants of Indochina or the Chinese, he surmised were mere "half-races," including hybrids between Indians, old Scythians, and Huns, or in the case of Native Americans, an "emerging race," that is, a Hunnish people who had not yet completely adapted to the American climate. Skin colour, Kant believed, was determined by the effect of climate on human blood: the red-brown of Native Americans was the effect of the acid air in the cold land of their origin, the olive yellow of Indians was a result of the gall secretion that was produced as a result of the dry heat and had entered the blood, a kind of permanent jaundice. Kant saw the generative stock of the species as originary white-skinned humans with brunette hair from the moderate latitudes with a favourable climate. He considered highly blond north Europeans, copper red Native Americans, black Senegambians, and olive yellow Indians to be degenerative descents produced by the combined influences of air temperature and humidity.[62] Ten years later in his "Determination of the Concept of a Human Race" (Bestimmung des Begriffs einer Menschenrace), these ideas were developed further, although modified as concerns the division of races. If a Moor, that is, a Mauritanian, grew up in a room and a Creole in Europe, Kant claimed, they would be indistinguishable from the inhabitants of our continent, because – in contrast to a Senegambian – they belonged to the white race. For Kant, there were "with certainty no more hereditary differences in skin colour than these: the white, the yellow Indians [from India], the Negroes and the copper-coloured, red Americans." The "yellow" people, as he literally named them, therefore did not live in East Asia, but rather on the Indian subcontinent. Kant seemed now no longer quite certain when it came to the Mongols, whom he had previously referred as "Huns," whether they should be classified as a separate race or simply as a variation of the whites. The distinctiveness of Mongols concerns "actually only the form," he remarked, "not the skin colour, which all previous experience has taught us is the inevitable feature of racial characteristics." He remained convinced, however, that the Chinese emerged from a mixing of Mongols "with southern peoples (presumably Indians)."[63]

From this it followed that the Chinese could no longer be all white, they had to have something yellowish about themselves. The influential racial theorist Johann Friedrich Blumenbach, a Göttingen professor of medicine known as the "father of anthropology," came to the same conclusion. Like Kant, Blumenbach had begun his research on the matter in 1775 with his *Dissertatio inauguralis de generis humani varietate nativa*. Four years later, in the first edition of his *Natural History Handbook*, he identified five races: the original and largest race comprised, according to his claims, all Europeans including Laplanders and Eskimos, North Africans, and Asians, west of the Ob, Caspian Sea, and the Ganges. "All these peoples have, by and large, a white colour," Blumenbach stated, "and, according to our concept of beauty, have the best form." The members of the second race consisted of the other inhabitants of the Asian mainland and are "mostly yellow brown." The remaining three races were organized as follows: Africans were characterized as "black," the Americans as "copper red," and the people on the South Asian islands, Australians, and Polynesians as "blackish brown."[64]

Blumenbach was initially careful with his judgments. He did not claim that all members of a particular race possessed the same skin colour, nor that there existed a generally valid aesthetic standard according to which the various peoples could be judged. He also emphasized that his theory was based on ideal types that stood in contrast to the countless gradations of individual skin colour in reality.[65] Nevertheless, the more he elaborated his theory, the more he believed that his own interpretation provided a successful synthesis of all previous theories on what produced the variations in human skin colour: if Buffon, for example, had stressed the influence of climate; Kant, qualities in the blood; and others still, the effects of the organs, especially the liver, then Blumenbach had combined them, to the extent that he asserted that liver diseases were much more common in the tropics. He also asserted that the children of Europeans who were born in India had a bilious constitution and shape. Through this type of reasoning, yellow skin colour was turned into a type of degeneration. Blumenbach suspected, after all, that "given that jaundice, even with the many forms of the disease, frequently colours the skin to different degrees, and given that the skin of coloured people is remarkably similar, this could be a permanent consequence of having once survived the illness."[66]

In this sense, he viewed the whites, whom he classified as "Caucasians," as the original race, from which extremes degenerated, on the one hand, the Mongol and, on the other hand, the Ethiopians, while the Americans and Malaysians were represented as transitional races. Blumenbach's statements about these five races became increasingly unambiguous and apodictic, in tandem perhaps with the growing agreement of his contemporaries. In the fifth edition of his *Handbook*, he writes laconically that the Caucasian race is "of a white colour," in the eleventh edition from 1825, it is of "more or less white in colour" – but no longer "mostly of a white colour." In contrast, the Mongol race is, according to the later editions, "mostly wheat yellow" (somewhat like cooked quince or dried lemon peel)[67] – only "mostly," of course, but through its "yellowish" tone it distinguished this race from Indians, who are described as "tawny or cinnamon brown," as well as from the "brown" Malaysians, or even the sun-tanned whites.

Every race is thereby standardized into a typology. This reflects the obsessive creation of categories in the eighteenth century. Linnaeus, for example, had already brought elements from the ancient theory of the four temperaments in relation to his "racial classification": *Americanus rufus, cholericus, rectus … pertinax, contentus, liber* (American red, choleric, righteous; black, straight … stubborn, zealous, free), *Europaeus albus, sanguineus, torosus … levis, argutus, inventor* (European white, sanguine, brawny … gentle, acute, inventive), *Asiaticus luridus, melancholicus, rigidus … severus, fastuosus, avarus* (Asian yellow, melancholic, stiff … severe, haughty, greedy), *Africanus niger, phlegmaticus, laxus … vafer, segnis, negligens* (African black, phlegmatic, relaxed … crafty, sly, careless).[68] *Völkertafeln* (charts of nations), on which various peoples were organized schematically by specific traits had become quite popular. Important philosophers contributed significantly to the construction of such typologies as well.[69] As much as David Hume warned at the start of his essay, "Of National Characters," against taking the concept of "national character" too far and ascribing to each individual the qualities of his nation, he nevertheless insisted that, in general, the Swiss were more honest than the Irish, the English better educated than the Danes. He also considered it appropriate to draw such distinctions about the character and abilities of the various races: "I am apt to suspect the negroes, and in general all the other species of men (for there are four or five different kinds) to be naturally inferior to the whites. There never was a civilized nation of any other complexion than white."[70] Kant wrote similarly, "The Spaniard is earnest, reserved, and honest," and "The Frenchman has an overwhelming feeling for moral beauty. He is polite, courteous and pleasing," yet he also wrote with direct reference to Hume: "The negroes of Africa have no natural feeling that rises beyond foolishness," which is why their difference from whites "is just as great with regard to mental capacities as it is in terms of colour." As he wrote in an early essay, "this guy was black from his head to his feet, a clear indication that everything he said was stupid." Orientals also fared badly in his comparison of the aesthetic feelings inherent to the individual nations: only the Europeans understood how to sublimate their sexual urges, claimed the lifelong bachelor philosopher of Königsberg, Orientals in contrast had no concept of the morally beautiful.[71]

Membership in a race or a nation became – though surely not without internal disagreements[72] – one of the decisive foundations that explained the intellect and emotions, as well as character. In regard to the Chinese, most travel writers, with a few more nuanced views,[73] had always marvelled at the uniformity of the ruling order, culture, and life forms in this vast kingdom. The well-regarded "China specialist," Abbé Grosier claimed, for example, in 1785: "Wander through the various provinces of France; you will find in each one individual nuances, character traits, that distinguish the diverse inhabitants ... Wander through the Chinese Empire: everything will appear to you as if cast in the same melting pot and poured into the same form."[74]

On account of such reports, David Hume, who traced the development of national character back to "moral" (in the sense of cultural and socio-economic) rather than to "physical" conditions, could declare triumphantly: "the Chinese have the greatest uniformity of character imaginable: though the air and climate in different parts of those vast dominions, admit of very considerable variations."[75] Georg Christoph Lichtenberg was not much different when he lamented, "heads and opinions all turned by the same lathe, everything the same, everywhere. With their little wax drop in the middle of their faces, they glide by sentences that bring us with our hooked and peaked noses to a halt a hundred times. If the command came from above: $2 \times 5 = 13$, then it became $2 \times 5 = 13$ from the Great Wall to Guangdong."[76] That such people could not possess an attractive appearance was considered self-evident in an age in which the Swiss Lavater sought to examine the relationship between character and physiognomy.[77] And thus, presumably with an ironic jab at Lavater, Lichtenberg portrays a Chinese mandarin in the following manner: "His face seemed sculpted from meerschaum and had almost that same colour, only a little more greenish, you could see his nose only if he sat in profile ... Whereby he only rarely looked at us with his softly slit pig eyes."[78]

There can be no doubt that those who held the Chinese in high regard classified them generally as "white," and those who looked down on them usually considered them as in some way "coloured."[79] Travellers in the sixteenth and seventeenth centuries, and those who worked with their reports, did not hesitate to classify the Chinese, in large part, as "white," because they saw the Chinese people as standing on the same cultural level if not higher.[80] Sixteenth-century authors such as Jean Bodin assumed a heliotropic movement of culture from east to west, and according to the impressions of the earliest China visitors, the Middle Kingdom exceeded both in terms of wealth and urbanity what anyone had seen in Europe.[81] In the seventeenth century Europeans came to learn more about and appreciate China's political system, and its moral and social philosophy. In this regard it was no coincidence that the admirer of China Leibniz represented two "middle" races in his racial organization, namely – in modern terms – Europide and Sinoide (Chinalike), in contrast to the other two races of humans, the Negro and Laplander, which he considered climatically conditioned degenerations.[82]

Montesquieu saw things already a little differently. In keeping with his exposition in *The Spirit of the Laws*, China was, like other Asian empires, an example of Oriental despotism – a charge that weighed all the more heavily as the critique of Absolutism spread through Europe. Montesquieu considered the Chinese to be the most deceptive people on earth.[83] And without invoking any racial theory, he asks himself in his then still unpublished "Thoughts": "if the yellow nations of Asia should spread themselves out across Europe, what would become of us?"[84]

Kant had as low a regard as Montesquieu of the character and the supposedly "Tartar shape" of the Chinese and that he did not consider them to be fully white was easily explained, given that his "Physical Geography," published in 1802, contained a clear judgment: "Humanity attains its greatest completion in the race of the whites. The yellow Indians already have a lower talent. The Negroes are far lower and at the lowest end are some of the American tribes."[85]

As regards the Göttingen professor Blumenbach, his colleagues included not only the famous historian and Enlightenment publicist August Ludwig Schlözer, who called China "the dumbest kingdom in the world,"[86] but also the philosopher Christoph Meiners, who in his *Foundation of the History of Mankind* proudly announced his new groundbreaking insight that the human species consisted of two main branches, the original white Caucasian and the original brown Mongol, and "that the latter is not only much weaker in body and spirit, but also much more evil and immoral than the Caucasian." The Mongol branch, which, according to his view, deserved "rightly to be called the ugliest," included also the Chinese. The "lack of genius" did not appear to be as fully formed among the Chinese as among the Burats of Siberia, which is why Meiners allowed that the Chinese were at least a "half Enlightened Nation."[87]

In the eighteenth century the Chinese were denied the predicate "white," because they were no longer considered to be cultural equals. If one believed in a necessary connection between skin colour and racial or national character, on the one hand, as well as in a cultural hierarchy from white Europeans down to black Africans, on the other, then every darker tone of skin had to reflect a cultural and characterologically inferior position. The inverse also held true: whoever did not attain the standard of the "progressive nations of Europe" could not also be white. The persecution of Christians in China starting in 1720, the fact that the Imperial court confined the growing European-Chinese trade exclusively to the southern harbour city of Canton, and the not always peaceful relations between Europeans and Chinese living in Manila and Batavia might have contributed to this darkened image of China as well.[88] Even though the ever declining number of missionaries in the country and the members of the individual European embassies overwhelmingly held to the view that the Chinese overall were light-skinned, over time the stories told by merchants and sailors who knew only Canton strengthened the impression that the Chinese were darker.

But why then did the Chinese not become "brown"? Linnaeus had after all characterized them originally as "dark," Blumenbach still used "brown-yellow" to describe them, and yet both in the end switched over to "yellow, pale yellow" or "wheat yellow?"

There is only one common denominator between the many divergent reports: they were looking for a colour between "brown" and "white." Enter the theory that, depending on natural tendency and local conditions, skin colouring induced by newborn infant jaundice would vary and could be weaker or stronger. Still the views on Chinese culture remained ambivalent: as much as it might seem to lag behind contemporary European culture, one could hardly deny its superiority when measured by the standard of other nations, nor reject the antiquity of its cultural history. Putting forward the new concept of progress, Hegel revived the old topos of a heliotropic movement of culture, which was now understood differently: while the Orient once had been the cradle of human culture, it was the West that recently had taken over the leading role. Accordingly, Hegel and Herder considered Chinese culture to be stuck in a childhood stage.[89] The Rotteck-Welckersche 1848 *Staatslexikon* made the same point when it stated: "China has no history, at least not in the usual sense."[90] In this manner, even the Indians, whose ancient culture had just been discovered by Europeans, became "yellow" for Kant – just like the Chinese – as a means of setting them apart from the more or less cultureless races.

Racist models of interpretation neatly served to explain the contradiction between contemporary primitivity and past cultural accomplishment with lingering echoes. In the middle of the nineteenth century, Arthur de Gobineau's judgment of the "yellow races" was extraordinarily harsh: "This race is generally speaking small. The structure of these people's limbs, the power of their muscles, are completely unlike what we see in whites. They are short and stocky, without beauty or grace, somewhat grotesque and, frequently, even hideous. In their physiognomy nature used but little design, just a few lines to trace the essential: a nose, a mouth, small eyes thrown into large, flat faces. These rudimentary disdainful lines seem to be hastily drawn. Clearly the Creator meant to sketch but a rough draft ... as to their intellectual qualities, they are just as odd ... a complete lack of imagination, a unique tendency to satisfy their bodily functions, much tenacity but which is then applied to down-to-earth or ridicules ideas ... little or no pursuits, no inquisitiveness." This race, originally emerging from the Americas had, according to Gobineau, settled in China among other places, where they had mixed with the Negroes in the south spreading northwards – an apparent attempt to explain the darker skin colour of southern Chinese. However, the first creators of Chinese culture, Gobineau claimed, still had been members of the white race, just like the Malaysian mixture of yellow and black races, had been civilized by the Aryans.[91] As an extension of these ideas, the influential German race theorist Ludwig Schemann still asserted at the end of the Weimar period, that the truly profound guiding principles of Chinese culture could not possibly have issued from Mongol brains, hence Aryan creative energy must have been the driving force here as well.[92]

As for the attribution of skin colour, it may be significant that for Europeans – as the colour psychologist Ingrid Riedel explains – "yellow tends particularly towards ambivalence" – something that Goethe concluded in his *Colour Theory* as well. A cold, harsh yellow with murky green undertones releases negative associations, even fear, and serves therefore as a warning symbol: from the yellow plague flag to its use in today's street traffic. Yellow, with which medieval prostitutes as well as Jews were marked, symbolized both shame and a certain protective function. A warm sunny yellow, that is, a kind of "golden," on the other hand, symbolized noble dignity, and indicated even heavenly spheres. When applied to skin colour, yellow means, to again quote Ingrid Riedel the following: "'The yellow,' a collective term for the far eastern races, above all the Chinese, has become in our consciousness a symbol for high intelligence, a will to survival, a toughness, above all a spiritual wisdom. Fear and envy are mixed in it as well when Europeans speak among themselves of the 'yellow peril': in this context the negative symbolism of yellow suggests cruelty, opacity, slit-eyedness and mendacity, along with the huge expansiveness of their numerical superiority."[93]

These ambivalent European perceptions, which hardly were captured in the colour symbolism of the fairly inexpressive "brown," were met by the Chinese, who understood themselves as a "yellow" people – admittedly in a completely different sense than European race theorists. "Whenever I think back on my childhood," wrote the last Emperor, Pu Yi, in his autobiography, "a yellow veil is covering my memories: The enamelled roof tiles were yellow; the sedans were yellow, the lining of my clothes and hats, the belt around my hips were yellow; the bowls and plates, from which I ate and drank were yellow ... there was nothing around me that was not yellow. This colour, the so-called 'gleaming gold,' was an exclusive privilege of the Imperial family and from an early age it made me aware that I was something extraordinary and possessed a 'heavenly' nature."[94] The great initiator of civilization in China was the mythological "Yellow Emperor," and Chinese culture is known to have emerged in the area around the "Yellow River." It is then no coincidence that, for the Chinese, the centre of the world, namely, the Middle Kingdom, had been traditionally combined with yellow in their colour mythology, whereas the north had been associated with black, the east with green, the south with red, and, very conveniently, the west with white. These colours reflected, at least approximately, not only the colours of the heavenly kings that watched over these horizons, but also the shadings of the people living there.[95] These Chinese colour symbols became known in Europe through the Jesuit Amiot who lived in Peking towards the end of the eighteenth century. Race theorists, such as the Frenchman Topinard, and the German Schemann, made direct references to them.[96] There is much to suggest, in other words, that the European as well as the Chinese colour symbolism contributed to the designation of the Chinese as the "yellow race," once they had been classified as "not-white" on account of their cultural inferiority.

If one were to look at the changes in the European perspective on Chinese skin colour, and then chart how these unfolded over time, one would get the impression that the newly emerging discipline of anthropology made little progress in firmly settling on racial criteria.[97] More recently, some authors have rejected the race concept altogether as unscientific and have pointed out that even the anthropologists of the nineteenth and twentieth centuries were never in agreement over which features were necessary to determine a race and which were not.[98] If we take, for instance, Topinard's comparisons of body weight, then Bavarians ought to be more closely related to black people than to Hungarians. That same, at the time well-regarded, anthropologist also boldly claimed that Bernier had already distinguished between Laplanders, white Europeans, black Africans, and yellow Asians. Topinard borrows Bernier's divisions, while replacing the Laplanders with red Americans, though he acknowledges that already among Europeans there are significant variations between the brown tones (south of the Loire) and the rose tint (in Scandinavia), and that there are even more variations of supposed yellow among Asians, some of which cannot be distinguished from white, whereas others appear more as an olive green or brown.[99]

Is race a mere myth? One should not throw the baby out with the bathwater. The author of this essay, for instance, has never been taken for an East Asian or a black African. There are unquestionably external differences, some of which are – *cum grano salis* – even of a collective nature. Historical experience with countless race theories has shown, however, that three things cannot be delivered by such distinctions: (1) They cannot provide a meaningful ideal type of one race or the other, because in order to do so, one must acknowledge upon which criteria they are based and which subjects are being considered. This is why modern anthropology feels itself compelled, to use the methods of serology to undertake statistical investigations, which are no longer based on ideal types but rather on reproductive communities, focusing on the distribution of the few differing genes, that are responsible for the external appearances of humans.[100] (2) Drawing any conclusions based on external appearances about the character and intelligence is so thoroughly problematic that it is not appropriate as a starting assumption for any scientific investigation. (3) Anthropology can never arrive at a hierarchy for external or internal human qualities, because it does not possess a universally acceptable standard – for beauty, for example. In this sense, Buffon was correct when he wrote: "in natural history all systematic distributions have their inadequacies, it simply is a matter of how many ... all methods of this type are arbitrary conventions that do not depend on nature or on reason, but only on the convenience and the motivation of those using a particular method," and a little later again, "these methods are but convenient conventions that are modified when needed, by multiplying the conditions as many times as there are singularities in nature, so that these determine the method."[101]

To summarize: The belief, which dates back to Blumenbach and continues to appear in some schoolbooks today, that there are five races, distinguishable through their skin colour, is untenable.[102] The existence of a "yellow race" has never been demonstrated convincingly. It surely is no coincidence that, for the period 1911–81, there is under this subject heading but one reference to be found ... in the catalogue of the Staatsbibliothek in Munich, the largest library in the German-speaking world. In the newer catalogue, beginning in 1981, the subject heading ... has disappeared altogether.

The yellow race did not originate in the wide spaces of Asia, but was invented in the narrow rooms, or to be more precise, in the brains of

European scholars. If from there – as it appears – it might someday disappear, no one would regret the loss. However, that will still take a considerable amount of time.

Translation by Bettina Brandt and Daniel Purdy

NOTES

1 Originally published in German as "Wie die Chinesen gelb wurden: Ein Beitrag zur Frühgeschichte der Rassentheorien," *Historische Zeitschrift*, 255/3 (1992): 625–66. The translation published here is slightly abridged.
2 Letter dated 6 Jan. 1515, in Gian Battista Ramusio, *[Delle] Navigationi et Viaggi*, vol. 1, 3rd ed. (Venice 1563, reprint Amsterdam: Theatrum Orbis Terrarum, 1970), 180 [incorrectly printed as 280]): "gli huomini sono molto industriosi, & di nostra qualità, ma di piu brutto viso, con gli occhi piccolo." See also Nigel Cameron, *Barbarians and Mandarins: Thirteen Centuries of Western Travelers in China* (New York: Walker, 1970), 132ff; Donald F. Lach, *Asia in the Making of Europe* (Chicago: University of Chicago Press, 1965–77), vol. 1/2, 731n3.
3 Letter dated 24 Oct. 1522, in Simon Grynaeus, ed., [Joannis Hutichij], *Novus orbis regionum ac insularum veterbibus incognitarum*, 2nd ed. (Basel, 1537), 586: "candidam gentem et ciuilem satis reperunt, Germanis nostris simile." See Walter Demel, "Antike Quellen und die Theorien des 16. Jahrhunderts zur Frage der Abstammung der Chinesen: Überlegungen zu einem frühneuzeitlichen Diskussionsthema," *Saec* 37 (1986): 199–211, here 204–5; Lach, *Asia*, vol. 1/2, 172.
4 Gaspar da Cruz, *Tractado em que se côtam muito por estêso as cousas da China* (Evora, 1569), 18ff, 85: "As molheres comunmente, tirando as do longo do mar & as dos montes, sam muito aluas & gentis molheres" (The women generally, excepting those from along the sea and from the mountains, are very white and gracious women). See also, Lach, *Asia*, vol. 1/2, 752. The assumption that China borders on Germany was also held by Gaspar Barzeu, as is shown in his letters to Ignatius Loyola, dated 16 Dec. 1551 and 1 Jan. 1553 (Antonio da Silva Rego, ed., *Documentação para a história das missões do padroado português do Oriente: India* [Lisbon, Agência Geral do Ultramar, 1952], vol. 7, 83, 172.
5 Pierre Du Jarric, *L'Histoire des choses les plus mémorables advenvës tant és Indes Orientales ...* (Valenchienne, 1611), 732ff (compare with the quote in n15 below); Carlos Sanz, ed., *Primera historia de China de Bernardino de*

Escalante [Seville, 1577] (Madrid: Victoriano Suarez, 1958): The Cantonese are described as "baços como los de Berberia" (31), whereas the Chinese living further north are "blancos y ruuios, como en Alemania" (white and blond, like in Germany) (42); the inhabitants of the southern coast are "amoriscados, como los de Fez y Marruecos" (like the Moors of Fez or the Barbery Coast); and the remainder are like the Spanish, Italians, and Germans – "blancos y ruuidos y de buenas disposiciones" (white and blond, and of good dispositions). Similarly, Juan González de Mendoza, *Historia de las cosas más notables, ritos y costumbres del gran reino de la China* [1585], edited by Felix Garcia (España misionera, vol. 2) (Madrid: Aguilar, 1944), 23, 38: The inhabitants of tropical Canton are brown skinned ("morenos" or "amoriscados") just like other people on the same geographical latitude such as the Moors of Fez or from the Berber Coast. The Chinese living in the interior, on the other hand, are "del color de alemanes, italianos y españoles, blancos y rubios [blond, golden yellow with perhaps a touch of red], y un poco verdinegros [deep dark green!]" One significant methodological problem this essay faces is the difficulty of translating foreign colour designations adequately.

6 Walter Demel, "Abundantia, Sapientia, Decadencia – Zum Wandel des Chinabildes vom 16. bis zum 18. Jahrhundert," in Urs Bitterli and Eberhard Schmitt, eds., *Die Kenntnis beider "Indien" im frühneuzeitlichen Europa* (Akten der Zweiten Sektion des 37. deutschen Historikertages in Bamberg, 1988, Munich 1991), 129–53. A shortened version appears in *Sino-Western Cultural Relations Journal* 9 (1989): 28–37.

7 Charles Ralph Boxer, ed., *South China in the Sixteenth Century* (Works of the Hakluyt Society, 2nd Ser., No. 106) (London: Hakluyt, 1953), 282. Report from Martin de Rada; da Cruz, *Tractado*, 76. Mendoza, incidentally, passes over these comments by his sources in silence.

8 Diego de Pantoja, *Carta del Padre – ... para el Padre Luys de Guzmã Prouincial en la Prouincia de Toledo: Su fecha de Pequin ... a nueue de Março de mil y seyscientos y dos años* (Seville, 1605), 78: "son comunmente todos blãcos, aunq' no tãto como los de Europa."

9 Alvaro Semmedo [a.k.a. Alvarez Semedo], *Imperio de la China i cvltvra evangelica en èl, por los Religiosos de la Compañia de IESVS*, edited by M[anuel] de Faria i Sousa (Madrid, 1642), 34: "La Gente de la China es blanca, assi como la de nuestra Europa; aunque en la Provincia de Cantam, por quedarle alguna parte debaxo del Tropico, se vè el color algo Moreno" (People in China are white, like those of our Europe; although in the Cantonese Province, which falls under the tropical part, their colour looks rather darker). Joan Nieuhof, *Het Gezantschap Der Neêrlandtsche Oost-Indische*

Compagnie, aan den grooten tartarischen Cham, Den tegenwoordigen Keizer van China ... (Amsterdam, 1665), part. 2, 56: white skin colour, "gelyk d'Europers," only in the south is it browner, and except for the population in certain provinces, the facial features are similar to those of Europeans as well. Giovanni Francesco Gemelli Careri, *Giro del Mondo* (Naples, 1700), vol. 4, 364: "Il color de' Cinesi è bianco, como quello degli Europei."

10 William Dampier, *A New Voyage round the World* (London, 1697), 407.

11 James Spedding, Robert Leslie Ellis, and Douglas Denon Heath, eds., *The Works of Francis Bacon*, 14 vols. (London, 1857–1874; reprint ed. Stuttgart-Bad Cannstatt: Frommann, 1963), here vol. 2, 577: "being olivaster." *Historische Verhael / Vande treffelijcke Reyse, gedaen ... door ... Cornelis Matelief de longe [1605–1608]*, in Isaac Commelin, ed., *Begin ende Voortgangh van de Vereenighde Nederlantsche Geoctroyeerde Oost-Indische Compagnie*, 2 vols., 2nd ed. (no location given, 1646; reprint ed. Amsterdam: Theatrum Orbis Terrarum, 1970), here vol. 2, 95: The Chinese on the coast "zÿn Swarte als die van Fez in Africa" (are black like those of Fez in Africa) otherwise "meesten deel witte / d'een doch meer als d'andere/ na datse deun aen de couwe Lan den ghebooren zÿn: want daar zÿn sommige die den Spanjaert ghelÿck zÿn/ andere den Duytschen / zÿnde wat blondt ende roodt" (most are white/though some more than others/given that some were born in cold countries: because there some are similar to the Spanish/others similar to the Dutch/being a bit blond and red). Daniello Bartoli, *Dell'Historia della Compagnia di Giesu, Terza parte dell'Asia: La Cina* (Rome, 1668), 22: The Chinese in the south are described as being "aliquanto piu vliuigno" (somewhat more olive-tinged) than those in the north as lighter.

12 François Valentyn, *Oud en Nieuw Oost Indien*, 5 vols. (Dordrecht/Amsterdam, 1724–26), here vol. 2, 258: The Chinese inhabitants of Ambon Island are "niet blank, maar uyt den bruyngeelen, en bleek; hoewel die gene, die om de Noord in China gebooren zyn, in blankheit niet veel van ons verschillen" (not white but more a brownish-yellow and pale; though those who were born in the north of China don't differ much in whiteness from us). The Chinese in the South are pale yellow ("bleekgeel"). Karl Rudolf Wernhart, *Christoph Carl Fernberger, Der erste Österreichische Weltreisende (1621–1628)* (Vienna: Europäischer Verlag, 1972), 3ff, quote on 124–5: "von persohn sein sie ein wenig gelb" (they are a little yellow in their personage). See also, Arnoldus Montanus, *Denckwürdige Gesandtschafften der Ost-Indischen Gesellschaft in den Vereinigten Niederländern / an unterschiedliche Keyser von Japan* (Amsterdam, 1670), 52: The inhabitants of the Japanese harbour city Nagasaki "are white compared with other Indian

peoples, however, yellow and without lively colours, when compared with Europeans."

13 Jean Baptiste Du Halde, *Description géographique, historique, chronologique, politique, et physique de l'empire de la Chine et de la Tartarie chinoise*, 4 vols. (Paris, 1735), here vol. 2, 80: "La couleur de leur visage n'est pas telle que nous le disent ceux qui n'ont vu de Chinois, que sur les côtes des Provinces Méridionales. A la vérité, les grandes chaleurs qui regnent dans ces Provinces ... donnent aux Artisans & aux gens de la campagne, un teint basané & olivâtre; mais dans les autres Provinces, ils sont naturellement aussi blancs qu'en Europe" (The colour of their face is not as those say who have only seen the Chinese on the shores of the Southern Provinces. In truth, the great heat prevailing in these provinces ... give craftsmen & people of the countryside, a swarthy and olive-coloured complexion; but in the other provinces, they are naturally as white as in Europe).

14 See, e.g., the quote from St Francis Xavier in Cameron, *Barbarians*, 150; Pedro Morejón, *Historia y relación de lo svcedido en los reinos de Iapon y China, ... desde el año de 615 hasta el de 19* (Lisbon, 1621), 104: "gente blanca" (white people); Nicolaus Trigautius, ed., *De Christiana Expeditione apud Sinas Suscepta ab Societate Iesu, Ex P. Matthaei Riccij Commentarijs*, book V (Augustae Vind., 1615), 65: "Sinica gens ferè albi coloris est, nam nonnulli è prouincijs ob vicinitatem zonae torridae subfusci sunt" (Chinese people are almost white, but some provinces because of the closeness from the torrid zones are dark). Letter of the Franciscan Paolo da Gesù to Pope Gregory XIII about the Chinese, whom he had seen primarily in Canton: "sono di color bianco" (they are white); qtd. in Marcellino da Civezza, *Storia universale delle Missioni Francescane*, vol. 7/2 (Prato, 1891), 899. Martino Martini, *De bello tartarico historia*, 3rd ed. (Cologne, 1654), 19: Tartars like the Chinese "albo colore" (of white colour); Henri de Feynes, *Voyage facit par terre depuis Paris jusques à la Chine* (Paris, 1630), 164, calls the skin of the Chinese "fort blanc" (very white); and along the same lines, Samuel Purchas, *Haklvytvs Posthumus or Purchas his Pilgrimes*, 4 vols. (London, 1625), vol. 3, 410: "very white." In the same manner, the compiler, Johann Christoph Wagner, *Das mächtige Kayser = Reich Sina / und die Asiatische Tartarey ...* (Augsburg, 1688), 139: Chinese women are "in general exceedingly beautiful, charming and graceful ... with white skin and brown eyes."

15 *Dictionnaire universel, historique et critique des moeurs ... des Peuples des quatre Parties du Monde*, 4 vols. (Paris, 1772), here vol. 1, 251: "le teint blanc et la phisionomie agréable & qui respire la gaieté."

16 Du Jarric, *L'Histoire*, 732–3: "Les enfants en leur bas âge sont fort beaux, & gentils: car beaucoup d'iceux sont aussi blancs que ceux d'Europe:

tellement qu'en la Prouince de Canton, ils sont de mesme couleur que les Espagnoles: & tant plus qu'on monte en hault vers le Septentrion, ils sont aussi plus blancs; de façon que à Paquin [Peking], ils rasemblent fort aux Italiens, ou aux François" (Children in their earliest years are very beautiful, & kind: because many are as white as those of Europe, so that in the Province of Guangzhou, they are the same colour as the Spanish: & the more that one goes up higher northwards, they are also more white, so that at Paquin [Peking] they resemble strongly Italians, or French). As adults the Chinese turned ugly.

17 Jan Huygen van Linschoten, *Itinerario: Voyage ofte schipvaert van – naer oost ofte Portuaels Indien, 1579–1592*, 2nd ed., edited by Heert Terpstra, vol. 1 (*Werken uitgegeven door de Linschoten-Vereenigen*, vol. 57) (The Hague: Martinus Nijhoff, 1955), 101: On the South coast, in the territory of Macau and Canton, "is het volck van coluer bruijnachtigh, ghelijck die witte Mooren in Africa ende Barbaria, ende eensdeels die Spaengiaerden; maer die van binnen in 't landt zijn ghelijck die Neerlanders ende Hooghduytschen, te weten van coluer" (the people are of a brownish colour, like the white Moors in Africa and in the Barbery coast, and also somewhat like the Spanish; but inside the country they are similar to the Dutch and the Germans in colour).

18 Léonce de Brotonne, *Les Sénateurs du Consulat et de l'Empire: Tableau historique des pairs de France (1789–1814–1848) – Les Sénateurs du Second Empire* (Paris, 1895; Geneva, 1974), 1–53.

19 Michael Baudier, *Historie de la cour du Roy de la Chine* (Paris, 1631), 10.

20 "In the history of ideas, it is noteworthy that, although there existed a wide range of travel literature, one cannot find a single use in any lexicon of the term 'race' in an anthropological context before the end of the eighteenth century." Werner Conze and Antje Sommer, "Rasse," in *Geschichtliche Grundbegriffe, Historisches Lexikon zur politische-sozialen Sprache in Deutschland*, eds. Otto Brunner, Werner Conze, and Reinhard Koselleck (Stuttgart: Klett-Cotta, 1985), vol. 5, 135–78, here 141.

21 See Nieuhof, *Gezantschap*, part 2, 188; Joseph Francois Charpentier Cossigny, *Voyage à Canton* (Paris, 1799), 280; Diogo de Couto, *Da Asia de – *, 14 vols. (Lisbon, 1778–88), vol. 2/2 (Dec. V, liv. VIII, cap. XII), 266: The Japanese are described as "homens mais alvos, que os Chins" (men whiter than the Chinese).

22 According to John Pollock, in *The Black Feet of the Peacock: The Color-Concept "Black" from the Greeks through the Renaissance* (New York: University Press of America, 1985), 219ff, already Herodotus had named two theories for the formation of black skin colour: either the semen were black or blackness was determined by climate – which can be recognized in the literal

meaning of Aithiops as sunburned. Aristotle rejected the first explanation, and medieval authorities (such as Isidore of Seville, Bartholomeus, Albertus Magnus) followed this line. In the literature about the first explorations, and their reception, one finds the idea that black skin colour is generally derived from the environmental influences.

23 Peter Osbeck, *Reise nach Ostindien und China, Nebst O. Toreens Reise nach Surate and C.G. Ekebergs Nachricht von der Landwirthschaft der Chineser* (Rostock, 1765), 219.

24 See the letter of the Austrian missionary Laimbeckhoven to his mother dated 14 Sept. 1741, in *Neuer Welt-Bott ... Allerhand So Lehr- als Geist-reiche Brief, Schriften und Reis-Beschreibungen: Welche von denen Missionariis der Gesellschaft Jesu aus beyden Indien ... angelangt seynd*, eds. Joseph Stöcklein, Peter Probst, and Franz Keller (Augsburg, 1728) vol. 5/1, 34, 37. George Staunton, *An Authentic Account of an Embassy from the King of Great Britain to the Emperor of China ... taken chiefly from the papers of ... the Earl of Macartney ...* (London, 1797), vol. 1, 47.

25 Adam Olearius, ed., *Des Welt-berühmten /... / colligirte und viel vermehrte / Reise-Beschreibungen /... / Wie auch Johann Albrecht Mandelslo / Morgenländischen und Jürg Andersens und Volq. Yversens Orientalischen Reise / Mit angehängter Chinesischen Revolution ...* (Hamburg, 1696), 105. In Mandeslos's report, which appears in the same collection, the Chinese are described as having a "blackish-yellow" skin colour (97).

26 Michael Banton, *The Idea of Race* (London: Praeger, 1977), 18, ascertained that this meaning was preserved in English as well as French up until this date and began to change only afterwards. Words such as "rassig" and "Rassepferd" (thoroughbred) still appear in German. On the etymology, see Conze and Sommer, "Rasse," 135ff. The term "race" as it has been used in Romance languages since the thirteenth century is derived from the Latin "radix," "generatio," and "ratio," as well as the Arabic "râz" ("head," "chieftain," and in its transferred meaning, "descent"), an interpretation that holds a high degree of probability according to Imanuel Geiss, *Geschichte des Rassismus* (Frankfurt: Suhrkamp, 1988), 16ff

27 In the sixteenth century Europeans interpreted the different Asian skin tones in this manner. See Lach, *Asia*, vol. 1/2, 827.

28 Anti-negroid prejudices do not seem to have existed in antiquity. See Geiss, *Rassismus*, 82ff

29 "Black," *Oxford English Dictionary*, vol. 2, 2nd ed. (Oxford: Oxford University Press, 1989), 238, 239. Winthrop D. Jordan, *The White Man's Burden: Historical Origins of Racism in the United States* (New York: Oxford University Press, 1974), 6.

30 Ingrid Riedel, *Farben: In Religion, Gesellschaft, Kunst und Psychotherapie*,
7th ed. (Stuttgart: Kreuz, 1989), 158ff; Rudolf Gross, *Warum die Liebe rot
ist: Farbsymbolik im Wandel der Jahrtausende* (Düsseldorf: Econ, 1981), 147;
Norbert Bernhard, *Tarzan und die Herrenrasse: Rassismus in der Literatur*
(Basel: Lenos,1986), 142ff. For the Renaissance, see Pollock, *Black Feet*,
212ff. On rare occasions, the colour black is considered a sign of good luck
(e.g., a chimney sweep): Hanns Bächtold-Stäubli, ed., *Handwörterbuch des
Deutschen Aberglaubens*, 9 Vols. (Berlin: De Gruyter, 1927–41), here vol. 7,
1431ff

31 The question raised by Jordan (*Burden*, 9) of why the history of the Noah-
curse, "which logically implied slavery but absolutely nothing about skin
color should have become a popular explanation of the Negro's blackness," seems not to require recourse to the "ancient associations of heat
with sensuality." Kusch, the founder of the black African Nubian empire,
was also considered a son of Noah. Additionally, another division has
Jafet as the progenitor of the lords, Sem of the clerics, Ham of the slaves,
which Aristotle's thesis about "born slaves" undoubtedly served to
reinforce. Léon Poliakov, *Le Mythe aryen: Essai sur les sources du racisme et des
nationalismes* (Paris: Calmann-Lévy, 1971), 19ff; Patrick von Zur Mühlen,
Rassenideologien: Geschichte und Hintergründe (Berlin: Dietz, 1977), 28.

32 In the Papal Bull, "Sublimis Deus," Indians were described as "veri hom-
ines fidei catholicae et sacramentorum capaces" (capable of being true
men in the catholic faith and of receiving the sacraments). Rüdiger Schoot,
"Die Folgen der europäischen Ausbreitung für die überseeischen Völker,"
in *Historia Mundi*, vol. 8, *Die überseeische Welt und ihre Erschließung*, ed.
Fritz Valjavec (Bern: Lehnen, 1959), 251–78. See also, Wolfgang Reinhard,
Geschichte der europäischen Expansion, vol. 2 (Stuttgart: Kohlhammer, 1985),
65; Urs Bitterli, "Auch Amerikaner sind Menschen," in *Die Natur des Menschen: Probleme der Physischen Anthropologie und Rassenkunde (1750–1850)*,
eds. Gunter Mann and Franz Dumont (*Soemmering-Forschungen*, vol. 6)
(Stuttgart: G. Fischer, 1990), 15–29.

33 Richard H. Popkin, "The Philosophical Basis of Eighteenth-Century
Racism," in *Racism in the Eighteenth Century*, ed. Harold E. Pagliaro
(Cleveland: Press of Case Western Reserve University, 1973), 245–62,
here 251. Leon Poliakov, Christian Delacampagne, and Patrick Girard,
Über den Rassismus (Frankfurt: Ullstein, 1977), 71–4; Conze and Sommer,
"Rasse," 143 with n54; Virgile Pinot, *La Chine et la formation de l'esprit
philosophique en France (1640–1740)* (Paris: Paul Geuthner, 1932), 246ff. The
problem became more pronounced with the first explorations, as it was
noted that Native Americans had not been in contact with the remaining,

previously known people. Therefore, Paracelsus claimed already in 1520 that they could not be sons of Adam, and on that basis Isaac de la Peyrere published his work *Præadamitae* in 1655. See *Histoire de la Science* (Paris: Gallimard, 1957), 1353.

34 Jordon, *Burden*, 8ff.

35 This distinction, used by many authors, refers to the process of turning these prejudices into science in the sense of the following, to my mind, accurate definition: "A fundamental characteristic of racist theories consists in the assumption of one superior and another inferior race's existence based on false scientific arguments." Maria Luiza Tucci Carneiro, *Preconceito racial no Brasil-Colônia: Os Cristãos-novos* (São Paulo: Brasilense, 1983), 17.

36 See the chapter, "Die Institution der Sklaverei als Erscheunungsform des Rassismus," in Ernstpeter Heiniger, *Ideologie des Rassismus: Problemsicht und ethische Verurteilung in der kirchlichen Sozialverkündigung* (Immensee: Neue Zeitschrift für Missionswissenschaft, 1980), 5.

37 Geiss, *Rassismus*, 33ff; Zur Mühlen, *Rassenideologie*, 20, 46, maintains that the European master mentality can be explained as the result of a self-awareness of the economic, transportation, and military-technical superiority over other peoples from whom the slaves were taken. Marvin Harris, *Patterns of Race in America* (New York: Walker, 1964), 70, assumes that racist prejudices were developed as ideological justification for the European interest in exploiting black labour. See more recently Otger Autrata, *Theorien über Rassismus* (Hamburg: Argument, 1989). This furthermore raises the question of why in the first half of the nineteenth century, "just as the battle against slavery was being won by abolitionists, the war against racism in European thought was being lost." Nancy Stepan, *The Idea of Race in Science: Great Britain 1800–1960* (London: Macmillan, 1982), 1. Another possible consideration was the spread of the classical standard of beauty to which European racists adhered. See George L. Mosse, *Toward the Final Solution: A History of European Racism* (New York: Howard Fertig, 1978), xii.

38 Poliakov, *Mythe*, 24ff. On Gilles André de La Roque's biological meaning of aristocracy, see the excerpts from "Traité de la Noblesse" (Paris, 1678), in Guy Chaussinand-Nogaret, *Une histoire des élites, 1700–1848* (Paris: Mouton, 1975), 24.

39 Charles Ralph Boxer, *The Portuguese Seaborne Empire, 1415–1825* (London: Hutchinson, 1969), 272: "If it is not true, it is a good story!" The historical context for this anecdote is supposedly based on the fact that in the Middle Ages the urban mercantile class was intermarried with and related to the Jewish community. The landed upper aristocracy maintained a

hostile relationship towards the urban merchants even though they were also often related through marriage with the nobility, particularly the lower strata. On the formation of "blood purity" as a concept in relation to power struggles with the ruling classes, see José António Saraiva, *A Inquisição portuguesa*, 2nd ed. (Lisbon: Publicações Europa-América, 1956), esp. 10ff, 106ff. It is certain that a large number of noble families could be shown to have had a blemish on their family tree, which they hid in constant fear of the Inquisition. They were even more driven to insist on their "pure blood" given that the lower classes, who had no hereditary fears because their ancestors were generally unknown, did the same as well. Whether at home or in the colonies, the "little people" could claim to have an old Christian heritage and thereby feel they belonged to an old noble stock. This self-image manifested itself as a sense of superiority over others, whether they were Jews, Moors, New Christians, Indians, or Blacks. On the problem of "pure blood," see Albert A. Sicroff, *Les controverses des statuts de "pureté de sang" en Espagne du XVe au XVIIe siècle* (Paris: Didier, 1960); Boxer, *Portuguese Empire*, 249ff. On the far-reaching consequences of the concept, even after they had been declared legally invalid under Pombal, see Tucci Carneiro, *Preconceito*, 92ff, 195, 254.

40 Charles Ralph Boxer, *Race Relations in the Portuguese Colonial Empire, 1415–1825* (Oxford: Clarendon, 1963), 19, 67ff. See also his *Portuguese Empire*, 258ff, 303ff. The intense conflict between the Roman Propaganda Office and the defenders of the Portuguese Padroado (Patronage) formed the background for this insult. Johannes Beckmann, "Die Glaubensverbreitung in Asien," in *Handbuch der Kirchengeschichte*, vol. 5 (Freiburg: Herder Verlag, 1985), 305–50, here 319. According to Henniger, *Ideologie*, 34, not a single Indio in Latin America was given priestly robes during the entire sixteenth century because of racist arguments, whereas at the beginning of the sixteenth century, Albuquerque and Cortés had encouraged mixed marriages between conquistadors and women from the Native upper class in Goa and Mexico.

41 Only in West Africa, where the climate proved to be unhealthy for the few missionaries who arrived there from Europe, so much so that they usually did not live long, did the utilization of mulattoes – or less frequently Negroes – turn out to be unavoidable. Elsewhere the recourse to native-born clerics did not take off until the middle of the eighteenth century, partially through the influence of Enlightenment ideas, and partially because missionaries from Europe increasingly stayed away. See, Boxer, *Race Relations*, 6ff, 33, 56ff.

42 That the Jesuit Order included numerous conversos among its founding
    members also played a role in these ordinances. See Sicroff, *Controverses*,
    270ff.

43 Boxer, *Race Relations*, 62ff; Boxer, *Portuguese Empire*, 250ff; Boxer, *The
    Christian Century in Japan, 1549–1650* (Berkeley: University of California
    Press, 1951), 84ff: "los Portugueses que estan acostumbrados a chamar
    negros aun a los Chinas y Japones" (the Portuguese who are accustomed
    to call even the Chinese and Japanese 'Negroes') (460n27). In the year 1555,
    the 110 cadets in the Jesuit College in Goa still included 15 mestizos, 5
    Chinese, 5 Bengals, 3 Bantus, and 6 Abyssinians.

44 Diego Aduarte, *Historia de la Provincia del Santo Rosario de la orden de predi-
    cadores en Philippinas, Japon, y China*, 2 vols. (Manila, 1640), here vol. 1, 109:
    "su buengovierno, rectitud, y limpieça que en los Chinos, por ser natu-
    ralmente cudiciosos, es virtud rara." For a complete overview, see Walter
    Demel, *Als Fremde in China: Das Reich der Mitte im Spiegel frühneuzeitlicher
    europäischer Reiseberichte (ca. 1550–1800)* (Munich: Oldenbourg, 1992), 212ff.
    The Chinese liturgy, which had already received Papal approval in 1615,
    was never implemented on account of the multifaceted resistance by the
    Propaganda Congregation and numerous missionaries. Francois Bontinck,
    La lute autour de la liturgie chinoise aux XVIIe et XVIIIe siècles (Louvain: Édi-
    tions Nauwelaerts, 1962).

45 Charles Ralph Boxer, *The Dutch Seaborne Empire, 1600–1800* (London:
    Hutchinson, 1965), 215, 217, 223. The Chinese were particularly mistrust-
    ing of the "red-haired barbarians," as they called the Dutch (as well as the
    British) in contrast to the more dark-haired southern Europeans. John E.
    Wills, *Pepper, Guns and Parleys: The Dutch East India Company and China,
    1622–1681* (Cambridge, MA: Harvard East Asian Studies, 1974), vol. 75,
    22. Various incidents at Chinese universities in the recent past have shown
    that the Chinese, too, hold racist prejudices against black Africans.

46 Thomas Beck, *Rassismus als Problemlösungsstrategie: Die ideologische
    Bewältigung indianisch-europäischer Konflikte im frühen Neu-England*
    (Kleine Beiträge zur europäischen Überseegeschichte, vol. 10) (Bamberg:
    Forschungsstiftung für Vergleichende Europäische Überseegeschichte,
    1991), 5–6n18.

47 Geiss, *Rassismus*, 113.

48 Margaret T. Hodgen, *Early Anthropology in the Sixteenth and Seventeenth
    Centuries* (Philadelphia: University of Pennsylvania Press, 1964), 213ff.

49 The authors discussed in the following section are included in countless
    histories of anthropology and racism: Bernier, Linnaeus, Buffon, Kant, Blu-
    menbach, and frequently Meiners as well. See, e.g., Wilhelm E. Mühlmann,

Geschichte der Anthropologie, 2nd ed. (Frankfurt: Athenäum, 1968); Conze and Sommer, "Rasse."

50 Francois Bernier, *Histoire de la dernière Revolution des États du grand Mogol*, 2 vols (Paris, 1670/71), here esp. vol. 1, 143ff, and vol. 2, 203ff, 260ff, 277. José Frèches, "François Bernier: Philosophe de Confucius au XVII siècle," in *Bullettin de l'Ecole Française d'Extrème-Orient* 60 (1973): 385–400.

51 François Bernier, *Nouvelle division de la terre*, in *Journal des sçavans pour l'annèe*, MDCLXXXIV, vol. 12. (Amsterdam, 1685), 148: "qu'il y a sur tout quatre ou cinq Especes ou Races d'hommes dont la difference est si notable, qu'elle peut server de juste fondement à une nouvelle division de la Terre." See also Bernier, *Copie des étrenes* [*sic.*] *envoyées à Mme De la Sablière* (Montpellier, 1688).

52 See Jörg Fisch, *Geschichte Südafrikas* (Munich: DTV, 1990), 30.

53 Bernier, *Division*, 149ff: "fort noirs, ou plûtost bazanez" (149); "veritablement blancs" (151).

54 Conze and Sommer, "Rasse," 142.

55 Karl Linné, *Caroli Linnaei ... Systema Natvrae ... Caroli Linnaei ... Natur – Systema [Latin – German]*, 3rd ed. (Halle, 1740). The order of the sequence is also noteworthy.

56 Urs Bitterli, *Die "Wilden" und die "Zivilisierten": Grundzüge einer Geistes- und Kulturgeschichte der europäisch-überseeischen Begegnung* (Munich: C. H. Beck, 1976, new ed., 1982), 332, 354. See also Werner Kraus, *Zur Anthropologie des 18. Jahrhunderts: Die Frühgeschichte der Menschheit im Blickpunkt der Aufklärung* (Munich: Ullstein, 1979), 131ff.

57 Carolus Linnaeus, *Systema Naturae* [9th ed.] (Lugduni Batavorum, 1756), 3; Carolus a Linné, *Systema Naturae* [13th ed.] (Vindobonae, 1767), vol. 1, 29. It is noteworthy that the German translator of the 1740 edition rendered *fuscus* as "yellowish." For the other connotations of *fuscus*, which include "morally dirty," see Karl-Ernst Georges, *Ausführliches Deutsch-Lateinisches Handwörterbuch*, 2 vols., 8th ed. (Hanover, 1913), here vol. 1, 2890; Reinhold Klotz, *Handwörterbuch der lateinischen Sprache*, 2 vols., 7th ed. (Graz: Akad. Druck und Verlagsanstalt, 1963), here vol. 1, 1611ff.

58 Carleton S. Coon, *Living Races of Men* (New York: Random House, 1973), 218ff.

59 George Louis Leclerc, Comte de Buffon, *Histoire naturelle, générale et particulière*, 44 vols. (Paris, 1749–1804), here vol. 3: "les petits enfants naissent fort blancs, & sont fort beaux, mais en grandissant, leur teint change d'une manière surprenante, l'air les jaunit, le soleil les brûle, & il est aisé de reconnoître un Espagnol de toutes les autres nations Européennes"

(371–2n422); "leurs enfants naissent blancs, ou plutôt rouges, comme
ceux des autres hommes, mais deux ou trois jours après qu'ils sont nés, la
couleur change, ils paroissent d'un jaune basané qui se brunit peu à peu,
& au septième ou huitième jour ils sont tout noirs. On sait que deux ou
trois jours après la naissance tous les enfants ont une espèce de jaunisse;
cette jaunisse dans les blancs n'a qu'un effet passage, & ne laisse à la peau
aucune impression; dans les Nègres au contraire, elle donne à la peau une
couleur ineffaçable, & qui noircit toujours de plus en plus" (522–3).

60 Ibid, vol. 3, 482.

61 Nicolle Abbé de La Croix, *Géographie moderne*, vol. 1, new ed. (Paris, 1769),
60ff; Joannes Hunter, *Disputatio inauguralis quædam de hominum varietatibus,
et harum causis exponens* (Edinburgh, 1775), 366ff; Georg Simon Klügel,
Encyclopädie… part 1 (Berlin, 1782), 327ff; Johann Daniel Metzger, *Die
Physiologie in Aphorismen* (Königsberg, 1789), 5; Ernst August Wilhelm
Zimmermann, *Geographische Geschichte des Menschen*, vol. 1 (Leipzig, 1778),
77ff; Johannes Christianus Polycarp Erxleben, *Systema Regni animali* (Leipzig, 1777), 1ff.

62 Immanuel Kant, "Von den verschiedenen Racen der Menschen (1775)," in
Kant's gesammelte Schriften, section 1, 29 vols. (Berlin: Deutsche Akademie
der Wissenschaft zu Berlin, 1902–83), here vol. 1/2, 427ff.

63 Immanuel Kant, "Bestimmung des Begriffs einer Menschenrace (1785)," in
Schriften, vol. 8, 91–2n93, 101.

64 Johann Friedrich Blumenbach, *Handbuch der Naturgeschichte* (Göttingen,
1779), 63–4n63.

65 Johannes Friedrich Blumenbach, *De generis humani varietate nativa*, 3rd ed.
(Göttingen, 1795), 119ff, 284.

66 Blumenbach, *De … varietate*, 123ff, citation 131–2.

67 Blumenbach, *Handbuch*, 5th ed. (Göttingen, 1797), 61ff, and 11th ed. (Göttingen, 1825), 56ff. In his *De … varietate*, the typical skin colour of the
Mongol people is given as "gilvus s[ive] buxeus" (yellow, olive tinge)
(120); and "gilvus" (pale yellow) is equated with "jaunâtre" (yellowish)
(299).

68 Linné, *Systema Naturae*, 13th ed., 29. The addition of cultural characteristics, now considered of equal rank as the somatic criteria appears first
in the 10th edition of 1758. Conze and Sommer, "Rasse," 145. Claude
Calame, "Nature humaine et environment: Le racism bien tempéré
d'Hippocrate," *Science et racism* (Lausanne: Payot, 1986) 75–99, here 77,
comments on Linnaeus's explanations as follows: "Les bases du racism
ordinaire sont desormais jetées. Il suffit d'un critère de distinction fondé
sur un caractère d'ordre physiologique et assorti – c'est là l'essentiel – d'un

jugement de valeur. La hiérarchie morale à l'apparence scientifiques est dès lors constituée. Désormais les critères de distinction peuvent varier à volonté" (The foundation for straightforward racism has been laid. All one needs is a distinguishing criterion based on a physiological character and accompanied by – that's the main thing – a value judgment. The moral hierarchy in scientific appearance is therefore incorporated. From now on the distinguishing criteria may vary at will).

69 See, e.g., the "Teatro critic" of the leading Spanish Enlightener Benito Jerónimo Feijoo y Montenegro, *Mapa intellectual y cotejo de naciones*, in *Obras escogidos de Padre Fray* (Bibliotheca de Autores Españoles, vol. 56) (Madrid, 1863), 86–93. See also the commentary of José Luis Abellán, *Historia crítica del pensamiento español*, vol. 1 (Madrid: Espasa-Calpe, 1979).

70 David Hume, *Essays, Moral, Political, and Literary*, 1777 ed., *The Philosophical Works of David Hume*, edited by T.H. Green and T.H. Grove (London, 1875), 244, 252n1.

71 Immanuel Kant, "Beobachtungen über das Gefühl des Schönen und Erhabenen (1764)," in *Schriften*, vol. 1/2, 245, 246, 253, 255, 254.

72 Along with Rousseau, who was considered the "most illustrious opponent" of Enlightenment pre-racism (see Léon Poliakov, "Brève histoire des hierarchies raciales," *Le genre humain* 1 (1981): 70–82, here at 75), one would have to include Helvétius. See Claude Adrien Helvétius, *De l'esprit*, in *Œuvres completes*, vols. 5 and 6 (Paris, 1795), 56, where he argues that the physiognomic differences between a Chinese person and a Swede have no influence on their respective intellectual abilities, and given that Locke said that ideas enter through the senses, then they must both possess the same intellectual abilities. The English novelist Oliver Goldsmith relativized the European concept of beauty when he had a fictional Chinese man cry out: "when I reflect on the small footed perfections of an Eastern beauty, how is it possible I should have eyes for a woman whose feet are ten inches long?!" (*The Citizen of the World; or, Letters from a Chinese Philosopher Residing in London, to his Friends in the East*, vol. 1, 3rd ed. [London, 1774], 8).

73 See Nieuhof, *Gezantschap*, part. 1, 71, 109, 128, on the different characteristics of the inhabitants of the various Chinese provinces. Tellingly, this differentiation was written in the seventeenth century.

74 Abbé Grosier, *Description génerale de la Chine, Histoire générale de la Chine, ou Annales de cet empire, traduites du Tong-Kien-Kang-Mou* (i.e., the Chinese text), edited by Abbé Grosier in cooperation with Le Roux Des Hautesrayes, vol. 13 (Paris, 1785), 688: "Parcourez les différentes Provinces de France; vous trouverez dans chacune, des nuances, des traits de caractère

qui distinguient leurs divers habitans … Parcourez l'Empire de la Chine; tous vous semblera fondu dans le même creuset, et façonné par le même moule."

75 Hume, *Characters*, 249.

76 Georg Christoph Lichtenberg's *Vermischte Schriften*, new ed., 8 vols. (Göttingen, 1853), here vol. 6, 94.

77 Johann Caspar Lavater, *Physiognomische Fragmente zur Beförderung der Menschenkenntnis und Menschenliebe*, 4 vols. (Leipzig, 1775–78), esp. vol. 1, 50ff.

78 Lichtenberg, *Schriften*, vol. 6, 98.

79 The exceptions here prove the rule. At the height of his Sinophilia, Voltaire wrote that it could not be doubted, "that whites, Negroes, albinos, Hottentots, Laplanders, Chinese, Americans are entirely different races." Voltaire saw Negroes as standing far below the other races in terms of intellect. Europeans, however, he thought possessed an entirely different white skin than albinos, namely, one that was mixed with brown. He does not explain why he considered the Chinese a separate race. François-Marie Arouet de Voltaire, *Œuvres complètes de Voltaire*, vol. 1, *Essai sur les moeurs et l'esprit des nations*, edited by Louis Moland, vol. 11 (Paris, 1878), reprint ed. (Nendeln: Kraus, 1967), 5ff, citation at 5. Elsewhere he claimed in no particular order: "There are yellow, red, and grey races." See his *Dictionnaire philosophique*, vol. 3, *Œuvres complètes*, vol. 19, 377: "Homme (1771)."

80 See, Christian Delacampagne, *L'Invention du Racisme: Antiquité et Moyen Age* (Paris: Fayard, 1983), 22f. See also Walter Demel, "Europäisches Überlegenheitsgefühl und die Entdeckung Chinas: Ein Beitrag zur Frage der Rückwirkungen der europäischen Expansion auf Europa," in *Kolumbus' Erben: Europäische Expansion und überseeische Ethnien im Ersten Kolonialzeitalter (1415–1815)*, eds. Thomas Beck, Annerose Menninger, and Thomas Schlaich (Darmstadt: Wissenschaftliche Buchgesellschaft, 1992), 99–143.

81 Heinz Gollwitzer, *Geschichte des weltpolitischen Denkens*, vol. 1 (Göttingen: Vandenhoeck & Ruprecht,, 1972), 75. See Loys Le Roy, *De la vicissitude ou variété des choses en l'univers …*, 3rd ed. (Paris, 1579), 12, who sees culture and civilization as existing only in the moderate latitudes. Bodin discovers that according to the observations of the Spanish, the Chinese were "the most ingenuous people and the most courteous in the world" – because they were the people who lived furthest east! Jean Bodin, *Les six Livres de la République*, 4th ed. (Paris, 1583), reprint ed. (Aalen: Scientia, 1961), book 5, chapter 1, 692. Johannes Althusius, *Politica: Methodicé digesta atque exemplis sacris & profanes illustrata*, 3rd ed. (Herborn, 1614) reprint ed. (Aalen: Scientia, 1961), 447; *Populi orientales caeteris naturá suá, sunt humaniores & urbaniores*.

82 Gottfried Wilhelm Leibniz, *Otium Hanoveranum Sive Miscellanea* ..., edited
    by Joachim Friedrich Feller (Leipzig, 1718), 159ff. In general, Leibniz was
    a convinced monogeneticist, as is shown clearly in his 1696 letter to the
    diplomat Sparvenfeld (37ff), though he clearly did not see all human spe-
    cies as equal; see, e.g., his allusion to Bernier: "Je me souviens d'avoir lu
    quelque part, mais je ne sçourois pas retrouver, qu'un certain voyageur
    avoit partagé les hommes en certains tribus, races ou classes. Il donnoit
    une race aux Lappons et aux Samojedes, une autre aux Chinois et aux
    peuples voisins, une autre aux Nègres, encore une autre aux Cafres, ou
    Hotentots. En Amérique encore il y a une difference merveilleuse entre les
    Galibis ou Caribes, qui ont beaucoup de valeur et même d'ésprit, & entre
    ceux de Paraquay, qui semblent être des enfants, ou des écoliers toute leur
    vie. Cela n'empéche [*sic*.] pas que tous les hommes, qui habitent ce globe,
    ne soient tous d'une même race, qui a été altérée par les differens climats,
    comme nous voyons, que les bêtes et les plantes changent de naturel &
    deviennent meilleure ou degenerent" (I remember reading somewhere
    (but I cannot recall where) that a certain voyager divided human beings
    into certain tribes, races, or classes. He assigned a particular race to the
    Lapps and Samoyeds, a certain to the Chinese and neighbouring peo-
    ples; another to the Negroes, still another to the Cafres or Hottentots. In
    America there is a marvellous difference between the Galibis or Caribbean,
    for example, who have a great deal of value and just as much spirit, and
    those of Paraguay, who seem to be children or youths all their lives. This
    does not prevent human beings who inhabit the globe from being all of
    the same race, which has been altered by the different climates, as we see
    animals and plants changing their nature and becoming better or degen-
    erating). On Leibniz's Sinophilia, see Donald Lach, *The Preface to Leibniz'
    Novissima Sinica* (Honolulu: University of Hawaii Press, 1957).
83 Charles-Louis de Secondat de Montesquieu, *De l'esprit des lois*, in *Œuvres
    complètes*, edited by Roger Callois, 2 vols. (Paris: Editions Galimard, 1949),
    here vol. 2, 570–1: "the most cunning people on the earth." In French,
    deception and fraud were traditionally associated with the colour yellow.
    Grand Larousse de la langue française, vol. 4 (Paris: Librairie Larousse, 1975),
    2848, in the entry "jaune," the term "race jeune" is attributed to Montes-
    quieu. I was unable to find the phrase on the page cited in *Esprit*
    (XVII, 3); however, Montesquieu speaks of "femmes jaunes" kept by the
    king of Morocco alongside white and black women in his Sérail (XVI, vol.
    2, 512ff).
84 Montesquieu, "Mes pensées" (Fragmente), *Œuvres*, vol. 1, 1350: "Si les
    peuples jaunes d'Asie se répendoient en Europe, de quoi deviendrions

nous?" (If the Asian yellow people were to spread in Europe, what would become of us?)

85 Immanuel Kant, "Physical Geographie (1802)," edited by Friedrich Theodor Rink, in *Schriften*, vol. 9, paras. 318 and 319, 377ff. The manuscript is derived from reworked lecture manuscripts dating back to the year 1764. Perhaps the absence of such a similar statement in the essay of 1775 indicates a distancing from his initial racial prejudices. It may also be that the immediate impact of Kant's relatively short writing on the subject was minor – Blumenbach nevertheless refers explicitly to Kant in his conceptual rationale. Conze and Sommer, "Rasse," 147ff. Yet when Rudolf Malter, "Der Rassenbegriff in Kants Anthropologie," in *Natur des Menschen*, eds. Mann and Dumont, 122, insists: "The Kantian racial theory does not speak in the voice of racism, instead it is an earnest, energetic rebuttal against it – against the worst madness," this judgment seems to me to be a subtle yet one-sided analysis of the scholarly view on Kant's late philosophy, which neglects the historical reception of his earlier statements.

86 August Ludwig Schlözer, *Vorstellung der Universal = Historie*, 2nd ed. (Göttingen, 1775), 122.

87 Christoph Meiners, *Grundriß der Geschichte der Menschheit* (Lemgo, 1785), preface, 24, paras. 43, 45, 67 89. The Caucasian branch, according to Meiners, still split into a Celtic and an inferior Slavic race. In his racial theory, Meiners presented an explanation for why the arts and sciences developed only among certain peoples, by saying that in some places freedom and in others despotism prevailed and that Europe, even in a state of barbarism, was still superior to other parts of the world in their state of barbarism. In many regards, Meiners was the forerunner of Gobineau. Mühlmann, *Geschichte der Anthropologie*, 61, 82. With regard to his colleague Blumenbach, Meiners's theories contradicted his basic assumptions, he disputed, namely, that physical features alone were sufficient selection criteria for the divisions between humans. He also moved from a monogeneticist to a polygeneticist position. See Frank W.P. Dougherty, "Christoph Meiners und Johann Friedrich Blumenbach im Streit um den Begriff der Menschenrasse," in *Natur des Menschen*, eds. Mann and Dumont, 89–111, esp. 99, 104, and Georg Lilienthal, "Samuel Thomas Soemmering und seine Vorstellungen über Rassenunterschiede," in the same volume, 35.

88 See Demel, *Als Fremde in China*; Johan Leonard Blussé van Oud-Alban, *Strange Company: Chinese Settlers, Mestizo Women and the Dutch in VOC Batavia*, Diss. Phil., Leiden 1986, 78ff, also emphasizes that aside from a few bloody confrontations "the Europeans actually had little problem

dealing with and accepting the Chinese within the 'European' urban societies of Manila and Batavia."

89 Georg Wilhelm Friedrich Hegel, *Vorlesungen über die Philosophie der
Geschichte*, in *Sämtliche Werke*, edited by Hermann Glockner, vol. 11
(Stuttgart, 1928), 88ff: "World history travels from east to west" (150);
"With China and the Mongols … history begins" (159); "Already early on
we see China growing into the condition in which it finds itself today"
(163). Herder rejected the division of humans into races as artificial, but
considered the existence of "peoples" as naturally given. Mühlmann,
Geschichte der Anthropologie, 62ff. Manfred Welzel, "Die Anthropologie
Johann Gottfried Herders und das klassische Humanitätsideal," *Natur des
Menschen*, 137–67. On Herder's conception, see his *Ideen zur Philosophie der
Geschichte der Menschheit (1784)*, part 2, book 6, in *Herders Sämtliche Werke*,
edited by Bernhard Suphan, vol. 13 (Berlin, 1887), 281ff. See also his *Des
Lord Monboddos Werk*, in *Werke*, vol. 15, 179ff. On the judgements of Herder
and on Hegel about China, see also Demel, *Abundantia*, 151; Franz Rudolf
Merkel, "Herder und Hegel über China," *Sinica* 17 (1942): 5–26; Ernst
Schulin, *Die weltgeschichtliche Erfassung des Orients bei Hegel und Ranke*
(Göttingen: Vandenhoeck & Ruprecht, 1958), 67ff.

90 Article on "Sina," in *Das Staats-Lexikon*, eds. Carl von Rotteck and Carl
Welcker, 12 vols., 2nd ed. (Altona, 1848), 155–91, here 155.

91 Arthur de Gobineau, *Essay sur l'inégalité des races humaines (1853/55)*,
in *Œuvres*, vol. 1, edited by Jean Gaulmier (Paris: Pléaide, 1983), 558ff.
Accordingly, the accomplishments of the ancient Indian culture were interpreted as the result of Aryan migration. Geiss, *Rassismus*, 163ff.

92 Ludwig Schemann, *Die Rasse in den Geisteswissenschaften: Studien zur
Geschichte des Rassegedankens*, 3 vols. (Munich, 1928), here vol. 2, 9ff.

93 Riedel, *Farben*, 71ff, 86; Gross, *Warum die Liebe rot ist*, 169, 178ff; Heinz
Gollwitzer, *Die Gelbe Gefahr* (Göttingen: Vandenhoeck & Ruprecht, 1962).
As Professor Gollwitzer explained to me, no one questioned anymore
whether the Chinese were yellow at the time when the phrase "yellow
peril" came into being.

94 Pu Yi, *Ich war Kaiser von China: Vom Himmelssohn zum Neuen Menschen*,
translated by Richard Schirach (Munich: DTV, 1973), 34.

95 Faber Birren, *The Symbolism of Color* (Secaucas, NJ: Citadel, 1988), 13ff.

96 Schemann, *Rasse*, vol. 2, 14, with n14 directly referring to Amiot and Paul
Topinard, *Éléments d'anthropologie générale* (Paris, 1885), 63, where the text
states without reference that according to Father Amyot the "Chinese had
grouped the known peoples of this earth into five groups, according to colour: a pale violet race, one leaning towards yellow, a flesh-coloured race,

one white and one black." Jean-Joseph-Marie Amiot [Amyot] (1718–1793), who had arrived in China in 1750, was an astronomer, and played a leading role in the late French Jesuit mission in the Middle Kingdom. As a result of his rich correspondence, the majority of which was printed in the *Mémoires concernant l'histoire, les sciences, les arts, les mœurs, les usages etc. des Chinois: Par les Missionaires de Pekin*, edited by Ch. Batteux and L.-G. Oudent Feudrix de Bréquigny, 15 vols. (Paris, 1776–91), he had a considerable influence on the history of Sinology and the European image of China. Joseph Dehergne, *Répertoire des Jésuites de Chine de 1552 à 1800* (Rome: Institutum Historicoum S.I. 1973), no. 35.

97 On the establishment of anthropology as an independent discipline, see Mareta Linden, *Untersuchungen zum Anthropologiebegriff des 18. Jahrhunderts* (Bern: Peter Lang, 1976). Norbert Hinske, "Kants Idee der Anthropologie," *Die Frage nach dem Menschen* (Munich: Karl Alber, 1966), 410–27, here 425ff, underscores that Kant did not have a firm concept of anthropology.

98 Jacques M. Barzun, *Race: A Study in Superstition*, 2nd ed. (New York: Harper and Row, 1965) [1st ed., 1937!], 1, 8, 203ff, quotation at 16: "To sum it up: a satisfactory definition of race is not to be had." Ruth Römer, *Sprachwissenschaft und Rassenideologie in Deutschland*, 2nd ed. (Munich: Fink, 1989), 17, concluded that up until today there exists no reliable marker and no classification schema to distinguish one race from another. In a similar vein, see Geiss, *Rassismus*, 9ff, who correctly notes that investigations into the phenomenon of racism are, unfortunately, confined to the black-white problematic and to anti-Semitism. See also, Ashley Montagu, *Man's Most Dangerous Myth: The Fallacy of Race*, 5th ed. (New York: Oxford University Press, 1974), 62ff; Mario Lopes Pegna, *La razze umane non esistono* (Florenz: Editoriale Toscana, 1971). Countless examples of different suggestions for dividing the races are to be found in Bernardino Del Boca, *Storia della antropologia* (Milan: Vallardi, 1961), 194ff.

99 Paul Topinard, *L'Anthropologie*, 5th ed. (Paris, 1895), 412, 200ff, 354ff.

100 See the contributions in Ilse Schwidetzky, ed., *Die neue Rassenkunde* (Stuttgart: Fischer, 1962); Geiss, *Rassismus*, 21.

101 Buffon, *Histoire naturelle*, vol. 4, 151, 161.

102 Carleton S. Coon, *The Origin of Races* (New York: Alfred A. Knopf, 1962), 11ff. See *Völkergeschichtliches ABC und Bilderbuch für Kindheit und Jugend, mit vielen gemalten Abbildungen*, 2nd ed. (Kissingen, 1835). During the Third Reich "racial science" was part of the school curriculum. See Karl Bareth and Alfred Vogel, *Erblehre und Rassenkunde für die Grund- und Hauptschule*, 3rd ed. (Bühl: Konkordia, 1939). The series starts in the

fourth grade with a picture of the spread of pollen and ends in the eighth grade with a chapter on "preserving racial inheritance" (including a subsection on "eradicating the genetically diseased"), "the Jews and the German people," and "the National Socialist racial idea." In contrast to Lamarck (1744–1829), who supposedly laid the groundwork for Liberalism and Communism, the book insists that environmental influences cannot alter genetic inheritance (79). Europe, in the eyes of the authors, is a besieged fortress: blacks infiltrate through the open gateway of Marseille; "in the East the yellow race is awakening. Can the advance posts of the whites hold out against the assault?" This is the "battle of the future," between "white or coloured humans" (101). That this conception continues to influence the present is shown by Ronald Segal, *Kampf der Rassen: Der Aufbruch der farbigen Völker* (Düsseldorf: Econ, 1968); original English: *The Race War* (London: Jonathan Cape, 1966).

2 Leibniz on the Existence of Philosophy in China

FRANKLIN PERKINS

The first major translation of Chinese texts into a European language was the *Confucius Sinarum Philosophus*, published in 1687. Credited to Phillipe Couplet as chief editor, it was the culmination of decades of work by Jesuit missionaries living in China, going back to Matteo Ricci, who first entered China in 1582 and remained there until he died in 1610.[1] Along with an extensive introduction and a chronology of Chinese history, *Confucius Sinarum Philosophus* contained complete translations of three of the "Four Books" (*Sishu* 四書) that were taken as the classics of early Confucianism: the *Lun Yu* 論語 (Analects), *Da Xue* 大學 (Great Learning), and the *Zhong Yong* 中庸 (Doctrine of the Mean).[2] Europeans for the first time could read key primary texts from the Confucian tradition, though refracted through Jesuit translations and commentaries. The Jesuits portrayed early Confucianism as compatible with Christianity, arguing that Confucius held a rational natural theology including belief in the one supreme intelligent being and in the immortality of the soul. They emphasized and exaggerated rational elements of the Confucian tradition while simultaneously minimizing what might look like religious practices, taking Confucian rituals, for example, as demonstrations of respect rather than religious ceremonies. All of these elements became central to the Jesuit position of "Accommodation" in the Rites Controversy.[3]

The *Confucius Sinarum Philosophus* became controversial for this portrait of a Confucianism compatible with Christianity, but calling Confucius a philosopher in the title (*Confucius, Philosopher of China*) was unremarkable. From the start, Matteo Ricci had referred to the Confucian literati simply as "the Philosophers."[4] In fact, until sometime in the latter part of the eighteenth century, everyone agreed that philosophy existed in cultures outside of Europe. Leibniz refers frequently to Chinese philosophy and to Chinese philosophers, and Christian Wolff's controversial lecture on the Chinese as virtuous non-theists, which led to his being expelled from Halle in 1723, was published with the title *Oratio de Sinarum philosophia practica* (*On the Practical Philosophy of the Chinese*).[5] A passing comment in Spinoza's correspondence suggests that the existence of philosophy outside of Europe was taken for granted. Albert Burgh writes to Spinoza in September 1675, arguing that Spinoza cannot know the truth of his own philosophy because he has not compared it with all others: "To say nothing of possible future philosophies, have you examined all those philosophies, both ancient and modern, which are taught here, and in India, and everywhere through the whole world?"[6]

Spinoza responds by saying that such comparisons are useless – the truth is known through itself not by comparison – but he does not question the assumption that there is philosophy in India and the rest of the world.[7] Even those critical of China and accommodation agreed that the Chinese had philosophy. Nicholas Malebranche published a text in 1707 entitled *Entretien d'un philosophe chrétien et d'un philosophe chinois, sur l'existence et la nature de Dieu* (*Dialogue between a Christian Philosopher and a Chinese Philosopher on the Existence and Nature of God*). Malebranche took the Chinese as atheists and materialists, and in the dialogue the Chinese Philosopher is largely a stand-in for Spinoza.[8] Nonetheless, Malebranche never doubts that his fictional Chinese interlocutor is a philosopher who can give and respond to arguments. For Malebranche, the problem is not that the Chinese lack philosophy but that their philosophy is wrong.

The recognition of philosophy in China would be unremarkable if philosophical common sense had not since reversed. Nowadays it is not only normal for new PhDs in philosophy to have learned nothing at all about cultures beyond Europe, it would be almost impossible for them to do so without going outside the department of philosophy. There are ironies about philosophers in an age of pluralism and globalization being less inclusive than philosophers living three hundred years ago. Here we see the ugly way in which we often remain in the legacy of racist and Eurocentric structures whose momentum leaves them in place until they are deliberately dismantled.[9] In fact, the claim that there is no philosophy outside of Europe is a key for resisting the demands of multiculturalism and globalization. We academics can no longer explicitly exclude China on the grounds of racism or irrelevance.

The only remaining defence is to say something like: of course the Chinese have important things to say and their ideas are worth reading, but not in our department, because it is not philosophy. The claim that something is not *real philosophy* differs crucially from the claim that is *bad philosophy*. The latter requires engagement, argument, and justification; the former is a way of evading those efforts.

My concern in this chapter is to look at the roots of this position, focusing on a philosopher writing before the shift took place – Wilhelm Gottfried Leibniz. I will argue that Leibniz's recognition of Chinese Philosophy followed partly from his conception of philosophy as a way of living wisely, and that the expulsion of Chinese thought from the discipline of philosophy corresponded with a break from this earlier view, replacing philosophy as a way of life with philosophy as a systematic science of concepts. Before turning to that moment in history, though, we should briefly consider the significance and complexity of the question: is there Chinese Philosophy? The question really is three questions folded into one. Most obviously, the question is about China – what were they doing there? From a historical perspective, the answer to the question will vary depending on what was known about China at a particular time. Such knowledge, however, has been least relevant to how the question is answered, and the answer is rarely seen to be in the hands of sinologists.[10] This suggests that the real question lies elsewhere, in a more fundamental question: what is philosophy? We can only say whether or not there is Chinese Philosophy once we have a definition of philosophy. Although philosophers sometimes act as if philosophy has an unchanging essence, the term is produced and employed in concrete contexts as a way of labelling human actions and social practices. As social practices and concerns change, conceptions of philosophy also change. Thus, a historical approach to the question of philosophy in other cultures must attend not just to the information available but even more to shifting conceptions of philosophy itself.[11] Even this, though, does not yet reach the heart of the matter, and those who say that there is or is not Chinese Philosophy rarely attend carefully to either of these questions. In practice, the question is raised almost only in one context – that of the power to include and exclude. The question is ultimately about institutional power, arising in discussions of who should get hired, what kinds of papers should be published, or what classes should be offered or required. These interests change over time and they exist on many levels – that of the state, that of its elites, that of particular institutions like universities, and that of individuals.[12] Thus, a history of the status of philosophy outside of Europe must attend to three dimensions: the information available on other cultures, the conception of philosophy used, and the various powers and interests at stake. While I have focused here on China and the discipline of philosophy, the same three levels apply to the attempt to incorporate any foreign practices into academic disciplines that were formed according to the particular contours and demands of European culture. Equally complex concerns apply, for example, to the global application of Religion or Literature.

When we consider the complex dimensions of the question of Chinese Philosophy, we can see that its significance for understanding the reception of China in the German Enlightenment is greater than we might initially think. On one side, to admit the existence of Chinese Philosophy was to grant a certain status to China and Chinese people. Superficially, it determined whether or not Chinese texts would be included in the canon of texts a philosopher was expected to know. On a deeper level – and it is easy to forget this now – the label of "philosophy" carried a kind of honorary weight, as philosophy was seen as the realization of what is most essentially and uniquely human, our ability for reason and self-reflection. The status of Chinese philosophy was inseparable from the status of the Chinese as human beings. Broadly speaking, we could divide the reception of China into two periods, the first running from Matteo Ricci to Christian Wolff and the second from Kant into the twentieth century. In the first period, the existence of philosophy in China was accepted, and in the latter it was not. Concomitantly, in the first period Chinese people were seen as equally human and in the second they were seen as racially inferior. That is not a coincidence. The denial of philosophy and the denial of full humanity went together.

Aside from its relevance for the status of China, the question of Chinese Philosophy was also a question about philosophy itself, and thus it has further significance for the formation of academic disciplines in Germany (and elsewhere in Europe). In particular, the problematic status of other cultures was crucial in reversing the ways Philosophy and Religion had been applied across cultures, resulting in our current exclusivist conception of philosophy and pluralist conception of religion.[13] That is, philosophers began to claim that only Europe had philosophy, while the newly emerging field of Religious Studies (Religionswissenschaft) claimed that every culture had religion.

Let me now turn specifically to Leibniz's writings on China. What is most striking in this context is that although Leibniz consistently refers to Chinese Philosophy, his contrast between Europe and China brings out the very differences that would later be used to exclude China from Philosophy: Europeans are skilled in theoretical reflection while the Chinese have practical observations and ethical rules.[14] We can begin with the comparison Leibniz makes in his preface to the *Novissima Sinica*. Leibniz first published the *Novissima Sinica* in 1697. As the title (*The Latest from China*) suggests, the book is a collection of news from China, gathering together various reports written primarily by the Jesuits. The preface Leibniz wrote for the volume explicitly encourages sending more missionaries to China and supports the Jesuit position of accommodation, but its main argument is for mutual cultural exchange. The value of this cultural exchange is based on Leibniz's view of China and Europe as having complementary strengths. In arts and practical skills, Leibniz says, Europe and China are about equal, but in profundity of knowledge and in theoretical disciplines, Europe wins. He explains:

> For besides logic and mathematics, and the knowledge of things incorporeal, which we justly claim as peculiarly our province, we excel by far in the understanding of concepts which are abstracted by the mind from the material, i.e., in things mathematical, as in truth demonstrated when Chinese astronomy comes into competition with our own. The Chinese are thus seen to be ignorant of that great light of the mind, the art of demonstration, and they have remained content with a sort of empirical geometry, which our artisans universally possess.[15]

In another passage, Leibniz claims that the reason the Chinese have failed to achieve excellence in science is precisely because they lack geometry. He adds that, aside from geometry, Europeans also have "First Philosophy," which allows "an understanding even of things incorporeal."[16] The lack of theoretical precision among the Chinese comes up throughout Leibniz's discussions of China. For example, he says that it is easier for the Chinese to learn from the Europeans, because European knowledge is public and consists more in reason, while Chinese knowledge is based on experience and is passed down by tradition among specialists.[17] Elsewhere Leibniz says that Europeans have the benefit of using logic, critical thinking, and mathematics, along with a more precise manner of expressing thoughts. Thus, he tells us, we should not be surprised that he was able to find the "true" meaning of the hexagrams of the *Yijing*, even though the meaning had been lost to the Chinese themselves.[18]

This division between Europeans as skilled in reason and the Chinese as skilled in practice has echoes in later dismissals of the Chinese, as in Kant's famous statement that the Chinese have fine ethical rules for guiding behaviour, but utterly lack "a concept [Begriff] of virtue and morality."[19] On such a view, it is no surprise that the Chinese would be denied philosophy. What is striking in Leibniz's use of the distinction, though, is that what the Chinese have is still called *philosophy*. Leibniz refers to "Chinese Philosophy" over and over again, and when speaking of European philosophy, he always refers to "our philosophers," implying that there are others. He calls Confucius (Kongzi), Zhu Xi, and the legendary figure Fuxi all philosophers, and he consistently refers to the Ming Dynasty collection of Confucian materials, the *Xingli Daquanshu* 性理大全書, as a "compendium of philosophy" or their "philosophical summa." What is Chinese Philosophy, though, if the Chinese lack precise modes of expression and the art of demonstration, and if they are – at best – weak in knowledge of incorporeal things? We get part of the answer in the same passage in which Leibniz points out Europe's strengths. He continues the comparison:

> But who would have believed that there is on earth a people who, though we are in our view so very advanced in every branch of behavior, still surpass us in comprehending the precepts of civil life? Yet now we find this to be so among the Chinese, as we learn to know them better. And so if we are their equals in industrial arts, and ahead of them in contemplative sciences, certainly they surpass us (though it is almost shameful to confess this) in practical philosophy, that is, in the precepts of ethics and politics adapted to the present life and use of mortals.[20]

Leibniz concludes that an expert in the excellences of peoples would have to judge the Chinese as superior, if it were not for Europe's possession of Christianity.[21]

Leibniz is here using China for his own purposes, as a way of criticizing and shaming Europeans, as when he says that the Chinese have accomplished more among the masses than religious orders in Europe can accomplish among their own members.[22] Whether or not this praise is exaggerated, though, does not alter the fact that the exchange Leibniz envisions is not between European *philosophy* and Chinese *practice*, but rather between two kinds of philosophy – "First Philosophy" and "Practical Philosophy." What does this practical philosophy consist of? In the passage above, Leibniz explains it as rules and political forms that deal with the actual condition of mortal human beings. He elaborates and gives examples through the next two paragraphs. Chinese laws are beautifully directed towards establishing public harmony and order.[23] Chinese obey their superiors, revere their elders, and respect their parents.[24] Chinese peasants and servants behave more lovingly and respectfully towards each other than even the most cultivated Europeans do.[25] The Chinese hardly ever offend each other, and "they rarely show evidences of hatred, wrath, or excitement."[26] Leibniz concludes that vice is universal and perfect virtue requires grace and revelation, but that the Chinese still manage to "temper the bitter fruits of vice," and "control many of the burgeoning growths of evil."[27]

From the perspective of contemporary academic philosophy, it is difficult to take Leibniz seriously when he calls such things *philosophy*. They certainly would not help anyone get tenure. The strangeness of his claim, though, illuminates how the meaning of "philosophy" has changed. Although we can already see the roots of our modern conception of philosophy in Leibniz himself, it is clear that Leibniz still considers living wisely to be part of being a philosopher. In a letter to the Jesuit missionary Joachim Bouvet, Leibniz calls such ways of living the *true* practical philosophy: "For the true practical philosophy (*true, not simulated philosophy as they say of our Roman Jurisconsults*) consists rather in these good orders for education, and for the conversation and sociability of men, than in the general precepts on the virtues and rights."[28] Such statements support Pierre Hadot's claim that the classical conception of philosophy as a way of life remained through the early modern period.[29] Our selective attention to early modern philosophers tends to obscure this element of their thought, but we need only consider that Descartes wrote *The Passions of the Soul* and Spinoza entitled his main work the *Ethics*.[30]

This conception of the philosopher as one who lives wisely also has a political dimension. Leibniz's praise for Chinese ethics is largely praise for the laws and customs by which the people live. These would have been designed by philosopher kings like Fuxi and philosopher teachers like Confucius, and when Christian Wolff lectured in 1730 on the ideal of the philosopher king, he took the Chinese as his prime example.[31] It is thus no surprise that Leibniz ends his praise for the practical philosophy of the Chinese with a description of Kang Xi, emperor of the Qing Dynasty. One must marvel at him, Leibniz says, because while his power is absolute, "he is educated according to custom in virtue and wisdom and rules his subjects with an extraordinary respect for the laws and with a reverence for the advice of wise men."[32] In this passage, we see another ideal of the philosopher – the "wise man" who would advise and educate the king. Although Leibniz could hardly claim such a role for himself in relation to his patrons in Hanover, it is difficult not to see this as an attempt to set up an ideal of the philosopher as a political adviser and even what we might now call a "public intellectual." It is precisely the role played, in theory at least, by the Confucian literati through much of Chinese history.

Leibniz's rationalism requires that "First Philosophy" and "Practical Philosophy" be connected. Leibniz links them even in the preface to the *Novissima Sinica*: "Now geometry ought not to be regarded as the sphere of workmen but of philosophers; for, since virtue flows from wisdom, and the spirit of wisdom is truth, those who thoroughly investigate the demonstrations of geometers have perceived the nature of eternal truths and are able to tell the certain from the uncertain."[33] Given the link between reason and virtue, the philosophy of the Chinese cannot be reduced merely to good behaviour. Leibniz's other main characterization of the exchange between China and Europe makes this clear: China should send missionaries to teach natural theology in Europe, just as Europe has sent missionaries to China to teach revealed theology.[34] The term "natural theology" was nearly interchangeable with the term "philosophy" in the early modern period, and Leibniz identifies the terms twice in his main essay on Chinese thought, which he entitled the *Discourse on the Natural Theology of the Chinese*. As his detailed analysis of Confucian metaphysics shows, Leibniz does not think the Chinese are incapable of reasoning. On the contrary, in distinguishing between natural and revealed theology, the exchange Leibniz envisions is close to an exchange of religion from Europe for philosophy from China. We see such a view suggested in a letter to Electress Sophie from April 1709, in which Leibniz characterizes the exchange in slightly different terms: while Europeans spread Christian religion and revelation to China, Europe needs the Chinese to send them "Missionaries of Reason ... to preach the natural Religion."[35] The claim that the Chinese need to bring *reason* to Europe appears also in the preface to the *Novissima Sinica*, where Leibniz says that Europeans are less ethical than the Chinese because Europeans are "not enough accustomed to act by reason and rule."[36]

This comparison suggests Leibniz sees China as a land of philosophy while Europe is dominated by religion, but Leibniz's view of natural theology in relation to Europe and China is more complex if not outright contradictory. In the *Discourse*, Leibniz praises and defends the natural theology of the Chinese, but consider the culmination of this defence:

> What we call the light of reason in man, they call commandment and law of Heaven. What we call the inner satisfaction of obeying justice and our fear of acting contrary to it, all this is called by the Chinese (and by us as well) inspirations sent by the Xangti [*Shàngdì* 上帝] (that is, by the true God). To offend Heaven is to act against reason, to ask pardon of Heaven is to reform oneself and to make a sincere return in word and deed in the submission one owes to this very law of reason. For me I find all this quite excellent and quite in accord with natural theology ... It is pure Christianity, insofar as it renews the natural law inscribed in our hearts – except for what revelation and grace add to it to improve our nature.[37]

As we see here, the ultimate defence of the natural theology of the Chinese is that it is the same as that of Europe. Thus, on this level, Leibniz thinks Europe has nothing to learn. On the contrary, Leibniz believes this same natural theology is expressed less clearly and systematically in the Chinese texts, since they lack a precise form of expression and have no art of demonstration. The learned among modern Chinese had lost it entirely, falling into a position close to that of Spinoza or the Stoics (all of whom, it should be noted, would certainly still be called philosophers).

If Leibniz thought natural theology in Europe was clearer and more complete than in China, then how are we to understand the claim that Chinese need to come to Europe to teach natural theology? Leibniz explains his meaning most fully in two letters written to Electress Sophie.[38] We have seen the letter from April 1709, in which Leibniz calls for Chinese missionaries of reason to come and teach natural religion. He explains: "the Religion of Reason is eternal, and God has engraved it in our hearts, [but] our corruptions have obscured it."[39] This religion of reason is obscure in Europe not so much on the theoretical side but rather as expressed in practice. Europe's natural theology lacks the clarity and immediacy that would inspire good actions. Here we see a kind of circularity – our moral weaknesses obscure reason, and the obscurity of reason makes us morally weak. Leibniz thought the Chinese had developed the most effective ways to limit such moral failings, an ability that is inseparable from their being philosophers and "missionaries of reason." Another letter written to the Electress nearly a decade earlier, on 10 September 1697, helps to further explain this relationship. The letter also voices Leibniz's call for missionaries of natural religion from China, but the failings of European morality are all explained as arising from conflicts between Christian factions. Leibniz took these conflicts as based on differing interpretations of doctrines that were peripheral to the key truths established by natural theology (that God exists, God is perfectly good, and there is justice in an afterlife). He explains: "For in effect, the government of the Chinese would be incomparably better than that of God, if God were like the bickering of the Sectarian Doctors, who each attach salvation to the chimeras of their party."[40] Although not explicit, Leibniz implies that, lacking revealed perplexities like the Trinity, the Chinese would be less tempted to allow such trivialities to obscure the basic truths of natural theology.

How does all of this fit together? Leibniz envisions philosophy as encompassing a continuum from the abstract truths of mathematics, logic, and metaphysics through general principles of politics and ethics down to actually being virtuous, which would include things like treating others with care and respect and freeing oneself from anger. All of these fall within the realm of philosophy. To some degree, Leibniz thinks that philosophy in both Europe and China covers this full range. The Chinese do have some systematic metaphysics, as the *Discourse* makes clear, and surely Leibniz would say that Europeans had at least a little success in being virtuous. Nonetheless, the Chinese were stronger in living wisely, while Europeans had gone further in abstract theoretical analysis. This may be the ultimate significance of his argument for exchange between China and Europe: the possibility of creating a complete philosophy running from abstract analysis all the way down to living with wisdom and virtue. There are some suggestions that Leibniz took the Chinese Emperor Kang Xi as having successfully made this synthesis. The emperor was distinguished not only for his justice, his charity towards the people, and his moderate way of life, but also for his love of learning.[41] This love of learning led the emperor to study geometry and trigonometry with the Jesuit missionary Ferdinand Verbiest. Leibniz tells us that this was in addition to a Chinese education that required a "discipline almost beyond the capacity of a private individual." Leibniz takes this combination of European and Chinese culture as the reason for Kang Xi's superior judgment, elevating him above other Chinese just as if one placed a European steeple on top of an Egyptian pyramid.[42] As this view of Kang Xi shows, Leibniz did not think the Chinese were by nature limited in their ability for abstract thought. The ability of the Chinese to incorporate European thought appears as well in Leibniz's frequent worry that China would absorb Europe's strengths, while Europe neglected to learn anything from China.

We should not let Leibniz's contrast between Europe and China mislead us into assuming that philosophy is divided into two distinct parts, the practical and the theoretical. The divide between theory and practice is itself a product of certain historical conditions and needs. Chinese philosophers would have rejected such a division, had it even arisen as something to reject. While Leibniz does distinguish the practical and the theoretical, the core of philosophy and reason lies within both. The significance of Leibniz's view of Chinese Philosophy is not that he values both sides of a divide (the theoretical and the practical) but that he does not divide them in the first place. We can clarify this view of reason by placing it in the context of two broader aspects of Leibniz's philosophy, both of which concern the unity and diversity of thought across cultures.

The first point is his assumption that all human beings have an instinct of reason, which expresses the innate ideas that all people share. The foundation lies in the principle of non-contradiction and the principle of sufficient reason, which are described as being like the muscles and tendons of human thought: "For general principles enter into our thoughts, serving as their inner core and as their mortar. Even if we give no thought to them, they are necessary for thought, as muscles and tendons are for walking."[43] Although the articulation of these principles in formal logical terms is an important step in the development of philosophy, it is not nearly as important as the fact that we all already use these principles in making sense of the world. Leibniz's analysis of Chinese Philosophy in the *Discourse* frequently relies on this commonality, which is ultimately what allows him to imagine engaging in dialogue with the Chinese as philosophers. He also uses it as a hermeneutic strategy. For example, when Antoine de Sainte-Marie says that the Chinese derive order from prime matter, Leibniz says this interpretation must be wrong, because the Chinese would not be "so stupid or absurd."[44] When we combine this instinct for reason with the fact that human beings find pleasure in gaining knowledge and that the truth itself has an inherent tendency to emerge into consciousness, Leibniz would say that all human beings have both the resources for and a natural tendency towards philosophy.

On the other side, Leibniz believes that human knowledge is always limited and perspectival. It is impossible to encounter the world other than from one finite point of view, and we remain necessarily distant from the ultimate structure of the cosmos. Even space and time are merely well-grounded phenomena, expressions of an inaccessible world of incorporeal monads that never interact. Human beings always reason *in media res*, in the midst of things. While we progress from our particular embodied situation towards greater and greater knowledge, our analysis of the world can go on infinitely in any direction, never coming to an end or an absolute foundation. As Leibniz tells us, even angels have more to learn.[45] Leibniz believes that some cultures have more knowledge than others – with Europe and China as the two concentrations of "human cultivation and refinement"[46] – but no view is ever complete. This renders Leibniz's philosophy inherently pluralistic and generates a need for dialogue and exchange. It would thus be a mistake to see the synthesis of the antitheses of European and Chinese philosophy as resulting in a final complete system. That system would only provide a new basis from which further questions would arise.

I hope to have shown that Leibniz's recognition of philosophy in China depends as much on his conception of philosophy as it does on his knowledge of China, his universalistic view of human nature, and his more favourable attitude towards other cultures. This is supported by the fact that the change in the conception of philosophy did not just affect the status of Chinese thought. Hellenistic Philosophy – which had been so important for the formation of philosophy in the early modern period – also faded into the background. Roman philosophers like Cicero and Seneca went the way of French *philosophes* like Voltaire, defined out of the discipline of philosophy (where they still remain). This is why, while racism played an important role in the elimination of Chinese Philosophy, the rise of racist views cannot be the whole story.[47] The details of how this conception of philosophy shifted requires further research, but a decisive moment is surely marked by Hegel, particularly his lectures on the history of philosophy. The introductions to these lectures are crucial because they put forth a new definition of philosophy and then use this definition to exclude cultures outside of Europe. A discussion of Hegel's view would exceed the scope of this essay and would require an analysis of many aspects of his thought. Here, I will just briefly note a couple of points as a contrast with Leibniz and as suggestions for further inquiry.

Hegel most of all argues for a *scientific* conception of philosophy, by which he means that philosophy must follow the necessary development of thought itself. In the introduction to the lectures on the history of philosophy from 1825 to 1826, he explains:

> The science [*Wissenschaft*] of philosophy is, accordingly, the development of the thought that is free. The whole [of this science] is the totality of this development, the circle that closes back upon itself, that remains wholly present to self, that is wholly itself, that seeks only to come to itself. In contrast, when we occupy ourselves with the sensible domain, we are present to something other and not present to ourselves. Only in thought are we present to ourselves. So philosophy is development of the thought that is untrammeled in its freedom, that develops itself freely. Philosophy, then, is a system.[48]

In arguing this point, Hegel makes a decisive break from the earlier Greco-Roman conception of *philosophia* as a way of life or a kind of political engagement. This is not to say that Hegel did not care about political involvement or living wisely, nor that he saw these as unrelated to philosophy. Philosophy is crucial for them, but it is still clearly distinct. Consequently, the actual lives of philosophers become irrelevant to the history of philosophy, which should only follow the necessary development of ideas.[49] This is the exact opposite of the Greco-Roman view: since philosophy had been conceived as a way of living and engaging the social-political world, *how* philosophers lived was of greatest importance. We see this most clearly in Diogenes Laertius's *Lives of Eminent Philosophers*, written around the third century CE, which in our modern view would not even fall within the genre of "the history of philosophy."

Perhaps the most important discussion for our purposes is in Hegel's attempt to distinguish Philosophy proper from what he calls popular philosophy ("Popularphilosophie"). Hegel singles out the writings of Cicero as an example: "His philosophizing can yield fine and admirable results as the philosophizing of a man who has been observant and knows what is worthwhile, what the world takes to be true. He presents his heartfelt experiences of the world, speaking with a cultivated spirit about the absolutely most important topics."[50] Popular philosophy does consist of independent thought derived from self-reflection, but what disqualifies it from being Philosophy proper is that it begins by assuming the human condition: "Here in the third sphere [i.e., popular philosophy] too the source is our natural being, our feeling, our disposition, our inner being as impelled toward God. The content that is called God, law, duty, and so forth, is in a merely natural state."[51] We can take this as a rejection of Leibniz's conception of philosophy as necessarily positioned *in media res*. Like Leibniz, Hegel believes there is "the instinct of reason," but this cannot count as Philosophy as long as this reasoning is only implicit.[52]

I would like to conclude this chapter by turning to what I labelled as the third dimension of the question of the existence of Chinese Philosophy, that of interests and power. Such shifting concerns partly explain both the change in the conception of philosophy and its application to other cultures. Leibniz was writing at a time when the very possibility of philosophy as distinct from religion remained in question. In fact, this distinction between philosophy and religion was conceived more as a distinction between "natural theology" and "revealed theology." From the beginning, the possibility of natural theology was linked to the thought of other cultures. Aquinas introduces the distinction in order to explain how pagans like Aristotle – whom Aquinas refers to simply as "the Philosopher" – could have said so many true things about the divine, human nature, and morality, all without the aid of revelation.[53] The answer was that our natural human capabilities allow us to reach such truths, which constitute natural theology. While Aquinas takes care to keep natural theology in the service of revealed theology, the same human ability to reach truths without revelation was later used to justify the possibility of philosophy for Europeans as well. Since Europe conceived its cultural identity as fundamentally Christian, the claim for philosophical independence from Christianity required arguing that philosophy could arise from acultural human abilities. Given this origin, it is not surprising that when philosophers began to claim independence from revealed theology, they appealed to the universality of reason and assumed or asserted that human beings in other cultures would also have philosophy. In this context, the belief that other cultures have philosophy is not a *result* of philosophy's orientation towards universalism but rather is a *premise* for the very possibility of philosophy. Thus, those who saw no value in Chinese thought – from the missionary opponents of the Jesuit position to the Pietist enemies of Wolff – generally did not deny that the Chinese had reason but rather denied the power of reason to lead to anything other than *splendida peccata*, "splendid sins."

By the time of Hegel, the division between philosophy and religion was more secure, even if their relationship and status were still under debate. The link between philosophy and universality remained, but this universality was seen as an *achievement* of European philosophy, fully compatible with the belief that no other culture had it. Indeed, Hegel inverts the earlier argument from the universality of reason to the possibility of philosophy. For Hegel, the only way the universality of Philosophy can be reconciled with the actual diversity of philosophies – over time and across cultures – is if philosophy reached its fully explicit form only in one place, which, not surprisingly, was his own.[54] At the same time that the status of philosophy was freed from the actual universality of reason, the political and economic importance of European hegemony became more and more clear, providing a strong incentive for any discipline to rationalize Europe's superiority. We must add, though, that the legitimacy of philosophy still faced challenges, but from a different direction – the demands of academia. The shifting structures of universities demanded that philosophy constitute itself as a *science*. Simply put, it would be difficult to create a scientific discipline oriented towards living wisely or training public intellectuals and political advisers, precisely what Leibniz and Wolff praised as the "practical philosophy" of the Chinese, and what indeed most classical Chinese "philosophers" had attempted to do.

We still remain in the legacy of this shift, and it creates a fundamental dilemma for applying the label of "philosophy" to what was done in pre-modern China. If we say it is not philosophy, we exclude it from the canon of a philosophical education; if we say it is philosophy, we risk fundamentally distorting what Chinese thinkers themselves were doing, ripping certain theoretical concerns from their place in a way of living wisely.[55] By revealing the historicity of this shift, though, we can at least see that the current exclusionary conception of philosophy is peculiarly *modern*. It is striking, for example, that Zhuangzi and Mengzi would fit pretty well in *Lives of Eminent Philosophers*; in fact, that they would fit much better than Kant or Hegel would. Of course, that our modern conception of philosophy emerged in a context of European imperialism and racism does not mean that this conception of philosophy itself is wrong. It does mean, though, that we cannot simply say something is or is not philosophy – we must also defend the conception of philosophy we wish to use. Certainly, the condition of the world has changed enough since the time of Hegel to justify a re-examination of our concept of philosophy, in hopes of a definition more adequate to the current world situation. That work, though, must be rooted in a more thorough investigation of the factors that led to the modern view of philosophy and the exclusion of other cultures. My hope is to have contributed one little piece to better understanding that history.[56]

NOTES

1 For an excellent discussion of the composition and content of the *Confucius Sinarum Philosophus*, see D.E. Mungello, *Curious Land: Jesuit Accommodation and the Origins of Sinology* (Honolulu: University of Hawai'i Press, 1985), 247–99.

2 A translation of the fourth book, the *Mengzi* 孟子, was published by François Noël in *Sinensis imperii libri classici sex* in 1711.

3 The Rites Controversy centred on two questions – were the Confucians theists or atheists, and were Confucian rituals secular or religious? The dominant Jesuit position argued for the former position on each question. On that view, Christianity was required as a supplement to Confucianism rather than as a complete replacement. Thus, the position was labelled "accommodation."

4 See, e.g., Matteo Ricci, *China in the Sixteenth Century: The Journals of Matteo Ricci, 1583–1610*, translated by Louis Gallagher (New York: Random House, 1953), 58.

5 The original text is published in Christian Wolff, *Oratio de Sinarum philosophia practica Rede über die praktische Philosophie der Chinesen*, translated and edited by Michael Albrecht (Hamburg: Felix Meiner, 1985). A translation can be found in, *Moral Enlightenment: Leibniz and Wolff on China*, translated and edited by Julia Ching and Willard Oxtoby (Monumenta Serica Monograph Series 26) (Nettelal, Germany: Steyler Verlag, 1992). For discussions of this lecture and the broader context of Wolff's interest in China, see Mark Larrimore, "Orientalism and Antivoluntarism: On Christian Wolff's 'Oratio de Sinarum Philosophia Practica,'" *Journal of Religious Ethics* 28.2 (2000): 189–219, and Donald F. Lach, "The Sinophilism of Christian Wolff (1679–1754)," *Journal of the History of Ideas* 14.4 (1953): 561–74.

6 Ep 67; Benedict de Spinoza, *The Letters*, translated by Samuel Shirley (Indianapolis: Hackett, 1995), 303 (translation modified); Ep 76, Spinoza, *Letters*, 342.

7 Ep 76, Spinoza, *Letters*, 342.

8 Those who claimed that the Confucians were atheists frequently made this link to Spinozism, which was the most prominent model for such a view in Europe at the time. For example, Pierre Bayle discusses Confucianism and Buddhism in his entry on Spinoza, and discusses Spinoza in his entry on Japan (Pierre Bayle, *Mr Bayle's Historical and Critical Dictionary*, translated by P. des Mazeaux [London: Routledge/Thoemmes Press, 1997; reprint from 1736], vol. V, 199, and vol. III, 550). For discussions of this connection, see Yuen Ting Lai, "The Linking of Spinoza to Chinese Thought by Bayle

and Malebranche," *Journal of the History of Ideas* 23/2 (1985): 151–78, and
Thijs Westseijn, "Spinoza sinicus: An Asian Paragraph in the History of the
Radical Enlightenment," *Journal of the History of Ideas* 68/4 (2007): 537–61.

9   For a discussion of the role of racism in the formation of the philosophical
canon, see Peter Park, *Africa, Asia, and the History of Philosophy: Racism in
the Formation of the Philosophical Canon, 1780–1830* (Albany: State University
of New York Press, 2013).

10   For example, in the most explicit recent attempt to argue that philosophy
is unique to Europe, Rodolphe Gasché makes no attempt to survey other
cultures; the only evidence given about any other culture is a second-hand
report of an unidentified Englishman residing in some African country,
who comments that the locals take criticism as a personal insult (Rodolphe
Gasché, *Europe, or the Infinite Task: A Study of a Philosophical Concept* [Palo
Alto: Stanford University Press, 2009], 349). For a critical analysis of
Gasché's *Europe, or the Infinite Task*, see Franklin Perkins, "Europe and the
Question of Philosophy: A Response to Rodolfe Gasché's *Europe, or the
Infinite Task*," *Comparative and Continental Philosophy* 3/1 (2011): 28–37, and
Gasché's response in the same volume.

11   On this point, see Robert Bernasconi, "Philosophy's Paradoxical Parochi-
alism," in *Readings of Cultural Imperialism: Edward Said and the Gravity of
History*, eds. Keith Ansell-Pearson, Benita Parry, and Judith Squires (New
York: St Martin's, 1997), 212–26.

12   The three dimensions of the question naturally influence each other. For
example, the redefinition of philosophy as a science followed from the need
to construct philosophy as an academic discipline within conceptions of the
university and of science. This redefinition of philosophy in turn led those
interested in promoting China to alter their presentation of it. The shift in
emphasis towards Buddhism and Daoism, for example, followed partly
because they seemed more capable of appearing as a science of concepts,
whereas Confucianism looked too much like simple practical guidance for
living well. On this point, see Anne-Lise Dyck, "La Chine hors de la philosophie: Essai de généalogie à partir des traditions sinologique et philosophique
françaises au XIXe siècle," *Extrême Orient, Extrême Occident* 27 (2005): 13–47.

13   This shift in the conception of religion has been well studied and makes
an interesting contrast with the field of philosophy, where the shift seems
to have gone almost unnoticed. See, e.g., Tomoko Masuzawa, *The Invention of World Religions, Or, How European Universalism Was Preserved in the
Language of Pluralism* (Chicago: University of Chicago Press, 2005), and
Richard King, *Orientalism and Religion: Post-Colonial Theory, India, and the
"Mystic East"* (London: Routledge, 1999).

14 I have avoided attempting to evaluate this general claim, which suffers from the flaws of overgeneralization and of definition by contrast or lack. The very isolation of abstract necessary truths from practice and experience is itself a product of European thought. In this essay, I make only the weak claim that, as in ancient Greece and India, what we would label as philosophical inquiry in China was integrated with practices of self-cultivation and living wisely, in a way that is difficult to assimilate into the modern practice of philosophy as an academic discipline.

15 *Novissima Sinica* (hereafter, *NS*), s. 2; translation by Donald Lach, in Daniel Cook and Henry Rosemont Jr, *Writings on China* (Chicago: Open Court, 1994), 46.

16 *NS*, s. 9; Cook and Rosemont, *Writings*, 50.

17 Leibniz to Bouvet, 18 May 1703; Rita Widmaier, ed., *Leibniz Korrespondiert mit China* (Frankfurt: V. Klostermann, 1990), 179.

18 *NS*, s. 68; Cook and Rosemont, *Writings*, 132–3. Leibniz thought the hexagrams of the *Yijing* represented a system of binary arithmetic similar to the one he had just invented.

19 Helmut von Glasenapp, *Kant und die Religionen des Osten* (Kitzingen-Main: Holzner Verlag, 1954), 103–4. Glasenapp cites Ms. 2599, which consists of lecture notes from Christian Friedrich Puttlich, probably from 1785. The manuscript seems to have since been lost.

20 *NS*, s. 3; Cook and Rosemont, *Writings*, 46–7.

21 *NS*, s. 10; Cook and Rosement, *Writings*, 51.

22 *NS*, s. 4; Cook and Rosemont, *Writings*, 47.

23 *NS*, s. 3; Cook and Rosemont, *Writings*, 46–7.

24 *NS*, s. 4; Cook and Rosemont, *Writings*, 47.

25 *NS*, s. 4; Cook and Rosemont, *Writings*, 47.

26 NS, s. 4; Cook and Rosemont, *Writings*, 47.

27 *NS*, s. 5; Cook and Rosemontv 48.

28 Leibniz to Bouvet, 2 Dec. 1697 (emphasis added); Widmaier, *Leibniz Korrespondiert*, 62.

29 Pierre Hadot, *What Is Ancient Philosophy?* translated by Michael Chase (Cambridge, MA: Belknap Press of Harvard University Press, 2002), 263–70.

30 Descartes makes his priorities clear in *The Passions of the Soul*: "But the chief use of wisdom lies in its teaching us to be masters of our passions and to control them with such skill that the evils which they cause are quite bearable, and even become a source of joy" (*The Philosophical Writings of Descartes*, translated and edited by John Cottingham, Robert Stoothoff, and Dugald Murdoch [Cambridge: Cambridge University Press, 1994], vol. II, 404).

31 The lecture was published as "De rege philosophante et philosopho regnante" (On the philosopher king and the ruling philosopher). For a translation of the lecture, see Ching and Oxtoby, *Moral Enlightenment*; for the original text, see Christian Wolff, *Gesammelte Werke* II, vol. 34/2 (Hildesheim: Georg Olms, 1983), 563–632.

32 *NS*, s. 6; Cook and Rosemont, *Writings*, 48.

33 *NS*, s. 9; Cook and Rosemont, *Writings*, 50.

34 *NS*, s. 10; Cook and Rosemont, *Writings*, 51.

35 Onno Klopp, ed., *Die Werke von Leibniz* (Hanover, 1864–84), vol. I, ix, 3, 301.

36 *NS*, s. 4; Cook and Rosemont, *Writings*, 47.

37 *Discourse on the Natural Theology of the Chinese*, s. 31; Cook and Rosemont, *Writings*, 105.

38 For a more detailed discussion of these letters, see Franklin Perkins, *Leibniz and China: A Commerce of Light* (Cambridge, MA: Cambridge University Press, 2005), 146–57.

39 Klopp, *Die Werke von Leibniz*, vol. I, ix, 3, 301.

40 G.W. Leibniz, *Sämtliche Schriften und Briefe*, edited by Deutsche Akademie der Wissenschaften (Darmstadt: Akademie Verlag, 1923–), series I, vol. 14, 72.

41 *NS*, s. 7; Cook and Rosemont, *Writings*, 49.

42 *NS*, s. 7; Cook and Rosemont, 49.

43 *New Essays on Human Understanding*, translated by Peter Remnant and Jonathon Bennett (Cambridge, MA: Cambridge University Press, 1981), book I, chapter i, s. 20, 84.

44 *Discourse*, s. 12; Cook and Rosemont, *Writings*, 85.

45 *New Essays* IV, xvii, s. 16; Remnant and Bennett, *New Essays*, 490.

46 *NS*, s. 1; Cook and Rosemont, *Writings*, 45.

47 For a persuasive argument on the role of racism in the exclusion of Chinese (and non-Western) philosophy, see Park, *Africa, Asia, and the History of Philosophy*.

48 *Lectures on the History of Philosophy 1825–6*, vol. I, *Introduction and Oriental Philosophy*, edited and translated by R.F. Brown and J.M. Stewart (Oxford: Oxford University Press, 2009), 54/219. Citations of Brown and Stewart include the page number followed by the corresponding page number in vol. VI of *G.W.F. Hegel Vorlesungen*, edited by Pierre Garniron and Walter Jaeschke (Hamburg: Felix Meiner, 1994).

49 Hegel says, "The events and actions of the history of philosophy do not have the kind of content that includes issues of personality and individual character" (Brown and Stewart, *Introduction*, 208/5). Hegel several times emphasizes that he is writing a history of philosophy, not of philosophers (e.g., Brown and Stewart, *Introduction*, 101/363, 261/318).

50 Brown and Stewart, *Introduction*, 227/187.
51 Ibid., 228/188.
52 Ibid., 84/259.
53 For a more detailed discussion of this point, see Perkins, *Leibniz and China*, 4–6.
54 Hegel makes this point consistently through his introductory lectures on the history of philosophy. See, e.g., Brown and Stewart, *Introduction*, 58–9/225–6 (from 1825–26) and 259–60/315–17 (from 1829–30).
55 For a Chinese perspective on the latter point, see Zheng Jiadong (鄭家棟), "The Issue of the 'Legitimacy' of Chinese Philosophy," *Contemporary Chinese Thought* 37/1 (2005): 11–23.
56 Versions of this essay were presented at the Pennsylvania State University, Fudan University, the National University of Singapore, and the Pacific Meeting of the American Philosophical Association. I am grateful for feedback and suggestions from these various audiences, particularly for comments presented at the APA by Ursula Goldenbaum.

3 Leibniz between Paris, Grand Tartary, and the Far East: Gerbillon's Intercepted Letter

MICHAEL C. CARHART

Language and *Origines Guelficae*

Leibniz was not always interested in China. Although he stands near the beginning of Europe's attempt to acquire systematic knowledge of its far eastern rival, Leibniz's interest in China emerged from a project much closer to home – the origins and migrations of the European nations. Early in his career Leibniz did share that general curiosity about the exotic civilization of the Far East characteristic of many orientalists and antiquarians of the seventeenth century, but it was not until he conceived of the second preliminary dissertation to *Origines Guelphicae* – entitled *Migrationes Gentium* – that he undertook a positive effort to acquire new knowledge of Asia and, by extension, of China. And then, once he had established what kinds of knowledge he wanted from Jesuit missionaries, making actual contact with them was anything but straightforward. Actual contact with the Jesuits of China was made less through design than serendipity – the acquaintance of a correspondent in Berlin, a diplomat stationed in the eastern Baltic, and a well-placed Russian of Flemish descent who forwarded through Leibniz's correspondence network a top secret document confiscated by the Moscow Ministry of Foreign Affairs.

Educated in law at the universities of Leipzig and Altdorf in the 1660s, with further informal study at Paris, London, and the Hague in the 1670s, Leibniz emerged as a polymathic scholar of encyclopedic interests and talent. Having found a patron in the Duke of Braunschweig-Lüneburg at Hanover, in the 1680s Leibniz was assigned the task of writing a genealogical history of that noble house. The specific purpose of that genealogy was to support the duke's bid to be elevated to the status of Elector, the highest rank in the Holy Roman Empire. But writing accolades of his noble patron stood to make Leibniz appear the most obsequious of courtiers, an image he was keen to avoid. So in early 1691 he came up with a plan to make a genuine contribution to scholarship. To the genealogy proper he would append two preliminary dissertations.

These preliminary dissertations would explain, respectively, the land of Lower Saxony where the House of Guelph ruled and the people whom they ruled. The first preliminary dissertation, on the land of Lower Saxony, would be a geohistory, an explanation of how the Harz Mountains came to be and the wonders they contained, like fossilized fish, sharks' teeth, and other "games of nature" that suggested that the face of the earth once looked very different. This first preliminary dissertation Leibniz finished in 1694 under the title of *Protogaea*. The second preliminary dissertation, on the people of Lower Saxony and how they had come into that country, was a story of ethnogenesis. Leibniz understood that the Low Saxons were not indigenous to that part of Europe but had migrated to it sometime in the prehistoric past. Leibniz hypothesized that the original homeland of the European nations was somewhere in the region of the Caspian Sea, possibly east in the steppes of Grand Tartary, or perhaps further west on the north shore of the Black Sea. But how to prove it? Historical documents existed only back to the Roman Empire, by whose time the Germanic tribes already occupied the forests of northern Europe.

In order to reconstruct the origins and migrations of the European nations yet lacking any documentary evidence, Leibniz turned to language. By comparing the vocabularies of neighbouring and widely separated nations, Leibniz thought he could establish how those nations were related to each other. Once the relationships were established, he might be able to explain European ethnogenesis – the original homeland of the European peoples and the course of their migrations to the west.

Historians of nineteenth-century comparative linguistics frequently pay lip service to Leibniz as an early example of the practice of their discipline. But where nineteenth-century comparative linguistics was based on structural grammar, Leibniz had no hope of learning the inflectional patterns of the languages of the nomads across the Central Asian steppe. His methodology instead was comparative vocabulary: word lists and the Lord's Prayer in various languages.

For Leibniz's purposes the Lord's Prayer contained a pretty good vocabulary of basic concepts: Our, Father, Sky/Heaven, Holy/Sacred,

Name, Kingdom, Will/Wish/Desire, Earth, Day, Bread; and the verbs to be, to do, to come, to give, etc. A set of Lord's Prayers in several languages would offer a means to recognize cognate terms in related languages as well as languages that differed completely from each other. This would give one the means to identify relationships between languages and, by extension, the relationships between the nations of Europe and Asia.

Brilliant in conception – impossible in execution. By the time Leibniz started his project, the Lord's Prayer had been collected in nearly a hundred languages. By the early nineteenth century, Johann Christian Adelung would publish the prayer in some five hundred world languages. Leibniz considered it an act of piety for a missionary to translate the prayer into a new language. Ideally, missionaries travelling across Asia to China would translate the prayer into the languages of the peoples through whom they passed. Leibniz hoped that those missionaries would send him copies of the prayer in those hitherto unknown languages.

Beginning in 1691, Leibniz built a network of correspondents he hoped would supply him with linguistic knowledge of the present inhabitants of various regions. That network of correspondents – many of them world-travelling Jesuit missionaries destined for China – is what brought him into contact with China and supplied him with the only real set of data with which he had to work. In other words, Leibniz's work on Confucian philosophy and the *I-Ching* with Joachim Bouvet, a Jesuit in China, was directly the product of his linguistic inquiries into the peoples and nations of northern and Central Asia.

It is true that at first glance Leibniz's linguistic inquiries appear to be bound up with an interest in China from the very beginning.[1] While on his grand tour of Italy seeking the genealogical origin of the House of Guelph in the House of Este, Leibniz chanced to meet the procurator of the Jesuit Vice-Province of China, Claudio Philippo Grimaldi, who was in Rome for a few months in 1689. Both Leibniz and Grimaldi were accomplished mathematicians, and it was the Jesuit community of mathematicians at the Linsei Academy at Rome, whose meetings Leibniz attended while in the eternal city, that opened the door to Grimaldi. Leibniz and Grimaldi met on a couple of occasions in July 1689, and some of Leibniz's notes from at least one meeting survive and have been published by Rita Widmaier.[2] Although their conversation centred on mathematics, Grimaldi related some curiosities about China, including the Oriental Tartaric language of the Manchus. As his thoughts on the subject matured over the next couple of years, Leibniz rued his neglecting to attend more carefully to Grimaldi's knowledge of Asiatic languages; but in 1689 he had not yet hit upon his plan for the second preliminary dissertation to *Origines Guelficae*. Twice – in 1691 and again in 1692 – Leibniz wrote to Grimaldi for samples of the languages of the peoples through whose lands he passed in his travels. And from Goa in India Grimaldi did respond to Leibniz's 1692 letter, but that response offered only promises, not actual data.

It is also true that while he was in Rome in November 1689 Leibniz wrote to the Jesuit Giovanni Laureati, exhorting him in the name of the public (and asking also for himself) to be mindful of the gravity of his task of promoting commerce between two distant worlds, a commerce, so to speak, of learning and mutual light.[3] But by 1692 Laureati, too, was on his way to China, and Leibniz never heard from him again.

When Leibniz appended to a broad encyclopedic request for knowledge of China a more specific request for information about languages, he made it clear that he required samples of the languages of Tartaric Central Asia, not those of China per se. In Andreas Müller and Christoph Mentzel, both at Berlin, Europe already had students of the Chinese language far more expert than what Leibniz himself aspired to be.[4] Leibniz, on the contrary, was interested in the languages of the lesser-known peoples through whose areas an overland traveller would pass on the way to China. Here is how he explained it in 1691 to a fellow mathematician, the Jesuit A.A. Kochanski of Warsaw:

> I wish very strongly that a brief but complete notice of the languages of most of the nations currently present in Scythia could be obtained for us. Your colleagues could do this quite easily. For those who have been to Muscovy could easily obtain the Lord's Prayer or certain other things expressed in the languages of the peoples of Siberia and of neighboring nations all the way to the Ob and beyond, as well as of the nations around the Caspian Sea. Merchants at the Black and Caspian Seas also might investigate without too much difficulty the peoples distributed between the Persians, Muscovites, and Turks, as well as of those who are settled between the Muscovites, Persians, Mongols, and China. This knowledge would bring much light regarding the Origins of peoples. For it is likely that many of the peoples now in Europe originally came from the North.[5]

Unfortunately, so strenuous were the logistics of seventeenth-century Asiatic travel that although overland missionaries passed through many nations and languages, there was less opportunity for conversation and contemplation than Leibniz seemed to think. Grimaldi assured Leibniz that there was no possibility of investigating curiosities linguistic or otherwise, saying, "I had to become more barbarous than those barbarians through whom I travelled."[6] And other Jesuit travel reports displayed in rich detail the hardship faced by travelling missionaries and the precarious circumstances in which European Catholics found themselves in Sunni, Shi'ite, and Orthodox empires.[7]

By 1695, when Grimaldi's response from Goa reached Leibniz in Hanover, Leibniz had figured out that Grimaldi, Laureati, and other world travellers were not going to come through for him. He turned instead to their superiors. Did not the Society for the Propagation of the Faith at Rome have a library of missionary vocabularies and grammars? These would contain the linguistic data that he sought to compare. Unfortunately, although he had access to a few Jesuit mathematicians in the eternal city, those connections were not sufficiently strong to induce someone in the Propaganda Office to do the legwork of assembling, digesting, copying, and sending to Leibniz the data he sought.

Failing the Italian Jesuits, Leibniz turned to the French Jesuits. In the 1680s the French assumed a de facto leadership in the Jesuit China Mission when Philippe Couplet brought a Chinese Christian to Versailles and Royal Confessor François d'Aix de la Chaise, also a Jesuit, persuaded King Louis XIV to support on royal stipends and with royal letters patent not one but six missionaries who travelled to the Far East (Guy Tachard stepped off in Siam and returned to France) plus two others who attempted to reach the Great Wall overland through Grand Tartary. Leibniz knew that the Jesuit Antoine Verjus directed the movements of those French royal missionaries, that Verjus reported directly to Father De la Chaise, and that Verjus must necessarily be sitting on a wealth of knowledge in the reports that his missionaries sent home. Moreover, Leibniz once had been acquainted with Verjus's brother Louis, ennobled as le comte de Crécy, a member of the noblesse du robe and the French diplomatic corps. Crécy had come to Hanover years before on official business. Thus, Antoine Verjus would seem to be plausibly in range through the Republic of Letters.

Verjus seemed all the more plausible a source of linguistic knowledge because in the autumn of 1693 Leibniz had received a gift that he attributed to Antoine Verjus of a new edition of published mathematical and astronomical observations made by Jesuit missionaries in Siam and China.[8] Leibniz repeatedly dropped Verjus's name to his other correspondents in order to display his Parisian and Far Eastern credentials.[9] But it is doubtful whether Verjus himself actually intended the volume as a gift in the way that Leibniz thought. Leibniz sent Verjus no thank you note acknowledging receipt of the book, a basic form of politeness in the early Enlightenment Republic of Letters. In 1694 Leibniz sent twenty-five copies of his newly published *Codex diplomaticus iuris gentium*, one of which he earmarked specifically for Verjus,[10] but there is no indication that he enclosed a specific note to the Jesuit. Once Leibniz did succeed in gaining the Jesuit's attention (as will be shown below) Verjus responded apologetically for neglecting to acknowledge receipt of Leibniz's *Codex diplomaticus*, and in recompense he sent Leibniz a recent publication of the Jesuits of the Far East: Goüye's *Observations physiques et mathématiques* (1692), precisely the book he supposedly had given him two years before. This exemplar Verjus clearly intended for Leibniz personally, as Verjus inscribed a dedication to him inside the cover.[11] If the volume received in 1693 was indeed from Verjus, then by early 1695 Verjus had forgotten that he had sent it to Leibniz. In any case, the miscommunication indicates the distance that separated the Paris Jesuit from Leibniz, despite Leibniz's attempts to bridge it. It is only in 1695 that Leibniz succeeded in attracting the attention of the Paris Jesuits; and it would be through them – specifically Verjus and Joachim Bouvet – that Leibniz entered into an effective correspondence with the missionaries of China.

Scholars celebrate the far-flung connections established by Europeans in the age of exploration. That Leibniz's long-shot letter across Asia to Grimaldi actually found its target at Goa is an example of the European travel and mercantile network. But extraordinary examples of success like this tend to obscure the real difficulty in acquiring systematic knowledge. Europe abounded in curiosities and exotica from the Far East, but for a scientific project like Leibniz's on linguistic evidence of European origins, acquiring the specific knowledge he required was very difficult. Through 1693 and 1694 Leibniz appealed to his contacts at Berlin, Warsaw, Stockholm, and Paris, but repeatedly he discovered his fellow literary republicans dead (d'Herbelot), imprisoned (Larroque), not responding (Kochanski), out of the country (Sparwenfeld), or simply lacking sufficient knowledge even if trying to be helpful (Spanheim).

Given the liaison between Berlin and Moscow, Leibniz thought that surely there must be an agent of Brandenburg in Muscovy who could procure the needed language samples. His closest contact at the

Brandenburg court being incapable of giving the assistance Leibniz sought, Leibniz tried another approach. For several months he had been using his *Codex diplomaticus iuris gentium* as an icebreaker (the same volume he had sent to Paris in twenty-five copies). In January 1695 he sent a copy of the volume to the prime minister of the Brandenburg court, Eberhard Danckelman. Courtly protocol being as it was, a courtier of middling rank like Leibniz could not write directly to the head of a privy council like Danckelman. Instead, he sent the volume to Danckelman's secretary, J.J.J. Chuno. He congratulated Chuno on his being promoted along with Danckelman. He then asked Chuno to ask Danckelman a question about law (Danckelman's expertise). And finally in a postscript Leibniz pitched his linguistic project, hoping that someone at Berlin would invite him to send a questionnaire he had formalized about Tartaric languages in and beyond the empire of Muscovy.[12]

As it turned out, Danckelman was the wrong person to ask about Asiatic languages. Moreover, Spanheim had been correct all along, that since 1689 (i.e., before Leibniz and Spanheim had begun to correspond) Brandenburg had had no resident or envoy in Muscovy. But Chuno was enterprising. He found Brandenburg's former envoy from 1689, then stationed at Königsberg. Over the course of January to October 1695, Leibniz and Chuno exchanged some two dozen letters. What began with a letter fishing for an invitation to send to Berlin a more formal inquiry into Asiatic languages rapidly developed into a correspondence network that stretched to Königsberg and Danzig, to Moscow and back to Paris, and ultimately to Nerchinsk in Transbaikal Siberia/Manchuria. It was during these months that Leibniz collected most of the documents that he would publish two years later in *Novissima Sinica*, the latest news from China. It was also on the basis of the material collected through this network that Leibniz finally got the attention of the Paris Jesuits and their mission in China.

In August and September of 1689, a month's journey beyond Lake Baikal and two months' journey from Beijing, negotiators for the Muscovite and Qing Chinese empires met to determine the boundary between their respective domains.[13] Skirmishes had already been fought between the two sides a few years earlier, one of them resulting in a Muscovite garrison being almost entirely wiped out. Inside the negotiating tent, abrupt manners and differing customs created tensions between the two sides that nearly scuttled the talks. Borders were fiercely debated as both sides tried to explain their intentions regarding remote forests, mountains, and rivers that were largely unknown to both of them. The Qing had brought an army and deployed it across the Nercha River, surrounding the Muscovite garrison. The Muscovites, only a few hundred strong but armed with cannons, refortified the interior of their stockade and were determined to go down fighting if it came to blows. And then there was the question of language: In what language could Manchus and Muscovites make themselves understood to each other? The answer, of course, was Latin. On behalf of the Qing, two Jesuit mathematicians were brought along as advisers and translators. One was the Portuguese Tomé Pereira, the other Jean-François Gerbillon, a Frenchman under the jurisdiction of Antoine Verjus. Present on behalf of the Czars Ivan and Peter was a Polish Latinist named Andrei Belobotskii. Over the course of several days in early September 1689, the French Jesuit Gerbillon engaged in shuttle diplomacy between the Qing encampment and the Muscovite fortress, first delivering proposals and counterproposals and then hashing out the precise language of the treaty once an understanding was reached. Finally, at the end of the ordeal, the Treaty of Nerchinsk successfully concluded, Father Gerbillon sat down to write a long letter to his superiors at Paris, the royal confessor François de la Chaise and his procurator for East Indies missions, Antoine Verjus. He sealed the letter and handed it to the Muscovite ambassador, who promised to carry it to Moscow and then forward it on to Paris.

In February 1695, J.J.J. Chuno, secretary to the prime minister of Brandenburg, took the initiative to forward Leibniz's postscriptum requesting knowledge of Asiatic languages to his colleague at Königsberg, Johann Reyer, Brandenburg's most recent envoy to Moscow. Chuno put the request in his own words and thus gave Leibniz's project a kind of official sanction. He wrote a similar letter to the abbot of a Cistercian cloister outside of Danzig, whom he knew to be in contact with the royal court of Poland. Copies of these letters Chuno sent back to Leibniz.[14] Chuno confirmed that Reyer did maintain a contact at Moscow, a certain Andreas Vinius, P.M. Chuno supposed that P.M. must stand for prime minister.[15]

Leibniz was elated! The prime minister of the Empire of Muscovy! After months – years – of nagging inquiries, finally he had found the acquaintance of an acquaintance who must have had specific knowledge of the peoples and languages of central and north Asia. Leibniz ordered his secretary to make two copies of a formalized request for languages that he had drawn up in the previous weeks, and these he enclosed with an exuberant letter of gratitude to Chuno.[16]

Within weeks, however, Leibniz's enthusiasm was dampened. Vinius, it turned out, was not prime minister but only postmaster.[17] Chuno warned Leibniz not to get his hopes up for substantial knowledge from Muscovy: Reyer had expressed to him, "I must warn that at present the Muscovite Nation is very much indisposed toward investigating such curiosities, for what does not smell to them directly of money and evident utility cannot bring them to lift a finger. I know this from experience, as I had the opportunity to explore their genius for eighteen weeks."[18]

Mere curiosity. Undaunted, Leibniz suggested to Chuno that even if Vinius were merely postmaster, nevertheless he directed the czars' diplomatic dispatches, and in such a position he "could easily furnish some knowledge concerning nations and languages." And "if it is true that [the Muscovites] intend to mount a better campaign against the Crimean Tartars, it would seem that news of that region would be more than mere curiosity."[19]

Through the spring of 1695 Leibniz pressed Chuno and Reyer for any specific knowledge of Tartaric peoples and languages that they might wring out of Muscovy: "Czeremise, Circasian, Nagaiskio, Calmuck, Uzbec, Mongol etc., which peoples all inhabit Tartary"; on the Black Sea from the Danube to the Don including Crimea; on the Caspian Sea and beyond towards the east and north; in Siberia, along the Ob and Irtysch Rivers, and all the way to China.[20] Unfortunately, even the Muscovites seemed to have little knowledge of the indigenous languages spoken on the margins of their empire. Nevertheless Vinius had something that he thought the Brandenburgers might find curious – a letter that had come under his jurisdiction, intercepted from a French Jesuit in the Far East.

More than twelve pages long, written by a French Jesuit *ex Tartaria orientali* somewhere near the Chinese wall, addressed to François de la Chaise, the royal confessor of Louis XIV of France, and dated 22 August 1689, the letter had been confiscated in Moscow. Reyer himself did not actually have the letter but its capture had caused such a sensation that he had heard of it. Chuno asked around and discovered that the Muscovite interpreter at Berlin had heard of the intercepted letter, too. Chuno told Leibniz that he would press his contacts to obtain that letter as well as anything else that might pertain to Leibniz's researches. Immediately upon receiving this report from Chuno, Leibniz wrote to Paris.

I have learned that a person whom I know has a copy of a letter of twelve sheets addressed to Rev. Fr. de la Chaise, but intercepted by the Muscovites. It is dated the 22 of August from a location in Oriental Tartary near the Great Wall. This is a bit old. Nevertheless if the equivalent has not been received by other means, I shall inform myself more particularly and try to obtain the same. It seems to contain something instructive and useful. Perhaps the Rev. Fr. Verjus will not be angry to learn this particularity.[21]

This letter Leibniz sent not to Antoine Verjus directly (although he was trying, he still had no direct commerce with the Jesuit) but to the resident envoy for Braunschweig-Lüneburg in Paris, Christophe Brosseau. Brosseau responded promptly with the news that Verjus was at Versailles, but as soon as he returned to Paris he would pass on Leibniz's notice.[22] Two days later Leibniz was in direct contact with Antoine Verjus.[23]

Antoine Verjus, procurator of French Jesuit missions to the Far East, knew the precise location of each of the missionaries whom the court of Louis XIV supported overseas. He was well aware of Gerbillon's lost letter. He even knew what it said. But he was very angry to know where it had gone: not only intercepted in the most impolite of ways but that it had been opened and even distributed for copies. He asked Leibniz to obtain a copy, or better yet, the original itself. Verjus knew that Gerbillon and his Portuguese colleague Tomé Pereira had been instrumental in mediating the negotiations between China and Muscovy. "The Ambassadors of Muscovy showed him extreme gratitude," Verjus explained, "and the least of their promises was to arrange the swift and secure passage of their letters to us by way of Grand Tartary, Siberia, Muscovy, and Poland." And not only the passage of their letters: Verjus understood that the court of the czars had promised passage of Jesuit missionaries themselves. "No less positively did they promise to give complete liberty to our missionaries for passage to China by way of their States."[24]

Keenly interested in finding an overland route from Western Europe to the Far East, Verjus had twice outfitted expeditions of missionary-astronomers who might map the locations and caravan routes through Central Asia. Although daunting in the extreme – to hike or ride the width of Eurasia from Paris to Beijing – the overland route would serve as an alternative to the dangerous prospect of sailing months at sea on tenuous, disease-ridden ships at the mercy of the monsoons that drove them. European political considerations motivated Verjus as well.

For Leibniz, an overland route through Muscovy and Grand Tartary offered the possibility of learning the locations and relationships of the Central Asian nations that he needed to write the second preliminary dissertation to *Origines Guelficae*. Thus, confessional differences aside, Leibniz and Verjus shared an interest in sending missionaries over land through Grand Tartary.

Unfortunately, both expeditions that Verjus had organized – those of Louis Barnabé and of Philippe Grimaldi – saw their passport applications rejected by the court of the czars at Moscow.[25] Verjus believed that the Muscovite court had reneged on a promise to permit Jesuits to pass through their realm. Philippe Avril (Barnabé's partner who wrote a travel report of the expedition) believed the Muscovite court to be motivated by greed and not wanting anyone outside its employ to see the vast region of Siberia teeming with game whose furs were Muscovy's principal export in the seventeenth century.[26] For their part, the Muscovites expressed their inability to guarantee safe passage through regions over which they exercised little or no control.[27] And Leibniz, too, in assuming that samples of Tartaric languages should have been easy to procure, overestimated the power that the czars could project beyond their core domain of Muscovy.

Verjus had not even responded to Leibniz before Chuno sent additional material that Reyer had brought back from Moscow. Gerbillon's intercepted letter turned out to be two letters, one for de la Chaise and another addressed to Antoine Verjus himself. Leibniz drafted a second letter to Verjus with this news. In that second letter he expressed the hope that the Jesuits would publish all the knowledge that they had of the Far East.

Leibniz was on the verge of sealing this second letter when the response to his first letter arrived from Verjus at Paris. He quickly dashed off a postscript affirming what he had already stated in the main body: that the Jesuits must not hoard their knowledge of the Far East but should share it with the European Republic of Letters. "Since your fathers are of the Royal Academy of Sciences and a great King protects them in their long voyages," Leibniz admonished, "I hope that the public will profit more from their discoveries." He reminded Verjus that a century earlier the Jesuits used to publish an annual volume of letters from Japan. From Rome he had since learned that the Jesuit General had determined that there was no need for such a series any more, but Leibniz hoped that the French branch of the Society might think differently. "The observations of the French Fathers could serve as a supplement," he proposed. Perhaps it was the case that already there was a comprehensive edition of notices from the Far East, but even the good work of the Royal Academy of Sciences, which was printed, was not distributed through booksellers in Germany. "It is only by chance that I have seen recently the third volume of Father J. d'Orléans, and this seemed a considerable book to me," he complained.[28]

There is no way to document precisely what effect the Protestant of Hanover had on the Jesuit of Paris, but in 1698 Verjus hired Charles le Gobien to edit for publication some of the reports of Jesuit missionaries in the Far East and around the world. Gobien's project first bore fruit in 1702. By 1708 Gobien's editions became the serial *Lettres édifiantes et curieuses*, a capital source of European knowledge of China through much of the eighteenth century.

Leibniz was not waiting for Gobien, however. Already in April 1695 his letters to Antoine Verjus suggest that in Chuno's Muscovite documents Leibniz caught a glimpse of a publication of his own. That spring and summer Chuno showered Leibniz with bits of knowledge that Reyer gathered from Moscow. Gerbillon's letter to Antoine Verjus came through in May, and in June Leibniz passed it on to Paris, keeping a copy for himself.[29] Later that summer Gerbillon's letter to François de la Chaise arrived from Chuno, and this gave Leibniz occasion to write to Verjus again in early October. By then the Paris Jesuits were deeply in his debt.

Beyond Gerbillon's intercepted letters, Reyer told Chuno that he possessed a copy of a manuscript treatise on the grammar of "the Tartar language." This, too, Reyer had obtained "par strategeme" from a Jesuit.[30] From which Jesuit and where and when Reyer obtained the grammar is not known, but Chuno was certain that this piece would satisfy some of Leibniz's curiosity about Tartaric languages. Leibniz wondered which "Tartar" language it addressed.[31] Later that summer of 1695, when Reyer sent the manuscript from Königsberg to Chuno at Berlin and Chuno to Leibniz at Hanover, Leibniz learned that it was the Manchu language of the Qing dynasty of "Oriental Tartars" who had conquered China.[32] Through 1696 and 1697 Chuno sent additional instalments, but it required a couple of years before Leibniz came to learn what he had – Ferdinand Verbiest's *Elementa linguae Tartaricae*.

Reyer was able to obtain a third bit of knowledge about Siberia, Grand Tartary, and China for Leibniz. Andrei Vinius, the postmaster at Moscow, evidently persuaded Adam Brand, a native of Lübeck who was working in Muscovite employ, to summarize the itinerary of an ambassadorial caravan he had accompanied from Moscow to Beijing in

1693, 1694, and 1695. The official account of the journey was housed at the Ministry of Embassies (later, Foreign Affairs) at Moscow, but Brand wrote up a six-page summary of the expedition specifically for Leibniz. Thus, through Chuno to Reyer to Vinius, Leibniz succeeded in making indirect contact with a German traveller on the ground in Moscow.[33]

These three pieces – Gerbillon's letters, Verbiest's Tartaric grammar, and Adam Brand's itinerary – constitute three of the six documents Leibniz would translate into Latin and publish in April 1697 as *Novissima Sinica*, his only publication specifically about China. At the last minute, Leibniz learned that Verbiest's *Elementa linguae Tartaricae* had been published at Paris in 1696,[34] so he substituted that work with another Verbiest treatise, *Astronomia Europaea*, a copy of which he had made at Rome during his grand tour of Italy in 1689.[35]

From Gerbillon's letters Leibniz learned that the French Jesuits were under a mandate to take scientific observations and to publish their findings. But he also learned that they were in no hurry to publish, preferring instead to take their time and to get it right.[36] But Leibniz's mandate was different. Charged with writing *Origines Guelficae*, and the first preliminary dissertation (*Protogaea*, 1694) already complete, Leibniz needed comparative linguistic knowledge for his second preliminary dissertation (*Migrationes Gentium*), and he needed it now. If the Jesuits would not publish what they knew, then Leibniz would do it himself. He had already hinted as much to Verjus in April 1695.

Novissima Sinica was read by Joachim Bouvet, the close colleague of Jean-François Gerbillon, who returned briefly to France in 1697.[37] Verjus instructed Bouvet to attend to Leibniz's desires for specific knowledge of China,[38] and, as Bouvet departed Paris for La Rochelle and the Far East, Verjus hired a secretary (Gobien) specifically to manage the correspondence coming in from Jesuit missions around the globe.[39] Claudia von Collani is correct when she points out that the "letters exchanged with Joachim Bouvet constitute certainly the highlight of ... Leibniz's correspondence with and about China."[40] But Leibniz did not set out to establish himself as an authority on all things Chinese any more than he set out to publish *Novissima Sinica* as part of a preconceived intellectual or cultural program. Instead, he stumbled onto the Jesuit mission in China in the course of his search for specific knowledge of the nations that inhabited the space between Europe and China. It was only because that project failed – in the sense that he never did acquire the linguistic data he needed to write the second preliminary dissertation to *Origines Guelficae* – that he turned the curiosities that his correspondents sent him into ends in themselves. The core of *Novissima Sinica* was two intercepted letters that Leibniz learned about through serendipity. Those letters he used as a tool to gain the attention of Antoine Verjus. Only once that relationship was established with Verjus, and once Verjus introduced Leibniz to Joachim Bouvet, did his collaboration with the Jesuits of the Far East begin in earnest.

NOTES

1 See Claudia von Collani, "The Exchange of Knowledge between Europe and China by Missionaries," in *Missionsgeschichte als Geschichte der Globalisierung von Wissen: Transkulturelle Wissensaneignung und -vermittlung durch christliche Missionare in Afrika und in Asien im 17., 18., und 19. Jahrhundert*, eds. Ulrich von der Heyden and Andreas Feldtkeller (Stuttgart: Steiner, 2012), 111–26; Claudia von Collani, *Von Jesuiten, Kaisern und Kanonen: Europa und China – eine wechselvolle Geschichte* (Darmstadt: Wissenschaftliche Buchgesellschaft, 2012).

2 Gottfried Wilhelm Leibniz, *Der Briefwechsel mit den Jesuiten in China (1689–1714)*, edited by Rita Widmaier, translated by Malte-Ludolf Babin (Hamburg: Meiner, 2006), nos. 1–4, 2–25.

3 A.I.5, no. 263, Leibniz to Giovanni Laureati, Rome, 12 Nov. 1689. The following convention is employed for citations of the Leibniz correspondence. "A." refers to the Berlin-Brandenburg Academy of Science edition of Leibniz's *Sämtliche Schriften und Briefe*. "I" refers to *Reihe I, Allgemeine Briefwechsel* (or below, n40, "IV" to *Reihe IV, Historische Schriften*). "5" is the volume number of the series. "no. 205" is the letter number within the volume. All dates are replicated from the Academy editors' suggestions. Dates in brackets have been inferred by the editors in lieu of an actual date written on the manuscript document. The double date indicates the ten-day discrepancy between the Old Style and New Style calendars at the end of the seventeenth century. If only one date appears, it refers to the New Style dating. Page numbers are given only when the letter is long. On the phrase "a commerce ... of light," see Franklin Perkins, *Leibniz and China: A Commerce of Light* (New York: Cambridge University Press, 2004).

4 See David E. Mungello, *Curious Land: Jesuit Accommodation and the Origins of Sinology* (Honolulu: University of Hawaii Press, 1989), chapters 6 and 7.

5 A.I.7, no. 267, Leibniz to Adam Adamandus Kochanski, Hanover Dec. 1691, 487–8.

6 A.I.9, no. 421, Claudio Filippo Grimaldi to Leibniz, Goa 6 Dec. 1693.

7 Philippe Avril, *Voyage en divers états d'Europe et d'Asie* (Paris: Barbin, Boudot and Josse, 1692); [Jacques Villotte], *Voyages d'un Missionaire de la Compagnie de Jésus, en Turquie, en Perse, en Arménie, en Arabie, et en Barbarie* (Paris: Vincent, 1730); George David, "Brevis Relatio revolutionis in regno Moscovitico, et expeditionis repentinae patrum Societatis Jesu," in Charles Daniel and Jean Gagarin, *Études de théologie, de philosophie et d'histoire*, vol. 2 (Paris: Julien, Lanier, and Cosnard, 1857), 418–27.

8 Thomas Goüye, ed. *Observations physiques et mathématiques pour servir à l'histoire naturelle: Envoyées des Indes et de la Chine à l'Académie Royale des Sciences à Paris, par les Pères Jesuites, avec les réflexions de Mrs de l'Académie et les notes du P. Goüye* (Paris: Imprimerie Royale, 1692). Leibniz mentions the book in A.I.8, no. 207, Leibniz to Adam Adamandus Kochanski, [Hanover, July 1692], but it is not clear that he yet possessed it. By Nov. 1692 Leibniz certainly possessed it when he wrote to Landgraf Ernst, "The Reverend Father Verjus has done me the honor to send me through the Comte Ballati the physical and mathematical observations of Jesuit missionaries gone to Siam and China" (editorial note to A.I.8, no. 207, on 349).

9 E.g., A.I.9, no. 152, Leibniz to Adam Adamandus Kochanski, [Hanover, 2nd half of Jan. 1693]; A.I.10, no. 98, Leibniz to Carlo Mauritio Vota, [Hanover, Dec. 1693]; and A.I.11, no. 205, Leibniz to J.J.J. Chuno, Hanover, 21 Feb./3 Mar. 1695.

10 A.I.10, no. 298, Leibniz to Reinier Leers, Hanover [2nd half of June 1694]; see the editorial note on 448 for Leibniz's list of the names of nineteen intended recipients.

11 A.I.11, no. 249, Antoine Verjus to Leibniz, Paris, 30 Mar. 1695.

12 A.I.11, no. 149, Leibniz to Johann Jacob Julius Chuno, Hanover, 20/30 Jan. 1695.

13 Jean-François Gerbillon, "Second voyage fait par ordre de l'Empereur en Tartarie par les Pères Gerbillon et Pereira ... en 1689," in *Description ... de l'Empire de la Chine*, edited by Jean-Baptiste Du Halde (The Hague: Scheurleer, 1736), vol. 4, 196–260. Also F.A. Golovin in *Russko-kitaiskie otnosheniia*, v. XVII, *Veke: Materialy i dokumenty*, eds. N.F. Demidova and V.S. Miasnikov, vol. 2 (Moscow: Nauka, 1972).

14 A.I.11, no. 176, Chuno to Leibniz, Berlin, 2/12 Feb. 1695; A.I.11, no. 180, Chuno to Leibniz, Berlin, 5/15 Feb. 1695; Reyer to Chuno, Königsberg, 18 Feb. 1695, in Woldemar Guerrier, *Leibniz in seinen Beziehungen zu Russland und Peter dem Grossen* (St Petersburg: Eggers, 1873), no. 3.

15 See Kees Boterbloem, *Modernizer of Russia: Andrei Vinius (1641–1716)* (New York: Palgrave Macmillan, 2013).

16 A.I.11, no. 205, Leibniz to Chuno, Hanover, 21 Feb./3 Mar. 1695.

17 A.I.11, no. 220, Chuno to Leibniz, Berlin, 2/12 Mar. 1695, reporting
    that the Desiderata had been sent to Reyer at Königsberg and Hacki at
    Danzig.
18 Reyer to Chuno, Königsberg 18 Feb. 1695, in Guerrier, *Leibniz*, no. 3.
19 A.I.11, no. 287, Leibniz to Chuno, [Hanover, 21–4(?) Apr. 1695].
20 A.I.11, no. 125, Desiderata circa linguas quorundam populorum; A.I.11, no.
    205, Leibniz to Chuno, Hanover, 21 Feb./3 Mar. 1695.
21 A.I.11, no. 224, Leibniz to Christophe Brosseau, [Hanover], 8/18 Mar. 1695.
22 A.I.11, no. 244, Christophe Brousseau to Leibniz, [Paris], 28 Mar. 1695.
23 A.I.11, no. 249, Antoine Verjus to Leibniz, Paris, 30 Mar. 1695.
24 A.I.11, no. 249, Antoine Verjus to Leibniz, Paris, 30 Mar. 1695.
25 François d'Aix de La Chaise to Ferdinand Verbiest, Paris 15 Jan. 1688, in
    *Correspondance de Ferdinand Verbiest de la Compagnie de Jésus (1623–1688)
    Directeur de l'Observatoire de Pékin*, eds. H. Josson, s.J., and L. Willaert, s.J.
    (Brussels: Palais des Académies, 1938), no. 78, 546–50.
26 Philippe Avril, *Voyage en divers états d'Europe et d'Asie*.
27 See Peter Perdue, *China Marches West: The Qing Conquest of Central Eurasia*
    (Cambridge, MA: Belknap Press of Harvard University Press, 2005), for
    Galdan's wars and state-building project in Zungharia.
28 A.I.11, no. 289, Leibniz to Antoine Verjus, [Wolfenbüttel], 15/25 Apr. 1695.
29 Gerbillon's letter to Antoine Verjus was probably enclosed with a lost let-
    ter of Chuno to Leibniz, Berlin, 11/21 May 1695; also enclosed was A.I.11,
    no. 317, Johann Reyer to Leibniz, Berlin, 11/21 May 1695, which survives.
    Leibniz sent the Verjus letter with A.I.11, no. 334, Leibniz to Antoine
    Verjus, [Hanover], 27 May/6 June 1695. Gerbillon's letter to François de la
    Chaise was sent with A.I.11, no. 483, Leibniz to Antoine Verjus, [Hanover, 4
    Oct. (?) 1695].
30 A.I.11, no. 284, Chuno to Leibniz, Berlin, 9/19 Apr. 1695.
31 A.I.11, no. 398, Leibniz to Chuno, Hanover, 15/25 July 1695.
32 A.I.11, no. 443, Chuno to Leibniz, Berlin, 24 Aug. /3 Sept. 1695.
33 A.I.11, no. 293. Chuno to Leibniz, Berlin, 16/26 Apr. 1695; A.IV.6, no. 58,
    Relation wie Isbrand seinen Weg nacher China genommen, [Mar./Apr.
    1695 (?)]. Muscovite Ambassador Isbrand Ides's official report is published
    in Demidova and V.S. Miasnikov, *Russko-kitaiskie otnosheniia v XVII veke:
    Materialy i dokumenty*; see also Gaston Cahen, *Histoire des Relations de la
    Russie avec la Chine sous Pierre le Grand (1689–1730)* (Paris: Alcan, 1912), cvi.
34 A.I.13, no. 366, Leibniz to Chuno, Hanover, 24 Feb./6 Mar. 1697; A.I.13, no.
    382, Johann Gabriel Sparwenfeld to Leibniz, Stockholm, 3 Mar. 1697.
35 See the Berlin Academy's very clever detective work at A.IV.6, no. 61,
    Novissima Sinica, 389, for Leibniz's copy of *Astronomia Europaea* on the

same paper as A.I.5, no. 263, Leibniz to Giovanni Laureati, Rome, 12 Nov. 1689.

36 Jean-François Gerbillon to François de la Chaise, Nerchinsk, 2 Sept. 1689, in *Magazin für die neue Historie und Geographie* (ed. A.F. Büshing) 16 (1782): 544; also Jean-François Gerbillon to Antoine Verjus, Nerchinsk 22 Aug. – 8 Sept. 1689 in *Magazin für die neue Historie und Geographie* 14 (1780): 407.

37 A.I.14, no. 358, Joachim Bouvet to Leibniz, Fontainebleau, 18 Oct. 1697.

38 A.I.14, no. 359, Antoine Verjus to Leibniz, Fontainebleau, 18 Oct. 1697.

39 A.I.15, no. 238, Bouvet to Leibniz, La Rochelle, 28 Feb. 1698.

40 Claudia von Collani, "Gottfried Wilhelm Leibniz and the China Mission of the Jesuits" in *Das Neueste über China: G.W. Leibnizens Novissima Sinica von 1697, Studia Leibnitiana* Supplementa 33 (Stuttgart: Steiner, 2000), 89–103, here 93. See also Claudia von Collani, *Joachim Bouvet, S.J.: Sein Leben und sein Werk* (Nettetal: Steyler, 1985).

4 The Problem of China: Asia and Enlightenment Anthropology (Buffon, de Pauw, Blumenbach, Herder)

CARL NIEKERK

Eighteenth-century scientific anthropology developed out of an epistemological need to find new ways of explaining human diversity. The literature of travel and exploration made it increasingly hard to believe that the non-European world was inhabited by strange and bizarre creatures and instead revealed that other parts of the world were populated by human beings in many respects very similar to those in Europe. Prominent natural historians and anthropologists such as Georges-Louis Leclerc, Comte de Buffon (1707–1788), Petrus Camper (1722–1789), Johann Gottfried Herder (1744–1803), and Johann Friedrich Blumenbach (1752–1840) advocated the view that humanity consisted of one species with a common ancestry (the so-called monogenism thesis[1]). Starting with Buffon's highly influential introduction to his *Histoire naturelle* – a text whose innovative power, as Ernst Cassirer has argued, is considerable[2] and has long been underestimated – Enlightenment anthropology sought to explain human diversity primarily as a function of space and time. Human difference, according to this line of thinking, can be explained by the heterogeneous climatological and geographical conditions in which humans live and by the different developmental patterns made possible by these conditions. All humans, according to Buffon, descend from one common ancestor.

The issue whether humanity has one or several roots, and whether biological and cultural differences can be explained through innate factors or through differences of place and time was a highly political one during the Enlightenment, as Blumenbach in particular shows. According to him, the assumption that humanity consists of several species can only be made out of "malignity, lack of attentiveness or thoughtfulness and a need to come up with new things" (Bosheit, Mangel an

Aufmerksamkeit und Neuerungssucht).[3] Blumenbach sees the unity of mankind as an issue of human rights[4] as does Herder[5]; those who question this unity do so to legitimate treating different categories of humans according to different standards. To explain the variety of the human species on the basis of climate and geography is emancipatory in that such attempts accept biological differences as logical consequences of circumstances of living and cultural differences as rational responses to those conditions. Such attempts also, though, as I will show in the following, introduce new forms of normativity in the shape of implicitly or explicitly prescriptive claims that undermine an otherwise descriptive discourse, hierarchies that may remain unarticulated, standards that are assumed to be ideal, or developmental trajectories that are given preference over alternative patterns of development.

In the context of the emerging anthropological sciences I would like to ask how the Enlightenment conceives of China. This is an interesting question, because, at least to some extent, China challenges many of the tacit assumptions underlying the epistemic foundations of Enlightenment anthropology. Chinese culture and society early on already achieved a relatively high level of civilization – something of which the Enlightenment as a whole was aware and which it respected. Nevertheless, Chinese society also appeared to be remarkably static and to resist development and, thereby, was at odds with the temporal model that the new anthropological thinking, following in the footsteps of Buffon, sought to introduce. And this represented a problem for Enlightenment anthropology.

The most precise (and detailed) identification of the problem of China that confronted Enlightenment anthropology can be found in the third volume of Johann Gottfried Herder's *Ideen zur Philosophie der Geschichte der Menschheit* (1787; the series of *Ideen* was published between 1784 and 1791), a book that builds on the climate- and geography-based theories of biological and cultural diversity espoused by Buffon, Blumenbach, and Camper.[6] China, Herder notes, is one of the oldest empires of the world (429)[7] and a nation that has "advanced to a splendid level of culture" (sich … zu einem vorzüglichen Grad der Kultur erhob) (442). Herder attributes this, indeed, to climate and geography. The key to understanding China according to Herder is its moderate climate; in comparison with the higher and colder north of Asia it has a less strenuous climate (430). To the eighteenth-century anthropologist's ear this immediately evokes associations with Europe, where a moderate climate supposedly led to a relatively high level of civilization.[8] Yet, this is not at all how Herder sees China. Herder is willing to admit that China's mild climate is at the root of "finer thought and dispositions" (feinere Gedanken und Anordnungen) (430). The problem, however, is that nature also gives its inhabitants too much leisure time ("Muße"), thus stimulating their drives, leading to "passionate behaviour and bad habits" (Leidenschaften und Unarten) (430). This, in turn, according to Herder, necessitates a series of "laws and institutions to constrain such drives" (Gesetze und Anstalten zu Einschränkung dieser Triebe) (430). China's problem is that of "despotism" (Despotismus) (430).

Herder's criticism of China, its institutions, culture, and people is part of a broader debate in the eighteenth century in which a view of China that originally was positive gradually comes under attack, and a predominantly negative view of China and Asia in general eventually starts to dominate.[9] On the one hand, this debate is conducted by philosophical means: Leibniz, Voltaire, Hume, Helvétius, and Holbach defend and idealize China primarily on philosophical grounds, while Diderot and the group surrounding Raynal are ambivalent.[10] But, on the other hand, the emerging discipline of anthropology, with its scientific ambitions in its descriptions of other, in particular also non-European peoples and their cultures, becomes increasingly important as well.

Buffon in his highly influential *Histoire naturelle* argues that humanity consists of only one species, and he seeks to explain biological and cultural differences through variances in climate, nutrition, ways of living, and epidemic diseases, in addition to the infinite number of individual differences among human beings.[11] Buffon's theories are important in the context of the epistemological paradigm underlying the Enlightenment's concept of knowledge because they allow both for a materialist explanation and a rational view of biological and cultural differences. The non-European world is no longer seen as populated by freaks and monsters, but by human beings very similar to Europeans. Anatomical collections in the eighteenth century are less about the monstrosity of nature's abnormalities, and more about gaining insight into developmental patterns.[12] Buffon sees human behaviour and culture as materially conditioned by climate and geography, while acknowledging humans' particular "way of living" (la manière de vivre), giving them a certain autonomy and allowing for individual differences as well; it is the "infinitely varied mixture of individuals who may resemble each other more or less" (le mélange varié à l'infini des individus plus ou moins ressemblans) that is also constitutive for human societies.[13]

Buffon's climate- and geography-based theories explaining anthropological variation are radical in that they conceive of the development of
European societies as one among many possible trajectories and by no
means as a model or the sole standard for the rest of the world.

Regarding China, Buffon, relying on travel reports by Jean Hugon
among others, notes that the Chinese are in general well built, tall, and
fat, and that their skin tone, due to climatological factors, in the southern provinces resembles that of Mauritanians and Spaniards, while the
skin of those living in the middle provinces is white like that of the
Germans[14] – insights that are more or less confirmed by several other
travellers to whom Buffon refers. Buffon explicitly cites Jean Chardin's
observation that differences in skin tone among the Chinese can be
explained by differences in climate and nourishment and that similarly
"regarding customs, difference is also based on the nature of the terrain
and its opulence, and whether it is more or less great" (à l'égard des
mœurs la différence vient aussi de la nature du terroir et de l'opulence
plus ou moins grande).[15] Even the Chinese themselves attribute dis-
similarities between their own people and the Tartars to "water and
earth, that is, the nature of the land" (ils disent que cela vient de l'eau et
de la terre, c'est-à-dire, de la nature du pays).[16] It is interesting to note
that climate theory was already a topic in travel literature before Buffon's seminal introduction to his *Histoire naturelle*,[17] but also that climate
and geography (earth and water) serve for the Chinese themselves as
tools to understand (and rationalize) their own societies, suggesting a
transcultural basis for these theories.

Among later Enlightenment anthropologists, Blumenbach is most
in line with Buffon, without a doubt influenced by a popular German translation of Buffon's work that had appeared between 1771 and
1774.[18] For instance, Blumenbach explains biological difference in line
with the *Histoire naturelle* on the basis of climate, nutrition, way of living, and the breeding of bastards ("Klima," "Nahrungsmittel," "Lebe-
nsart," and "Bastardzeugung") as reasons why the "formative drive"
("Bildungstrieb" or "nisus formativus") in humans is modified.[19] Blumenbach distinguishes five main varieties among humans, taking skin
colour and anatomy as his main criteria and pointing out that such categories by necessity are artificial and overlap with each other. Because
of their yellow skin tone the Chinese belong to the Mongol variety.[20]
Blumenbach here corrects Buffon by arguing that humankind consists
not of six main varieties, but five; he also asserts that Buffon confuses
Tatars and Mongols, by using the name of the former for the latter and

not distinguishing between the two, even though the Tatars belong to the Caucasian variety.[21] Throughout the different editions of his anthropological text, Blumenbach attempts to be primarily descriptive. Nevertheless, his theories do contain normative elements: by claiming that the Caucasian variety is the original race, Blumenbach establishes a clear genealogy that easily could be interpreted normatively; also his emphasis on the beauty of the Caucasian race and the observation that a white skin colour must be the original colour of all humans, on which he bases his claim that this is the original race,[22] can easily be abused for normative purposes. Like Buffon, however, Blumenbach seeks to avoid explicit value judgments about the Chinese.

This is different in the cases of de Pauw and Raynal. In its negative view of the Chinese people and their culture, and through its emphasis on climate and geography, Herder's four-volume *Ideen* follows the scepticism of anthropologist Cornelis de Pauw. In his preface to his two-volume *Recherches philosophiques sur les Égyptiens et les Chinois* (1773), with which Herder was familiar, de Pauw cautions that his account of the Chinese will by no means back up popular opinion, which is based on enthusiastic missionary reports and the missionaries' easy infatuation with what is or may appear as miraculous, but will focus, instead, on "the facts" (les faits).[23] De Pauw , too, claims to take as his point of departure an analysis of terrain and climate, in line with Buffon (vol. 1, III). Indeed, de Pauw greatly contributed to the popularization of Buffon's thinking,[24] even though in the case of *Recherches philosophiques sur les Égyptiens et les Chinois* the analysis of climate and geography quickly moves to the background and in most of the text is tangential at best.

Despotism is a key word also in de Pauw's work (vol. 1, VI; see also vol. 2, 187–8, 198, 216, 227). De Pauw seeks to distance himself from the far more favourable account of the Chinese in the 1770 edition of the *Histoire philosophique et politique des deux Indes*, written by the Abbé Raynal and his team (which from the fourth volume of the 1770 edition on also includes the Radical Enlightenment thinker Diderot[25]) – an account to which de Pauw refers explicitly in his introduction (vol. 1, VII). One of the key issues for de Pauw is whether bondage or serfdom exists among the Chinese.[26] Raynal's text argues that it does not and, moreover, that nobility in China is not inherited, but granted as a personal reward, while the majority of magistrates and those elevated to the first ranks of society are chosen from families of labourers, who tend to be well educated.[27] This is part of a larger argument in Raynal's *Les deux Indes* that seeks to read China as a model of natural law.[28]

In particular, de Pauw's chapter on the Chinese political system, "Considerations about the Government of the Chinese" (Considéra- tions sur le gouvernement des Chinois) (vol. 2, 187–232), reads like a point-by-point rebuttal of the ideas articulated in *Les deux Indes*. Among other things, de Pauw attacks Raynal's suggestion of a society without hierarchies. The emperor, according to de Pauw, is not elected, but the position is inherited even if the male line is extinct (vol. 2, 187). All viceroys have the right to decide over life and death of their subjects, without any possibility of appeal to a different juridical instance (vol. 2, 193; see also 226–8). Entire families are punished for the crimes of one of their members (vol. 2, 198).[29] De Pauw points out that there are many different kinds of serfdom among the Chinese (vol. 2, 205–8). Taxation is excessive, chaotic, and corrupt (vol. 2, 214). The army is comprised of slaves (vol. 2, 221–2). Magistrates are organized in nine separate orders, but otherwise according to entirely unclear principles (vol. 2, 222). Chi- nese writing is so complex that it is hard to figure out whether someone can read or not (vol. 2, 222–3). The Chinese are stuck in an ancestor cult; this explains their love for their region of birth (vol. 2, 229). In the same context, de Pauw traces "the pride of the Chinese" to "their ignorance and subservience" ("L'orgeuil des Chinois provient de leur ignorance & de leur servitude") (vol. 2, 229).

What we are witnessing in Raynal's and de Pauw's texts is the influ- ence of an anthropological paradigm that participates in the politici- zation of the discourse on China in the 1770s. Raynal, de Pauw, and later Herder, each in his own way, distance themselves from an earlier scholarly paradigm, represented in an exemplary way in texts by Buf- fon and Blumenbach (although both actually are their contemporaries), who in their deliberations on China intend to be primarily descriptive and far less feel the need to be explicitly normative – even though the kinds of developmental and aesthetic hierarchies they construct may ultimately have normative consequences. Interestingly, Herder, in the *Ideen* (and elsewhere in his work) only mentions de Pauw's (reaction- ary) texts and not Raynal's (progressive) *Les deux Indes*, even though it is assumed that he was familiar with this text as well.[30] This does not, however, mean, as we will see, that Herder unconditionally subscribes to de Pauw's theories and ideology.

To some extent Herder seeks to find his own way between overly negative and overly positive models of conceptualizing China – a con- flict that is, in an exemplary way, visible in the last three decades of the eighteenth century in the contrasting views of China articulated by Raynal and de Pauw. Herder is at great pains to explain why the positive climatological conditions in China that he and many fellow anthropologists have identified nevertheless necessitate an authoritarian regime.

Herder does have positive things to say about China. It is not a very materialistic country, for instance, the Chinese are not interested in digging for gold, in spite of its presence in China (431).[31] That China has been able to achieve and maintain a high level of culture and civilization, including an impressive urban and regional infrastructure (roads, bridges, and canals), can be attributed to the "patient industriousness" (geduldigen Fleiß) of its citizens, which in turn relies on an abundant agriculture and the presence of large supplies of fish and animals (431). Here, too, Herder's text, illustrating Buffon's ideas in an exemplary way, provides an analysis of culture and society based on geography and climate. Herder follows Raynal in his claim that nobility is not inherited in China, but, at least in principle,[32] is based on merit (432). Also, nobody is forced to adhere to a specific religion and no religion is persecuted,[33] a principle that even protects Jews and Jesuits in China (432). The country's legislation ("Gesetzgebung") is based on the teachings of habits and customs ("Sittenlehre"), which in turn build on "the holy books of the ancestors" (die heiligen Bücher der Vorfahren) (432), affirming Birgit Tautz's thesis that "the imagined permanence and stability of China" in Europe's eyes "evolved from texts"[34] that, according to Herder, for a long time have been admired by European philosophers and statesmen as "almost" (beinah) exemplary (432).

In citing these positive examples, emphasizing the model function of Chinese culture and society, Herder follows Raynal's positive views of China. But then Herder starts to question such a one-sided view, following the writings of de Pauw. In particular, the generally assumed stability of Chinese society is problematized by Herder. This stability can also be conceived as an obstacle to the country's further development – it is the reason "why it could not develop further" (warum es nicht weiter kommen konnte) (433). Herder's historicism has trouble coming to terms with this. He attributes the indolence of Chinese society to the roots of its people in the cultures of the Mongols and Tatars in the primitive northeast of China (433–4). China's despotism can be linked to the Tatars (433). Here, Herder picks up on Buffon's differentiation between Chinese and Tatars who, according to the *Histoire naturelle,* live among their horses and are fierce, belligerent, hunters, who like to be fatigued, enjoy their independence, and are tough and rough, while the Chinese, in contrast, are meek, peaceful, indolent, superstitious, submissive, dependent (in an almost slavelike manner), ceremonial, and courteous.[35] Buffon, too, speaks of a mixing of Tatars and Chinese,[36] although, as Blumenbach shows, Buffon lumps Tatars and Mongols together,[37] a mistake that Herder does not make. The argument that attributes China's despotism to it having been conquered by Tatars and Mongols can be found in de Pauw as well.[38]

Interestingly, in the context of the diverse backgrounds of the Chinese people, Herder speaks of an "innate tribal character and complexion" (angeborne Stammart und Komplexion) and "natural inclination" (Naturbildung) that that have remained virtually unchanged, in a way similar to the unchanged physical appearance of the Chinese (434), and that work against the climatological and developmental potential identified in Buffon's and Blumenbach's anthropologies. Here, too, Herder follows de Pauw's ideas. Even in their highest political achievements, the Chinese are still "nomadic Mongols" (ziehende Mongolen) (435). Herder here seeks to historicize his readers' views of China by showing how the Chinese people and their society are a composite of various historical developments. However, in order to do so he has to make assumptions about the "biological origins" of their customs and society that ultimately move in the direction of a racialization of his discourse on Asian alterity[39] by assuming an inalterable essence inherent to certain communities.

It is the Chinese language that according to Herder demonstrates most clearly the stagnation of Chinese society and its inability to develop further. The Chinese language is an expression of "unwholesome finesse in its details" (unselige Feinheit in Kleinigkeiten), but on the whole also lacks inventiveness ("Erfindungskraft im Großen") (434). That, in turn, is indicative of the Chinese national psyche: the Chinese are as in love with the superficial splendour of gold paper as they are with their ornamental language (435). The Chinese lack an appreciation "of nature's true relations" (an wahrem Naturverhältnis) and have neglected their ability to feel ("Empfindung") (435). The Chinese, in other words, have lost touch with their natural environment. They are an exemption from Buffon's theory of climate because of this alienation from their surroundings.

Herder proceeds, in a rather unexpected turn, to compare the Chinese to Europe's Jews. The Chinese are the Jews of East Asia: "that the Chinese in their corner of the world, like the Jews,[40] have managed to stay free of mixing with other peoples shows their idle pride"[41] (daß die

Sinesen in ihrer Erdecke sich, wie die Juden, von der Vermischung mit andern Völkern frei erhalten haben, zeiget schon ihr eitler Stolz) (436).[42] In an interesting way Herder here anticipates thoughts on which he will further elaborate in book 4 of *Ideen* when he discusses "Foreign Peoples in Europe" (Fremde Völker in Europa) (699–703), among them the Jews, who are characterized, in an infamous passage, as a "parasitic plant" (parasitische Pfanze), a people that latched on to European cultures, profited from them financially, even though, to their credit, they did also contribute to the preservation of ancient Hebrew literature and helped spread wisdom from Arab cultures (702). What this passage makes clear, in line with his deliberations on China in general, is that Herder has a problem accommodating mobile cultures in a model that understands a people's culture in line with Buffon as a result of geography and climate.[43] The difference between nomadic and sedentary peoples is fundamental for Herder; it is also clear that Herder tends to favour sedentary cultures that organically have developed as a product of their specific climate and geography, although he does also caution, as one critic has pointed out, against privileging one type of society over others.[44]

In the text immediately following the passage that characterizes the Chinese as Asia's Jews, Herder seeks to explain what he characterizes as the superficiality of the Chinese through the fact that they are in origin a mobile and nomadic (instead of a sedentary) culture. The Chinese have never been able to shake off the "Mongol nomadic way of living" (Mongolische Nomadenart) of their ancestors (436). In the case of the Chinese, Herder uses this fundamental trait, their nomadic background, to explain, for instance, the polite pre-emptive conduct ("jenes höfliche Zuvorkommen") of the Chinese and their childish obedience ("kindlicher Gehorsam") (436), a clear comment on Christian Wolff's attempts earlier in the eighteenth century to make "filial piety" into the basis and core of China's superior form of societal organization.[45] The Chinese behave submissively because they feel like outsiders. They are in need of an artificial order to compensate for their lack of affinity with the natural order. This order is provided by their language. Its language is a "dictionary of its morals, i.e., of politeness and good manners" (ein Wörterbuch der Moral d.i. der Höflichkeit und Guten Manieren) (439).

Seen negatively, the childish obedience of the Chinese people is, in turn, linked to what Herder perceives as this people's "lack of masculine power and honour" (Mangel an männlicher Kraft und Ehre) (437). Activity has a positive and masculine connotation; passivity is characterized not as effeminate, but as childish and infantile, and is in need of, but simultaneously also lacks masculine oversight (438). China is like an embalmed mummy or a hibernating animal (438). It is as if ancient Egypt were still a presence among Herder's contemporaries (440). Other peoples and nations, in contrast, either "progressed or perished and intermingled with others" (sind fortgerückt oder untergegangen und mit anderen vermischt worden); China, however, "like a relic from prehistoric times is at a standstill in its half-Mongol constitution" (ist wie eine Trümmer der Vorzeit in seiner halb-Mongolischen Einrichtung stehen geblieben) (440). The Chinese people are stuck "halfway in their education, as if it were in its boyhood" (mitten in seiner Erziehung, gleichsam im Knabenalter stehen geblieben) (441).[46] This could have changed should a second Confucius have emerged who might have restored a freedom of spirit ("den freien Fortgang des Geistes") (441).[47] Herder's statement is an interesting compromise: it allows for maintaining the positive view of Confucius that was characteristic for the early rather than the late Enlightenment, while at the same time incorporating the increasingly negative view of China characteristic for the last three decades of the eighteenth and also for the nineteenth century.[48]

In the end, Herder's view of China is paradoxical. Interestingly, on the one hand, Herder problematizes China's self-chosen isolation and its lack of interest in learning about other nations: it is a nation "that compares itself only with itself, and it neither knows nor loves what is outside of itself" (sich nur mit sich selbst vergleicht und das Auswärtige weder kennet, noch liebet) (439). This goes against Herder's idea that cultures all gain when engaging with each other,[49] an idea that is already present in Buffon's understanding of culture as the product of an "infinitely varied mixture of individuals who resemble each other more or less," as analysed above.[50] On the other hand, however, Herder points also to the advantages of such a self-chosen isolation. The fact that it has closed itself off from European nations – Herder names the Dutch, the Russians, and the Jesuits as examples – "has to be approved politically" ([ist] politisch zu billigen) in view of the behaviour of these nations in the countries surrounding China (442). It is their colonial abusive practices that make this a wise choice. Herder's text here echoes a statement in Raynal's Les deux Indes by Diderot in which he characterizes the closure of the country as a decision that is politically bad, but not unjust since Europeans are bad guests.[51] The Chinese despise the merchant who has left his country, but they nevertheless profit from him by trading tea – a beverage that Herder sees as harmful for Europe – for silver (442).

What do these early anthropologists' thoughts and deliberations on China tell us about the Chinese people and their culture?

Each of the thinkers discussed here seeks to distinguish between factual knowledge about China and the kind of half-mythological or pseudoscientific material that long had passed for anthropological knowledge – especially if they, and this goes in particular for Herder, have trouble identifying the exact boundaries between what is factual and what is not. The Enlightenment is in possession of a notion of Otherness that assumes that ways of living are in essence rational responses to conditions of time and place. The notion of alterity as used by the Enlightenment anthropologists discussed here assumes that humans are both similar and different across the globe: all humans have common biological roots, a common ancestor, but they have developed in diverse ways under the influence of the varying local circumstances under which peoples live. The climatological-developmental model proposed by Buffon, and further developed by Camper, Blumenbach, and Herder, however, also creates its own new normativities. In particular, the developmental aspect of Buffon's restructuring of natural history has normative implications. That China not only early on had achieved a high level of civilization, but also had managed to stabilize that level of civilization for a long time, was seen as a major achievement by the early Enlightenment. Gradually during the eighteenth century this started to change, as Enlightenment thinking in general, and anthropology in particular, started to become more interested in historical process.[52]

Herder is representative in this respect of the later eighteenth century. Herder's problem with China is that it seemingly does not want to follow the developmental pattern for which it is destined: either to follow its natural path of development further or perish as an autonomous culture by becoming part of another (stronger) culture. An additional problem is that Chinese culture is perceived by Herder as nomadic, which does not allow for the natural interaction of culture, society, and their "natural" environment. The Enlightenment has a model of alterity, but it neither has space for mobility nor does it have a model for cultures interacting with each other. Herder's understanding of culture is sedentary, not nomadic.

In the debate between de Pauw and Raynal that raged throughout the 1770s, Herder in general sides with de Pauw's more negative views of China, seeing it as a nation ruled by despotism and also copying de Pauw's view that the Chinese inherited negative character traits from their Tatar and Mongol ancestors, the implication being that such character traits resist change because of climate or geography.[53] The result is a civilization that goes its own way and ignores the eighteenth century's rapidly increasing awareness of the world. Nevertheless, Herder, at the end of his deliberations on China, does point to an advantage of China's isolationism: China's refusal to admit Europeans protects it from the kind of colonial abuse to which its neighbours in Asia are submitted (echoing similar statements by Diderot in his contributions to *Les deux Indes*). In spite of this emancipatory motif in Herder's thinking, his anthropology is fraught with contradictions that may translate into respect for China's autonomous cultural tradition, but that also articulate an inability to see that same tradition as of equal value to that of Europe – in spite of Herder's often proclaimed principle that each culture needs to be judged on its own merits. Although Herder is often credited with a cultural approach that emphasizes the incommensurability of cultures, one should not forget that his notion of culture is firmly anchored in theories of biology and geography and their power to shape human activity.[54]

In addition, Herder's contradictory statements about China may have something to do with the fact that to some extent Enlightenment anthropology's reflections on China are more about Europe itself than about China. In particular, China's moderate climate invites this comparison. Because Europe and China share a relatively mild climate, they do present alternate trajectories for each other's development. When Herder writes about China, he also writes about Europe, and vice versa. His fascination with the Other – and this goes for many of his contemporaries as well – is in the end also a fascination with the Self.

A NOTE ON ONLINE RESOURCES:

This essay would have been impossible without many online resources, most of which were not yet available a decade ago.

A complete facsimile French edition of Buffon's works can be found at the website of the Centre national de la recherche scientifique (CNSR): http://www.buffon.cnrs.fr.

A very useful bibliography of Blumenbach's works, including an almost complete set of digital scans of those same works, can be found at http://www.blumenbach-online.de/fileadmin/wikiuser/

Daten_Digitalisierung/Bibliographie/Bibliographie.html. The website of the Göttinger Digitalisierungszentrum also hosts a collection of texts and editions by Blumenbach: http://gdz.sub.uni-goettingen.de/dms/colbrowse/?tx_goobit3_search%5Bextquery%5D=ISWORK%3A1&DC=blumenbachiana. Scans of original editions of texts by many of Blumenbach's contemporaries are accessible through the Digitalisierungszentrum as well. Volumes 3–5 of Blumenbach's correspondence can be downloaded at the website of Norbert Klatt publishers: http://www.klatt-verlag.de/frank-wp-dougherty/; information about volumes 1 and 2 of the same edition can be found there as well.

The Bibliotheca Sinica at the University of Vienna offers a comprehensive list of the main editions of Raynal's *Histoire des deux Indes* published between 1770 and 1781, including electronic versions of facsimile copies of the originals of most of these editions: http://www.univie.ac.at/Geschichte/China-Bibliographie/blog/2010/12/25/raynal-histoire-philosophique/. A bibliography of the 49 editions of Raynal's *Histoire des deux Indes* published between 1770 and 1843 can be found at http://www.abbe-raynal.org/histoire-des-deux-indes.html. De Pauw's texts on Egypt and China can be found at the Bibliotheca Sinica as well: http://www.univie.ac.at/Geschichte/China-Bibliographie/blog/2011/01/15/pauw-recherches-philosophiques-sur-les-egyptiens-et-les-chinois/.

NOTES

1 For an overview of the debate on monogenism and polygenism in eighteenth-century anthropology, see Miriam Claude Meijer, esp. the chapter "Monogenism versus Polygenism: Adam and Eve," in *Race and Aesthetics in the Anthropology of Petrus Camper (1722–1789)* (Amsterdam: Rodopi, 1999), 81–5. Regarding the foundational importance of monogenism for Buffon's theories, see, e.g., Michèle Duchet, *Anthropologie et histoire au siècle des Lumières* (Paris: Albin Michel, 1995), 162, 166–8, and 173, and Tzvetan Todorov, *Nous et les autres: La réflexion française sur la diversité humaine* (Paris: Seuil, 2001), 141–2.

2 See Ernst Cassirer, *Die Philosophie der Aufklärung* (Hamburg: Meiner, 1998), 64, 102–6; see also Wolf Lepenies, *Das Ende der Naturgeschichte: Wandel kultureller Selbstverständlichkeiten in den Wissenschaften des 18. und 19. Jahrhunderts* (Munich: Hanser, 1976), 71–3, 75. The argument that Buffon's introduction provided the roots for modern anthropology has been made (powerfully and convincingly) by Frank W.P. Dougherty in his essay "Buf-

fons Bedeutung für die Entwicklung des anthropologischen Denkens im Deutschland der zweiten Hälfte des 18. Jahrhunderts," in *Gesammelte Aufsätze zu Themen der klassischen Periode der Naturgeschichte / Collected Essays on Themes from the Classical Period of Natural History* (Göttingen: Norbert Klatt, 1996), 70–88, 323–51. Even though the perception of non-European cultures by European authors and the concept "anthropology" in general have become very fashionable among scholars of the eighteenth century, a systematic overview and genealogy of eighteenth-century European anthropology that acknowledges Buffon's and Blumenbach's importance remains to be written.

3 Johann Friedrich Blumenbach, quoted by Gruber in *Über die natürlichen Verschiedenheiten im Menschengeschlechte*, translated and edited by Johann Gottfried Gruber (Leipzig: Breitkopf und Härtel, 1798), 287. Gruber quotes the second, Latin edition of the text: "Malitia quidem, negligentia et nouitatis studium posteriori opinioni fauebant" (They indeed gave a preference to malignity, negligence and a busying oneself with the newest opinions). See *De generis humani varietate nativa*, 2nd ed. (Göttingen: Vandenhoek, 1781), 47. Blumenbach ends his *Über die natürlichen Verschiedenheiten* with the statement that "all varieties of man known thus far belong to one and the same species" (alle bisher bekanntgewordene Abarten des Menschen nur zu Einer und derselben Gattung gehören) (224). Interestingly, *Über die natürlichen Verschiedenheiten* is dedicated to Herder.

4 "For a few years I have been collecting [material] on all that concerns humanity's varieties and divergences; an enterprise that in particular wants to defend the rights of humanity and to fight the laughable mixing of the true ape, the Orangutan, with diseases of the human body[,] and with the white Moor " (Seit einigen Jahren sammle ich zu allem was Verschiedenheiten und Abweichungen im Menschengeschlecht betrifft; ein Unternehmen das besonders die Rechte der Menschheit vertheidigen und die lächerliche Vermengung des wahren Affen des Oran ootans mit Krankheiten des menschlichen Körpers[,] mit dem weissen Mohren [...] bestreiten soll). Blumenbach, letter to Albrecht von Haller, 23 Feb. 1775, in *The Correspondence of Johann Friedrich Blumenbach*, vol. I, *1773–1782, Letters 1–230*, edited by F.W.P Dougherty; revised, augmented, and edited by Norbert Klatt (Göttingen: Norbert Klatt, 2006), 12–16, quote at 14.

5 "You, human, honour yourself. Neither the pongo nor the longimanus is your brother; but the American, the Negro, is. Him you should not repress, not murder, and not steal from; because he is a human like you; you should not fraternize with apes" (Du aber Mensch, ehre dich selbst. Weder

der Pongo, noch der Longimanus ist dein Bruder; aber wohl der Amerikaner, der Neger. Ihn also soll[s]t du nicht unterdrücken, nicht morden,
nicht stehlen: denn er ist ein Mensch, wie du bist; mit dem Affen darfst du
keine Brüderschaft eingehn). *Ideen zur Philosophie der Geschichte der Menschheit*, in *Werke*, vol. 6 (Frankfurt: Deutscher Klassiker Verlag, 1989), 255.

6 Regarding the importance of Buffon's introduction for the temporaliza-
tion of Herder's view of nature, see Ralph Häfner, *Herders Kulturentsteh-
ungslehre: Studien zu den Quellen und zur Methode seines Geschichtsdenkens*
(Hamburg: Felix Meiner, 1995), 56–7 (the author in the same context also
points to Diderot for the acceptance of this paradigm). The importance of
climate theory for Herder is also recognized by Anne Löchte, *Johann Gottfried Herder: Kulturtheorie und Humanitätsidee der* Ideen, Humanitätsbriefe
und Adrastea (Würzburg: Königshausen and Neumann, 2005), 15, 38, 66,
and 222.

7 All parenthetical page numbers refer to the following edition: Johann
Gottfried Herder, *Ideen zur Philosophie der Geschichte der Menschheit*, in
Werke, vol. 6 (originally published in 1784–91).

8 This argument can be traced back to Aristotle who argued that Greece's
moderate climate led to an early blossoming of human culture, an observation with which Herder and many other eighteenth-century anthropologists agreed (see Löchte, *Herder*, 66 and 15). The argument can be found in
Buffon's writings as well (see Duchet, *Anthropologie et histoire*, 255
and 275).

9 The increasing criticism of China can be documented in an exemplary way
by comparing the three different editions of Raynal's *Histoire philosophique
des deux Indes* (1770, 1774, 1780), as is done by Jonathan Israel in *Democratic
Enlightenment: Philosophy, Revolution, and Human Rights 1750–1790* (Oxford:
Oxford University Press, 2011), 558–72.

10 Cf. Israel, *Democratic Enlightenment*, 558–62.

11 See [Georges-Louis Leclerc de] Buffon/ [Louis Jean-Marie] Daubenton,
Histoire naturelle générale et particulière, vol. 3 (Paris: Imprimerie royale,
1749), 530: "there is originally only one species of humans that having
itself multiplied and expanded across the entire surface of the earth has
undergone different changes through the influence of climate, differences in nutrition, its way of living, epidemic diseases, and also through
the infinitely varied mixing of individuals who may resemble each other
more or less" (il n'y a eu originairement qu'une seule espèce d'hommes,
qui s'étant multipliée et répandue sur toute la surface de la terre, a subi
différens changemens par l'influence du climat, par la différence de la
nourriture, par celle de la manière de vivre, par les maladies épidémiques,

et aussi par le mélange varié à l'infini des individus plus ou moins ressemblans). Scholars today often associate eighteenth-century climate theory with Montesquieu, who in book 14 of part 2 of *De l'esprit des lois* (1748) discusses the effects of climate on society's legal system. This preference may be explained by the fact that Montesquieu's text among scholars and the general public today is more frequently read than Buffon's methodological introduction to his *Histoire naturelle*. However, among the eighteenth-century natural historians and anthropologists discussed here (Blumenbach, Camper, de Pauw, Raynal and his circle, and Herder) Buffon was far better known and also more frequently quoted and referred to, while Montesquieu was rarely mentioned in these discussions (without a doubt in part because he was primarily a legal scholar and political scientist, and not an empirical scientist). Also the intentions of both scholars' climate theories are quite different: Climate in Montesquieu is supposed to explain the backwardness and irrationality of certain peoples, their stasis of body and mind (*De l'esprit des lois*, vol. 1 [Paris: Garnier-Flammarion, 1979], 378), and thus the negative impact of climate needs to be overcome (378–9; see also Tzvetan Todorov, *Le jardin imparfait: La pensée humaniste en France* [Paris: Grasset, 1998], 95–6). Buffon, as I will show below, seeks to prove how different peoples rationally adapt to the climate surrounding them and thereby emphasizes the rational potential of all humans.

12 See Michael Hagner, "Enlightened Monsters," 213, in *The Sciences in Enlightened Europe*, eds. William Clark, Jan Golinski, and Simon Schaffer (Chicago: University of Chicago Press, 1999), 175–217.

13 Buffon, *Histoire naturelle*, vol. 3, 530.

14 See ibid., 385: "those [the Chinese] who live in the southern provinces are browner and have a darker tan than the others; in colour they resemble the people from Mauritania and the darkest Spaniards, while the people who live in the middle of the Empire instead are white like Germans" (ceux [les Chinois] qui habitent les provinces méridionales sont plus bruns et ont le teint plus basane que les autres; ils ressemblent par la couleur aux peuples de la Mauritanie et aux Espagnols les plus basanez, au lieu que ceux qui habitent les provinces du milieu de l'Empire, sont blancs comme les Allemands).

15 Chardin, quoted by Buffon, *Histoire naturelle*, 388; the quote is from *Voyages de Mr Le Chevalier Chardin, en Perse, et autres Lieux de l'Orient*, vol. 9 (Amsterdam: Jean Louis de Lorme, 1711), 6–7. An earlier version of the text was published in 1686. The bibliographical information provided in Buffon's text (388; referring to vol. 3, 86, of the same 1711 Amsterdam edition of Chardin's work) is not correct.

16 Buffon, *Histoire naturelle*, 388.

17 As Dougherty points out, Enlightenment climate theory has roots in antiquity, more specifically Hippocrates's treatise "On Airs, Waters, Places" (Περί αέρων, υδάτων, τόπων). See "Buffons Bedeutung für die Entwicklung des anthropologischen Denkens," 341n40; the same note sketches the Enlightenment's reception of Hippocrates's ideas before Buffon.

18 See Buffon, *Allgemeine Naturgeschichte: Eine freije mit einigen Zusätzen vermehrte Übersetzung nach der neuesten französ: Außgabe von 1769*, 7 vols. (Berlin: Joachim Pauli Buchhändler, 1771–74).

19 *Über die natürlichen Verschiedenheiten* (3rd ed., 1798), 73, 77, 79 and 80; see also 69. Climate was already a key term in the first edition of Blumenbach's text; see *De generis humani varietate nativa*, 1st ed. (Göttingen: Vandenhoeck, 1776), esp. 7–9. In addition Blumenbach lists "way of living and upbringing" (vitae genus et educatio) and the "mating of diverse species" (diuersae ... speciei connubio) (8, 9) to explain biological diversity.

20 *Über die natürlichen Verschiedenheiten* (1798), 206–7.

21 Ibid., 209–10, 214–15. In the first edition of his text, Blumenbach argues that mankind consists of four varieties (see *De generis humani varietate nativa*, 1st ed. [1776], 41–2); in the second edition he argues for five varieties ([1781], 51).

22 *Über die natürlichen Verschiedenheiten* (1798), 204, 206, 213.

23 [Cornelis] de P[auw], *Recherches philosophiques sur les Égyptiens et les Chinois*, 2 vols. (Berlin: G.J. Decker, 1773), here vol. 1, V. Subsequent parenthetical references in the text refer to this edition. Herder cites de Pauw once in his *Ideen*, where he mentions de Pauw's book on Egypt and China as useful preparatory work for a history that still needs to be written (458). That de Pauw's name is misspelled as "Paw" may have something to do with the fact that de Pauw's complete name is not listed on the title page of the 1773 edition. According to Wolfgang Pross, Herder derived the idea (for his anthropology foundational argument) that civilization moved from east to west (from Asia to Egypt, Greece, and Italy, and eventually to France and Germany) from de Pauw's *Recherches philosophiques sur les Américains* (1768/69); see "Herder und die Anthropologie der Aufklärung," 1156, in Johann Gottfried Herder, *Werke*, vol. 2 (Munich: Carl Hanser, 1987), 1128–16.

24 See Susanne Zantop, *Colonial Fantasies: Conquest, Family, and Nation in Precolonial Germany, 1770–1870* (Durham: Duke University Press, 1997), 13.

25 Regarding the complex authorship of the anonymously published *Histoire philosophique*, which included Guillaume-Thomas Raynal (1713–1796) (often listed as its principal author), Denis Diderot (1713–1784), Alexandre

Deleyre (1726–1796), Jean de Pechméja (1741–1785), Jacques Paulze
(1723–1794), and Paul Henri Thiry d'Holbach (1723–1789), several of them
contributors to the *Encyclopédie* as well, see Israel, *Democratic Enlightenment*, 421–3. Buffon for a while was part of d'Holbach's salon and therefore
conversed with other Radical Enlightenment thinkers. See Philipp Blom,
A Wicked Company: The Forgotten Radicalism of the European Enlightenment
(New York: Basic Books, 2010), 59–61. In the debate between de Pauw
and Raynal, Buffon sides clearly with Raynal when he attacks de Pauw's
views of Americans and cites Raynal as a counterexample. See *Histoire
naturelle, Supplément*, vol. 4 (Paris: Imprimerie royale, [1777]), 525–39; see
also Duchet, *Anthropologie et histoire*, 265–6. Buffon remarks about de Pauw:
"je suis fâché qu'un homme de mérite, et qui d'ailleurs paroît être instruit,
se soit livré à cet excès de partialité dans ses jugemens, et qu'il les appuie
sur des faits équivoques" (I am angry that a man of merit, and who by the
way appears to be learned, would give in to such excessive partiality in his
judgments, and supports them with such dubious facts) (527). On the one
hand, de Pauw sought to copy the model of the materialist anthropologist
in the style of Buffon; on the other hand, he was a "Schreibtischgelehrter"
(desktop scholar) who had trouble deciding (like Herder) to what extent
the written sources available to de Pauw were reliable or not. See Werner
Krauss, *Zur Anthropologie des 18. Jahrhunderts: Die Frühgeschichte der Menschheit im Blickpunkt der Aufklärung* (Frankfurt: Ullstein, 1987), 74, 109).

26 De Pauw attacks Raynal's claim that there is no slavery in China: "There
is neither real existing serfdom nor personal slavery" (Il ny'a ni servitude
réelle, ni servitude personele). *Histoire philosophique et politique des établissements et du commerce des Européens dans les deux Indes*, vol. 1 (Amsterdam,
1770), 90. China is first discussed in *Les deux Indes* as part of Raynal's history of the European colonization of non-European worlds (82–101).

27 *Les deux Indes*, vol. 1 [1770], 90. Later on (92–3) *Les deux Indes* explicitly lists
reasons that limit despotism in China.

28 See, e.g., *Les deux Indes*, vol. 1 [1770], 92, where the Chinese are described
as "a people sufficiently enlightened to feel that respect for the right
of ownership and the submission to laws are nothing but duties of the
second order subjugated to the unlimited rights of nature that had to
build societies only for the needs of all the people composing these societies" (un peuple assez éclairé pour sentir que le respect pour le droit de
propriété, que la soumission aux loix ne sont que des devoirs du second
ordre subordonnés aux droits imprescriptibles de la nature, qui n'a dû
former les sociétés que pour les besoins de tous les hommes qui les
composent).

29 Raynal, in contrast, argues that punishment in China is moderate: "On punit le crime par des peines douces & modérées" (Les deux Indes, vol. 1 [1770], 96–7).

30 See Günter Arnold, commentary at 978, in Herder, Adastea (Auswahl): Werke in zehn Bänden, vol. 10 (Frankfurt: Deutscher Klassiker Verlag, 2000), 965–83. Herder refers to texts by de Pauw not only in the Ideen, but also in Älteste Urkunde des Menschengeschlechts and Über die menschliche Unsterblichkeit.

31 According to Les deux Indes, the Chinese only collect gold when rivers have deposited it in the sand, but they do not go and look for it (vol. 1 [1770], 85).

32 Note Herder's use of the word "should" (soll) in the following passage: "No inherited nobility; only nobility based on merit should count in all ranks; men who have proven themselves should get honorary posts" (Kein erblicher Adel; nur Adel des Verdienstes soll gelten in allen Ständen; geprüfte Männer sollen zu Ehrenstellen kommen) (432). This may indicate that Herder is not entirely convinced that this is how it works in practice. See also Raynal, Les deux Indes, vol. 1 [1770], 90, for similar observations about China.

33 This, too, is part of the general positive view of China among early Enlightenment thinkers; see Israel, Democratic Enlightenment, 558–9.

34 See Birgit Tautz, Reading and Seeing Difference in the Enlightenment: From China to Africa (New York: Palgrave Macmillan, 2007), 4. According to Raynal, "The Chinese are the people on earth with the most regulations for the most ordinary actions" (Les Chinois sont le peuple de la terre qui a le plus de préceptes sur les actions les plus ordinaires) (Les deux Indes, vol. 1 [1770], 96).

35 Cf. Buffon, Histoire naturelle, vol. 3, 381 and 385: "The Chinese have customs entirely opposed [to those of the Tatars]; they are meek people, peaceful, indolent, superstitious, submissive, dependent (in an almost slavelike manner), ceremonial, and courteous in an overly flattering and excessive way" (Les Chinois ont des mœurs tout opposées [aux Tartares], ce sont des peuples mous, pacifiques, indolens, superstitieux, soûmis, dépendans jusqu'à l'esclavage, cérémonieux, complimenteurs jusqu'à la fadeur et à l'excès) (385).

36 Buffon, Histoire naturelle, vol. 3, 384.

37 See n21.

38 Cf. Recherches philosophiques sur les Égyptiens et les Chinois, vol. 2, 189–90; see also 205–6. Diderot, in contrast, in a section in the 1780 edition of Raynal's Histoire philosophique that seeks to address and debunk many of

de Pauw's observations, downplays the influence of the Tatars for numerical reasons: for every Tatar there were 50,000 Chinese; therefore their influence cannot have been great. *Histoire philosophique et politique des établissements et du commerce des Européens dans les deux Indes*, vol. 1 (Geneva: Jean-Leonard Pellet, 1782), 145. Already in the 1770 version Raynal points out that the Tatars adopted the Chinese spirit as articulated in its canonical texts (vol. 1, 98).

39 See Tautz, *Reading and Seeing*, 185–6.

40 The comparison of Chinese and Jews is also made by de Pauw, where the point of comparison is the necessity of the Chinese and Jews to negotiate deals with those in power to circumvent their corrupt practices and buy themselves protection (*Recherches philosophiques*, vol. 2, 211–12).

41 See also de Pauw's link between "pride" as a character trait of the Chinese and their ignorance and subservience, discussed above (*Recherches philosophiques*, vol. 2, 229).

42 Buffon attributes the high level of Chinese civilization to the fact that China borders on the sea enabling commerce with other nations, while the Tatars in their deserts are isolated from other peoples by mountain ranges (*Histoire naturelle*, vol. 3, 391).

43 For Herder's theory of climate, see "Was ist Klima? Und welche Wirkung hats auf die Bildung des Menschen an Körper und Seele?" in *Ideen*, 263–70. The critique that Herder does not leave room for "cultural mobility" and sees "cultural migration" as negative can be found in Sonia Sikka, *Herder on Humanity and Cultural Difference: Enlightened Relativism* (Cambridge: Cambridge University Press, 2011), 9.

44 See Sankar Muthu, *Enlightenment against Empire* (Princeton: Princeton University Press, 2003), 238–9, 243–4.

45 See Tautz, *Reading and Seeing*, 70–3. Raynal comments on the centrality of the model of children's love for their parents for understanding Chinese society as well (*Les deux Indes*, vol. 1 [1770], e.g., 94).

46 This illustrates what Löchte describes as Herder's "age analogy" (Lebensaltersanalogie) when describing the developmental stages of other, non-European cultures (Löchte, *Herder*, 13–14). The idea has, of course, highly normative consequences.

47 Confucius and Confucianism were central for European – and more specifically, German – views of China since the mid-seventeenth century, as Eun-Jeung Lee shows in *"Anti-Europa": Die Geschichte der Rezeption des Konfuzianismus und der konfuzianischen Gesellschaft seit der frühen Aufklärung* (Münster: Lit Verlag, 2003).

48 Eun-Jeung Lee argues that Western views of China changed around 1770, one of the reasons being that China isolated itself from international trade, for which it was criticized as backward (141). Lee also discusses Herder's ambivalent views of China (esp. 246–51) and criticizes his eurocentrism (259).

49 See Löchte, *Herder*, 131–3; Herder sees Europe as a model for such productive exchanges.

50 See n11 above.

51 Cf. Raynal, *Les deux Indes*, vol. 4 [1782], 160. Attempts by the Portuguese to colonize China are discussed in Raynal, *Les deux Indes*, vol. 1 [1780], 161–3, a section that was added in 1780. The text also points to tea having taken over Europe and "having become so necessary for the northern nations" (devenu si nécessaire aux nations du Nord) (162).

52 See in this context Maike Oergel's differentiation between Herder's "awareness of historicity" and his continued grappling with the questions this awareness raises in terms of understanding historical process. *Culture and Identity: Historicity in German Literature and Thought* (Berlin: De Gruyter, 2006), 7.

53 The assumption of the persistency of these traits prefigures racial thinking in de Pauw's work. De Pauw's reactionary reinterpretation of Buffon's environmental theory can also be seen in his views of blackness, which he saw as inferior, ingrained, permanent, and hereditary. See Andrew S. Curran, *The Anatomy of Blackness: Science and Slavery in an Age of Enlightenment* (Baltimore: Johns Hopkins University Press, 2011), 127; see also the discussion of Raynal, ibid. 194–9. Sikka discusses the vicinity of Herder's thought to aspects of racial thinking in spite of his opposition to the term (*Herder*, 130–9) without, however, claiming his theories to be racist. Herder's deliberations on China function as one of Sikka's examples (132–3).

54 See my argument in "The Romantics and Other Cultures," in *The Cambridge Companion to German Romanticism*, ed. Nicholas Saul (Cambridge: Cambridge University Press, 2009), 147–62.

5 Localizing China: Of Knowledge, Genres, and German Literary Historiography

BIRGIT TAUTZ

No Way past Goethe?

When Johann Wolfgang Goethe died in 1832, his unpublished papers contained the outline for an essay on China, the contours of which Anne Bohnenkamp describes in her editorial commentary on Goethe's "Chinesisches" (Chinese Matters).[1] A part of Goethe's last literary journal project, *Über Kunst und Altertum*, "Chinese Matters" was published in one of the last volumes of his works (VI, part1) and consists of three poems and a few interpretive paragraphs. It represents a piece of the puzzle that Goethe's notion of world literature has become, not a return to his intense phase of reading and reflecting upon China which had culminated, a decade earlier, in *Chinesisch-deutsche Jahres- und Tagzeiten* (Chinese-German Seasons and Times of Day; 1816–17). Most importantly, in this short work Goethe appropriates well-worn, late eighteenth-century images of China and ends up sealing in perpetuity a textual archive that enshrined German cultural beliefs about the Asian country.

In "Chinese Matters," Goethe turns his attention to thirty poems "by beautiful women" that had appeared in an English-language anthology by Peter Perring Thoms, *Chinese Courtship in Verse* (1824). Working through Thoms' translation and reinterpretation of these poems,[2] Goethe further adapted the material and offered a transposition that sought to render a reflection or image of common humanity generally rather than of Chinese peculiarity. To his mind, the poems were "Eine Dichtung, die ächte" (poetry, the real one; *Kunst und Altertum*, V, 3, 270) – an example of what he called *Weltpoesie* (world poetry). Unlike *Weltliteratur* (world literature), which implied exchange and communication across national boundaries, world poetry denoted a universal essence.[3]

No matter what Goethe's intention, today the poems in "Chinese Matters" are especially interesting for what they conceal: the prehistory of Goethe's Chinese imagery. By turning to the binding of women's feet, the subject matter of the first poem, Goethe varies an allegory that represented China in the eighteenth century. He swaps bound feet for the Great Wall of China and century-old books; each of these images stands for confinement and stagnation. And yet, by presenting these "Chinese Matters" in poetic form, he marks a crack that runs not just through poetry, but through all literary fiction, and that has shaped cultures of reading: "Chinese Matters" stands both for an *intercultural* circulation of texts centred on the images of elsewhere that the poems convey, and for the *pure* nature of poetry that Goethe sought to compose (and fantasized about).

Although "Chinese Matters" allows for both of these readings, one – poetry's allegorical universality – obscures the other by hiding the cultural prehistory of Goethe's poetic musings. What were contested, and ultimately changing, references to China fade into oblivion while marking the invention of modern literature and its historiography and, ultimately, of literary hermeneutics. For the poems suggest a way of reading that proceeds from, and simultaneously reinforces, the merger of actual China and textual China. In other words, to read about China meant to understand China. Goethe's poems thus resonate with broader cultural discourses, while setting themselves apart as *literature*. Echoing epistemological shifts that had altered textual representations of China and that marked what we today call *modern knowledge formation*, a new China manifested itself in the emerging, academic disciplines in the first decades of the nineteenth century.

Genres that we no longer associate with the lasting *literary legacy* of the time chronicle these *epistemic transformations*. They include the encyclopedia as well as the dictionary, which like no other genres had defined (and in some ways bracketed) the eighteenth century, as well as a number of small forms or genres that appear on the verge of losing critical importance in the early 1800s. Commonly published in journals, these include anecdotes and riddles, instalments of philosophical treatises, and even book reviews. Frequently, they claimed to be translations and referred to foreign-language texts as originals, while insisting on authenticity of experience and reliance on facts. Thus, acknowledging the interplay of text and fact, representation and referent, these texts make for the rich material from which literary history is fashioned. For, as Eric Hayot, Haun Saussy, and Steven Yao claim, such interplay exceeds the somewhat simplifying binary of China's reality and the perception of China; such interplay readily concedes that even facts are textually produced.[4] And yet, while insisting on their factuality and conveyance of knowledge, these genres embraced fiction. They thus enabled global literary modernity, and they do indeed tell the prehistory of Goethe's "Chinese Matters" – as well as of the other, modern academic disciplines.

The Burying Effects of Sino-Philosophy

Goethe's poems share this prehistory with another grand narrative that caps the story of China in eighteenth-century German texts: the place of China in Idealist philosophy. It, too, "purifies" and essentializes what had begun with diverse and complex images of the distant country in the early eighteenth century, before these cohered into a rather abstract concept or rhetorical figure, the "Chinese Cipher."[5] Deploying a series of metaphors that signified stagnation (e.g., the Great Wall, age-old books, a mummy), China took on a fascinating rhetorical life in Western philosophy around 1800 and, even more so, in readings and appropriations of philosophy since then. Often declared the proverbial Other of philosophies of history, China remained outside historical progress and, as Robert Bernasconi argues, outside of philosophy.[6] But China also served as a cognitive figure to imagine modern history's beginnings, thus complicating the spatial underpinnings of its unique role. Featuring prominently in stories that projected "Enlightenment as a narrative,"[7] China signalled stability. Acting as a unifier of the divine and the human, China thus legitimized a quest for natural order that ultimately led towards secularization. The result was a constellation flawed with tension, even contradiction, as temporal image and spatial dichotomy collided.

This "turn to narrative"[8] correlates with shifting cultural sentiments, with what has been described as *Sinophobia* replacing erstwhile *Sinophilia*. But the outward negativity in representing China proves to be about as invalid a model in asserting a fact about China, and about German attitudes towards China, as any attempt to affix different viewpoints to individual philosophers. For example, Adrian Hsia attempts to link Sinophilic and Sinophobic attitudes to German writers' embrace of Voltaire and Montesquieu, respectively; more comprehensively, Jonathan Israel proposes similar legacies of influence in his tome *Democratic Enlightenment*.[9] Franklin Perkins proceeds from the nexus between cultural difference and philosophical truth – a philosophical absolute akin to Goethe's world poetry – that seemed to unite the early modern world. In taking recourse to Michel de Montaigne, Perkins outlines the limits of philosophical universality, because "Montaigne's arguments about the diversity of opinions easily shifted into an argument against the existence of innate ideas, so that whether or not there are universal innate ideas became linked to whether or not cultures were utterly diverse."[10] In other words, where culturally specific ideas took hold, skepticism was born and undermined philosophical universals. To account for an actually existing China meant to put the authority of philosophy at risk, though it had barely begun to rival Christian theology as the hitherto unchallenged prism of Western knowledge production. Philosophy marshalled new guarantors of truth: reason and, later on, space and time. Consequently, while "China" served as an indicator of universal reason, it also came to symbolize a difference that placed it outside all models of thinking about Western history. Subsequently perpetuating the all-encompassing narrative that has East opposing West – and that ultimately projects Orient as Occident's Other – this constellation poses a challenge that lies at the heart of retelling the story of China and its place in German, and European, literary and cultural history.

David Porter has approached the ensuing methodological problem by pointing out the pitfalls of comparisions of East and West. He cautions against the pervasiveness of binary oppositions in intercultural theory and global literary discourse.[11] Recalling their historical contingencies, Porter introduces the term "instrumental amnesia"[12] to describe a phenomenon that has Eurocentrism "result from the intentional occlusion of a previously visible and viable alternative."[13] In commonly used theoretical models for telling the global history of literature, great philosophers, and specifically Hegel, define image-making, facts, and representation. Yet, as scholars probe East-West binaries against imaginary constructs of a global eighteenth century, the self-obscuring dimension of "instrumental amnesia" inevitably comes to the fore. If amnesia serves a purpose, the act of forgetting appears all too deliberate. Similarly, despite casting in a problematic light the philosophical narrative in which innate ideas shape and eradicate whatever cultural diversity may exist, "instrumental amnesia" in this case implies that, although we are able to assert a vanishing complexity of the eighteenth-century image of China, we fall short in knowing what led to its disappearance. In an effort to acknowledge the latter, instrumental amnesia ends up raising the spectre of deliberate acts of forgetting.[14] Playing with the idea of the return of the repressed *avant la lettre* – i.e., previously existing representations of cultural diversity appear as the temporal or racial Other of a Western Self – Porter underscores the need for historicizing the act of forgetting. For instrumental amnesia erases discursive traces that point to the impersonal forces of forgetting. Therefore, we must turn to eclipsed stories, and to the objects (e.g., tea, porcelain, silk) that were recast as mere luxuries, in order to interrogate the making of cultural and intellectual domination. We find these stories in genres that seem marginal today, in encyclopedia entries and varying forms of popular literature.

Complete and Compounded Knowledge: Zedler's *Universallexikon*

To focus on a philosopher's individuality implies accepting choices as well as one-directional arguments; they come at the expense of often messy and obscure material and suppress dense, multifaceted accounts that show formal richness. Philosophical narratives do not consider the diffusing impact of texts, especially their anonymous working through genres that exist to collect, archive, and disseminate knowledge and that possibly undermine the stabilizing impact of philosophical master narratives. In these genres, individuals fade into the background – as do traces of a particular kind of network and knowledge economy they maintained through the exchange of letters, compilation, and collaboration. One such genre, at least in the German-language context, is the encyclopedia.[15] Moreover, all over Europe, encyclopedias defined the epistemic and literary world of the eighteenth century, that is, before it was imagined to be a world of the individually authored book. At the same time, encyclopedias were instrumental in promoting the idea that knowledge exists in books and thus they have evolved as an important medium in its transmission. The encyclopedic genre embodied comprehensive knowledge in a perfect alignment of content and form, while gesturing to the fragile nature of this unity. Encyclopedias harboured "common knowledge." Considered "beyond factual reproach," they generated new genres while exposing epistemological fault lines.[16] Whereas other genres gave rise to the modern author, the encyclopedia depended on compilers. It frequently took its name from editors and publishers, while styling itself as a work not to be read but to be consulted.[17] Stylistically, encyclopedias resemble a convoluted amalgamation: they bear traces of a labouring quest for new knowledge, all the while preserving the derivative recording practices of a past that was considered epistemologically safe and that guaranteed an established tradition. For example, Johann Heinrich Zedler's *Universal-Lexikon* (Universal Encyclopedia; 1732–52) merely collected and compiled, shying away from presenting new systems for the categorization of knowledge. But encyclopedias also chronicle innovative efforts to appeal to the public. The multivolume *Universal-Lexikon*, often referred to simply as "the Zedler," invited users to leaf through the entries, because its compilers had a particular reader in mind: one who engaged in non-linear reading. Having read newspapers and journals, he or she moved on to consulting the encyclopedia on one special topic of interest.

Most importantly though, encyclopedias provided new models of global representation of knowledge, claiming to hold on to the conceptual ideal of organizing universal knowledge while imparting proven (as well as unknown) facts about particular places of the world. Transcultural knowledge and various transfer techniques among encyclopedias (e.g., adaptation, translation) intersected with an increasingly nationally conceived reservoir of symbolisms, which manifested itself in the vernaculars rather than the lingua franca, Latin. Balance, comprehensiveness, and entertainment were key to the encyclopedia's popular success in the eighteenth century. Jeff Loveland observes that "Zedler seems to have felt no concern about ignoring the boundaries between kinds of encyclopedias: just as he gambled that a market could be found for an encyclopedia larger than any yet printed, so he gambled that readers had little stake in maintaining genres of encyclopedias as they then stood – and his intuitions were vindicated."[18] Zedler had pursued an even more radical shaping of his public, reaching – almost literally – for the world. The lengthy preface sets apart the *Universal-Lexikon*, and its focus on facts and events, stories and histories, from competing lexica and dictionaries that, the author claims, should be called glossaries, because of their focus on words.[19] "The Zedler" represented distant countries and cities, despite the fact that readers and users were unlikely to travel there, drawing sharp distinctions from specialized reference works.[20] While having little use value, the entries therefore fostered the idea of valuable, "disinterested" knowledge – just like the authoritative preface helped pave the way for an individual author as guardian of knowledge.

The very nature of encyclopedias led to the implosion of any differences among its various types. Although they were tasked with informing and preserving (rather than with inventing or storytelling), encyclopedias enabled (and eventually necessitated) narrative organization. They swallowed small genres such as legends, chronicles, anecdotes, and travel accounts, while empowering grand narratives that infuse the epic, dramatic, and poetic forms of canonical literature. Ultimately, the encyclopedia embodies both a fragile corpus of genres straddling multiple lines – between fact and fiction, between knowledge and non-knowledge – and an engine for new poetic production and epistemic organization. Successful encyclopedias maximized the impact of all of the aspects detailed here, rather than simply giving way to articulating the impossibility of "universal knowledge" and drifting towards "disciplinary knowledge." While the latter sealed, I believe, the fate of encyclopedias and lexica in the early nineteenth century,[21] the amplification of embedded genres, creative innovation, and the quest for narrative order inevitably led to the genre's demise.

The representations of China circulating in the *Universal-Lexikon* express this general pattern,[22] appearing complex and fizzled, at times even contradictory, as writers and compilers attempt to pack more and more layers – knowledge – into the description of the country. The encyclopedia's main account of China comprises roughly twenty columns and starts out by naming the entry: linguistically, through common, multiple spellings of "Sina, China, Tschina" (vol. 37, 1556) and politically, by adding its form of government, which is "ein Kayserthum" (empire; ibid.). Immediately, though, the entry reverts to another system of classification, namely, and here I paraphrase, to what China was known for in German lands in the mid-eighteenth century: The author first recalls China's "sonderbaren Fruchtbarkeit" ([*sic*]; strange, odd fertility; ibid.). (Only as we read on, does it become clear that the talk is about vegetation and, to a lesser degree, agriculture, and not about mammal or human reproduction.) To that, the writer adds "grossen Reichthums, schöner Städte, vielen Einwohner" ([*sic*]; great wealth, beautiful cities, many inhabitants; ibid.). Although the clearly articulated categories could give structure to the entry, it nevertheless unfolds rather chaotically, adding themes and abandoning others, embellishing and thus imploding the initial categories of organization. Beginning with names and designations – chosen by the Chinese but more often than not imposed by their neighbours – the entry comments on geographical borders. Leaping ahead by crossreferencing the entry on the Great Wall of China,[23] there is an account of the political-geographical partition into provinces and, eventually, a basic interpretation of Chinese history: The entry distinguishes between the actual China and the Chinese Empire, describing the latter as encompassing the old country as well as the Tartar-occupied zones and ultimately amounting to a "a unified territory of terrifying size" ("einiges Reich ... von einer ganz entsetzlichen Grösse"; 1557). A description of natural topography follows. After three columns of meandering prose, the entry eventually returns to commenting upon agriculture. In about fifteen short lines, agricultural products, harvesting cycles, and preferred growing areas are listed, only for the compiler to conclude: "In short, it is impossible to find the words to describe the fertile Chinese Empire" (Kurz zu sagen: Es kann die Fruchtbarkeit des Reiches China mit keener Feder beschrieben werden; 1559). Short passages about individual provinces intersect accounts of mining; comments on family values and hierarchies give way to ideals of masculinity and femininity. Chinese ideals of female beauty are introduced; they meander into information about marital customs and laws and culminate in expressing surprise about males having to provide a dowry at the wedding – only to be followed, in the next sentence and without transition or section break, by an extensive linguistic commentary on the nature and development of Chinese characters (1562). Evidently, the dispersing, indeed exasperating effects of the entry on China arise from its internal organization or lack thereof. Although different thematic strands and excessive details interrupt the description, thus diverting the reader's attention, the author adds even more complexity by introducing new aspects (and ordering systems) such as the sciences (1564). Barely scratching the surface of complex topics such as religion, social stratification, and government, the compilation concludes with a lengthy table of Chinese emperors followed by a brief commentary on imperial government.

Allowing a glimpse at the discursive matrix of early eighteenth-century European historiography, in the *Universal-Lexikon* at the end of the entry on China borrows from the genre of chronicle. It thus alludes to the conventional, albeit increasingly obscured, belief in the divine legitimacy of the ruler. Yet here the entry oscillates between using the established small form of the chronicle and making a philosophical intervention in the debate on enlightened despotism which, though not raging, was omnipresent in eighteenth-century Europe and influenced Zedler's accounts of encyclopedic knowledge. After all, the first German encyclopedia did not share the critical tasks of the French *Encyclopédie*, which Hans-Jürgen Lüsebrink reads as a symptomatic sign of probing and challenging the boundaries of secure knowledge.[24]

As these attempts remained largely confined to the French tradition, the *Encyclopédie*'s critical and emancipatory impact was not exported.

In crafting the entry on China, the compiler-author of "the Zedler" did not pick up the unifying role that Chinese language had played in early modern Europe.[25] Rather than extending this role and applying it to the image of China, for example, by presenting it as a model state, or reflecting on the earlier function of Classical Chinese through comparison and contrast,[26] the language now denotes Chinese uniqueness. The entry explains the idiosyncrasies of both country and language by insisting on them being derivatives of the thing, the object to be named (vol. 37, 1164). According to the entry on "Sinesische Mauer" (Chinese Wall), Athanasius Kircher had introduced European geography as a means of comparison, hoping to stimulate readers' imagination of the world, its scale and expansion. Nevertheless, the monumental nature of China's territory escapes the imagination (vol. 37, 1615). Neither does the author-compiler turn to the wall as a sole or prevailing metaphor for delineating a clear-cut image of China's seclusion. Instead, he succumbs to a plethora of sources and images. According to Zhengxiang Gu, the sources for all the "Chinese entries" in the *Universal-Lexikon* amount to approximately 200 texts. Examining Gu's bibliography, I have determined that 85 of those were written in Latin, 55 in German, 24 in French, and the remainder in Dutch, Spanish, and Italian.[27] "The Zedler" turns this information into a composite of unorganized facts and anecdotes, complete with literature review, pseudo-citation, and paraphrasing. As a result, the entry on China in the *Universal-Lexikon* bundles different, often diametrically opposed authorities of narration, ultimately projecting to the culture of translation, without actually being a translation. It popularizes discourses and languages that counteract the trend that Lüsebrink describes as the spread of French encyclopedic knowledge across Europe. Accordingly, through the *Encyclopédie*'s translation into other languages, French thought penetrated, shaped, and amended national imaginations across Europe.[28] Though the circulation of encyclopedias through translation practices did indeed expose gaps in knowledge and, consequently, the need for supplements, expansions, and alternate languages, the resulting products are often unique. And while the multivolume "Zedler" instigates a push towards a linguistically unifying monument, a more fluid epistemic situation emerges. Though safely *contained* in the medium of the book and exemplifying a genre that insists on its ability to articulate universal knowledge – the encyclopedic entry can barely *contain* the build-up of images. The details that make up textual China threaten to disrupt and undermine what is considered secure, albeit bound knowledge. As such, the *Universal-Lexikon* reveals the distant country's uncertain status in the epistemological network of the German-speaking world: at once vague and complex, "textual China" entails both factual illusion and representational markers; it resembles an aggregate account.

Proving to be more complex than scholarship to date suggests,[29] the "textual China" of Zedler's *Universal-Lexikon* serves as a cultural reservoir. It contains knowledge, but undermines (in part) the purpose of an encyclopedia, that is, to *organize* knowledge as *information* – rather than just presenting facts in an additive manner.[30] Zedler's China threatens to fall apart. But as a generator of texts, the encyclopedia spins off alternate genres – including those that may account for the eighteenth-century shift in perceiving China and that preserve an alternate "textual China": reaching beyond the scope of Idealist philosophy, pure poetry, and Orientalizing fiction, the encyclopedia simultaneously escapes the disciplinary shape that "textual China" takes in early nineteenth-century encyclopedias.

Two textual practices shape this constellation, and they are at the core of making the eighteenth-century European encyclopedia: (1) translation from and into other languages, of sources as well as the complete encyclopedic work, and (2) the act of writing the encyclopedia in a language that was not Latin and that therefore enabled the circulation of knowledge beyond the narrow republic of scholars. Both practices come with contradictory effects. Translingualism and transnationalism morph into a unifying monolingualism that insinuates, at least rhetorically, the national. Indeed, the *Universal-Lexikon* represents an often remarked upon, curious instance of proclaimed universality that glosses over, yet at the same time exposes, tensions that reach beyond the universal and Germanness. Though the author of the preface, Johann Peter von Ludewig, praises "the Zedler" for its monopoly in German lands (or elsewhere for that matter),[31] he observes that no nationalizing intent forced the publisher's actions. Instead, the publisher preserved expertise in the face of dilettantism ("Halbgelehrten"), all the while recognizing the necessity of specialized labour and the limitations of simply translating existing encyclopedias.[32] Although fostering the idea of an enduring and comprehensive knowledge of the world amid nationalizing linguistic cohesion, the *Universal-Lexikon* "forgets" about both the non-existent nation and local interests in German lands.[33]

It is precisely in local contexts, however, that the other "textual China" survives. Populating small genres that, not coincidentally, hibernate in the margins of literary and cultural life, localized images of China remain eclipsed in early nineteenth-century efforts to reorganize the world epistemologically and encyclopedically. Pointing less to purposeful acts of forgetting than to pragmatic recall and bustling creativity, local genres constitute loose ends in an emerging narrative of modernity. Although the latter has divided the world into nations to be interpreted along the lines of West and East, and supplemented with fictions of Occident and Orient, local genres construct a China that interrupts the ensuing, stabilizing narrative of Enlightenment uniformity.[34]

Localized Genres, Localized Knowledge: Of Tea Poems, Chinese Anecdotes, and Agricultural Wisdom

Occasional poetry, anecdotes, and small agricultural treatises represent but three of the genres that I will depict as local genres, while seeking to capture their origins, impact, and resonance in the eighteenth century as well as their literary legacy in the centuries since then. For example, tea poems point to the conversational sentimentalism of the northern German salon culture. They tell the stories of luxurious indulgence and consumption, of cultivating sociability, and the rehearsing of virtue and taste. However, they stand for a lot more than expressions of Hamburg's access to the world, including the city's familiarity with the origins, export, and reputation of tea.[35] Elisa Reimarus's poem "Der Thee" (Tea at Teatime; 1757) condenses tea's import into a tale of poetic, communal, and ethical innovation, reminding readers – or, as it were, listeners to the poem's performance – of China's pride and flair of superiority vis-à-vis the Western world.[36] At the same time, another image, "Peckings Quell" (Peking's Spring), alludes to more than the origins of tea, because it anticipates expressions – not to say metaphors – of poetic inspiration. Fusing knowledge about China's alleged status in the Enlightenment republic of scholars with its future place in the Orientalist image of the world, the poem's figuration intersects the emergence of tea as an object. A special drink that harmonizes with nature, tea is brought into focus as an object of luxury, by praising its beauty and elevating its qualities through detailed descriptors (stanzas 1–4). Yet what develops as objectlike qualities dissolves into a dream or intoxication, only to be reawakened from magic and blissful loss of consciousness by a sigh; this poetic movement foreshadows the object's role in the literary imagination of modernity. Eventually, though, Reimarus's poem returns listeners and readers to their values of virtue, taste, and meaningful leisure activities. By casting aside the qualities of tea in favour of the sociability of drinking tea, the poem captures and restores its eighteenth-century environment: "As virtue calms the fiery temperament/they find pure taste and agility in themselves" (Dann finden noch zur Tugend feur'ge Seelen/Geschmack an sich, und in sich Zeitvertreib).[37]

At first glance, Jens Baggesen's poem "Theelied" (Song of Tea; before 1800?) augments the aspect of sociability. But underneath, it celebrates tea's export history, while enacting a tale of Orientalism that conflates geography with mythical Woman. Using the guise of a social poem (*Trinklied*), the poem tells the story of global exploration. Planted and cultivated by mythical women in distant Asian lands, tea arrives in Europe where it becomes more popular than wine; at the same time, it makes for an exotic consumer product whose allure the poem underscores by linking its possession to poetry's mythical inspirations. A narrative poem to its core, "Song of Tea" fuses Orient and myth as places of poetic origin, while transcending the object tea – its material, economic, and historical value – with the help of poetic language. Although "Theelied" was included in Baggesen's 1802 collection of poems,[38] "Der Thee" hibernated in archives; thus, bearing the unadulterated traces of salon performances in the mid-eighteenth century, both poems illustrate how objects (things) vanished from the literary and cultural canon before re-emerging in modernism.

For things are inevitably tied to processes of (de-)mystification, especially once they become valuable for literary imagination and production.[39] It is then that their hidden side of encapsulating and radiating cultural memory breaks out into the open. But things stand for more than simply the opposite of imagination. They surpass crude and simple materiality, thus transitioning, in the parlance of scholars, from being mere "objects" to somewhat elusive and mysterious "things."[40] Following Barthes, Ulrike Vedder delineates the status of things in literary texts, observing a mystique and proneness to self-fashion as a riddle, thus differentiating literary things from mere "epistemic objects" (to be found in experiments or exhibited in museums). She also insists on a narrative potential that allows things to generate stories. Things are indicators of both reality and fiction; in oscillating between pointing to one or the other, they circumscribe both a crisis of perception and a path towards eloquent representation.

The tea poems express this dual role of things: While Reimarus's poem preserves the magical qualities of the thing and its circulation in an oral culture, Baggesen's poem directs us towards the act of remembering by resurrecting tea's origins in the Far East and articulating them in a trade narrative that creates a mythical, feminized Orient. While both poems and poets were forgotten, the rhetoric and poetic form of Baggesen's poem was not. As trade, export, and material things were relegated to the realms of archives and, eventually, historiography, Orientalism emerged as the new narrative and poetic paradigm. Object and orality vanished temporarily or permanently, respectively, from European literary history. With the exception of so-called *Dinggedichte* (thing poems), which, by aspiring to duplicate content in form, achieved realist acclaim, objects became the purview of other, nonliterary discourses. Yet, object and orality, in linking tea poems, agricultural wisdom, and anecdotes with one another, illustrate the power and limitations of small, or as I shall call them, local genres vis-à-vis the dominant cultural narratives.[41]

To explore this dimension, a turn towards the rich archive of eighteenth-century German-language journals proves instructive. Here "textual China" figures prominently; at least 145 titles allude to the country, with many of them referring to (reviews of) travel texts.[42] The vast majority of these texts appears to have been published in northern German journals such as the Hamburg-based *Historisch-politisches Magazin, nebst literarischen Nachrichten* (Historical-Political Magazine, with Literary News), Berlin's *Deutsche Monatsschrift* (German Monthly), or the *Hannoverisches Magazin* (Hanover Magazine). Whereas the latter published mostly translations from the *Mémoires concernant les Chinois*,[43] and implied that readers know that this is the text it translates from, the former two journals rarely mark the "China texts" as translations. The Hamburg- and Berlin-based journals relay information and commentary on the Chinese population, finances, law, and administration. In at least one instance, they claim to publish a text by the Chinese emperor in translation,[44] whereas the *Hannoverisches Magazin* introduces historically verifiable figures and allusion to Chinese government in the form of anecdotes.[45] The preponderance of thematic clusters suggests a heightened interest in administrative, demographic, and economic issues in the places of publication, while at the same time preserving the legacy of textual China and its model state. Yet, belief in the authenticity of the latter is shattered, not just because many "Chinese texts" are conceded to be fragments, thus forfeiting the authority that comes with narrative completion and wholeness. More importantly, they relegate the authoritative presence of historically verifiable individuals to the anecdote, an amorphous genre that in the late eighteenth century explodes onto the German literary scene where it quickly takes on a vexing presence. In these journals, the transformation of popular belief into knowledge centres on anecdotes, as does the transposition of oral cultures into literary fact. Anecdotes frequently stake their legitimacy on an English or French original; Thomas Guillaume François Raynal's collections of historical and literary anecdotes serve as a model.[46] However, in extracting the anecdote from the collection and bringing it into the new context of the journal, the genre's intended role collapses: it no longer serves an integrating and informing function, but opens itself to invention and fiction. As their narrative authority vanishes before it has been established, anecdotes appear minor in more than one sense: small in terms of length, they insist upon boundaries between fact and fiction while simultaneously blurring these boundaries. Often entertaining, anecdotes elude the dynamics of the Enlightenment's institutions and the manner of narrating their stories. If institutions indeed negotiate the relationships between various motivations and purposes in societies, as Albrecht Koschorke claims, their narratives, too, strive to achieve, above all, stability and harmony.[47] But anecdotes can elude restrictive narrative patterns, as the example of the "Chinese anecdotes"[48] shows. Hinging upon Sinophilic images of the early eighteenth century, they feature a cast of characters that appear embellished and uncertain through the oral transmission of their stories; they introduce uncertainty into the process of narration. Thus, lending themselves to becoming the reservoir of fiction, anecdotes lose their epistemic authority. Instead, as they deviate from narrative norms and expectations, anecdotes create (and communicate) new modes of storytelling by *literalizing orality* and by toying with *invention*.

In introducing the practical sciences of the Chinese, as well as Chinese objects, the *Hannoverisches Magazin* proceeds quite differently. Here the authority, indeed the quasi-institutional character, of translation guards against any invention that anecdotes enable. By harking back to the original written in another language, the texts limit their degree of innovation. Especially agricultural knowledge catches the eye of the translator Anton Christian Wedekind. His "Chinese texts," published in instalments, deal mainly with the cultivation and breeding of trees, with greenhouses, natural fertilizers, and the medicinal qualities of plants. They point both to the intermediary status of translators in eighteenth-century networks of knowledge production, where they emerge as translator-*authors* and guarantors of knowledge, and to the local formation of genres and discourse. Wedekind's material has been narrated before; it represents the certainty of knowledge waiting to be communicated, popularized, and thus proliferated. It is unlikely that the translator-author would isolate the material free of its stabilizing context and establish a new narrative authority by insisting on his own creativity and invention. Wedekind was the head administrator of an estate in Bentheim, with family members employed in forestry planning and medical sciences. But the themes spoke to the interests of the journal's readership in Hanover and the vast agricultural, rural areas surrounding that city. Aside from the activities of the *Celler Landwirtschaftsgesellschaft* (Celle's Agricultural Society), the journal emerged as the most important venue for the popularization of knowledge in the area,[49] collaborating with the society and establishing new epistemic genres. By isolating records of knowledge from their encyclopedic or foreign contexts – in this case a monumental book – and rewriting them for the local audience in piecemeal fashion, the *Hannoverisches Magazin* supported the quest for implementing practical knowledge locally.

China Reorganized: The Encyclopedia in the Early Nineteenth Century

"Textual China" thus indicates not only divergent disciplinary contexts, but also generic and discursive fractures. It exposes the rifts between the emergence of narratives that unfold binary oppositions (of Universal and Particular, of Self and Other, of literalization and orality) and alternate stories, which I have contoured as local genre or knowledge. The latter are local not just because of their place of publication, local readership, and limited transregional impact, but also because they present an epistemic object in its momentous or situational configuration. The stories block their own sublimation in narrative temporality, insisting instead, again, on the particular constellation of the moment in which they are told. Often they do so by capturing aspects of orality or by rupturing a presumption of alternate truth. In this respect, "textual China" points to the unique role of fiction, namely, its complicity with a general operation of narrative – for example, in Orientalist fantasies of Other – while rupturing the latter's stabilizing impact and producing new forms such as situational poetry or anecdotes.

Frequently, however, local genres end up engaging in a play of metonymic transference and metaphorical condensation, thus preparing and supporting the epistemic reorganization we see in epistemic genres at the beginning of the nineteenth century. Although China's original import into the Enlightenment narrative – as both origin and proof of the universalizing language of reason – appears lost by around 1800, the alignment of China with a universally signifying capacity is preserved, albeit in the local realms of disciplinary divisions of knowledge. For example, Chinese origins were forced upon a plant that had no origins in the Far Eastern country whatsoever but whose healing power was widely described in popular medical texts. These texts introduced quinine to the German-speaking public under a very descriptive name: "China-Rinde" (China root). Although there were already mentions of the plant's South American origin in the 1750s, the name – which coexisted with "Fieberrinde" (fever root) – was only fully corrected to "Peru-Rinde" (Peru root) in the nineteenth century.[50]

Thus, in popular medical texts, Chinese objects come close to preserving and codifying their essence as a thing with nearly magical powers. Their associative links to the human body come full circle in the very extensive discussion of Chinese medicine in Johann Samuel Ersch and Johann Gottfried Gruber's *Allgemeine Encyklopädie der Wissenschaften und Künste* (General Encyclopedia of Sciences and Arts; 1818–89). "The Ersch-Gruber," as it is also known, has an informative, richly detailed, and meticulously organized section on the subject matter and connects medicinal effects of plants and herbs to theories of magnetism, energy balance, and body temperature. While the entry references du Halde as a source and authority, it quickly abandons the recourse to a textual tradition and turns to a new focus, namely, the consistent impact of Chinese natural medicine in German lands.[51] In that, the *Allgemeine Encyklopädie* locates China in different discourses than earlier encyclopedic writing. It distributes "textual China" across different entries, documenting greater interest in Chinese medicine (and in natural science in general, equated here with medicine in the first sentence) than in Chinese language and linguistics, which had been at the centre of encyclopedic writing about China in the early eighteenth century. In contrast, Ersch-Gruber separates the discussion of language, combining it with that of Chinese literature and music. Although the latter entry is extensive, the study of the Chinese language is now relegated to a place within *modern* scholarly institutions consistent with the beginning of institutionalized Orientalism. After all, "the Ersch-Gruber" also harbours China Studies in "Orientalische Studien" (Oriental Studies; vol. 28, 194). Moreover, the study of the Chinese language takes place abroad, namely, in London and Paris. German scholars are described as having very little desire to study Chinese or, for that matter, Japanese (vol. 28, 217–18). Home-grown philology merely dabbles in Sinology, with a prominent example being the bilingual Hager, who – German-born – grew up in Italy and, around 1800, after developing a fascination with Chinese, returned to a very early moment in the scholarly preoccupation with the Chinese language, namely, the *Clavis Sinica* (vol. 28, 171–2). But the shining example of Leibniz's linguistic universe is forgotten.

By including Orientalism in the encyclopedic representation of knowledge, "the Ersch-Gruber" also distinguishes itself from other dictionaries and lexica constituting the increasing variety of encyclopedic genres. In contrast, the first and second editions of Brockhaus's *Conversations-Lexikon* (Brockhaus's Encyclopedia; 1811–19) represent China in a truly conversational and amalgamated manner, by confining the entry on China to condensed travel stories, interwoven with vaguely referenced political events.[52] Stylistically, "the Brockhaus," therefore, preserves, and even revives, allusions to older accounts and genres that imparted images of China in the eighteenth century, suggesting a popular discourse of knowledge formation. Moreover, it formed a counterpoint to the cultural and political legitimacy that came with documenting institutional forms of Orientalism (China Studies) in an encyclopedia such as "the Ersch-Gruber."

Reading locally, that is, in accordance with genre and non-national interests, helps uncover eighteenth-century representations of China that today have faded into oblivion but that tell alternate stories of cultural history. They complicate not only the image of China as marker of temporal and spatial difference, but also any narrative linearity within the literary and cultural historiography of German lands. Reading locally reveals what is lost in a larger philosophical narrative such as Hegel's, which was, after all, conceived as a regional (i.e., European/Germanic) or hemispheric (i.e., Western) narrative and that promised universality. Reading locally also unveils a prehistory of literary imagery before Goethe's pure poetry and literary hermeneutics, one that has the intercultural circulation of texts as a constituent of world literature. In this way of reading the poems of "Chinese Matters," women perform ethnicity and symbolize something essentially Chinese. In Goethe's understanding of pure poetry, ethnicity dissolves into universality: women channel the idea that poetry per se is feminized.

Harmonizing the forces of nature while being an inspiring muse, the speech of women waits to be shaped by the poet. Although the former reading alludes to a well-defined, static image of China – an impenetrable, confined place – prevailing throughout the eighteenth century, the latter allegorizes this image completely. Suggesting, instead, that poetry is universal and translatable, pure poetry assumes an ultimate essence within a broader network of world literature that transcends any specific locale, time, and space. Seemingly universally comprehensible, pure poetry marks the advent of literature's modernity and of literary hermeneutics.

As reading locally underscores the epistemological complexity of Chinese traces in these local genres, it challenges us to consider whether images of China are more than a metaphor to discuss philosophical and historical progress. Instead, these local genres expose Idealist philosophy, literary Orientalism, and Goethe's pure poetry – and the images of non-Western worlds these narratives conjured up – as events in the history of mediation.[53] Although processes of mediation always leave something out, these local remnants are highly readable. These local instances of knowledge point to epistemic constellations – networks – that emerged as a cognitive gesture. Replacing, in the discourse on China, the quest for a universal language to which Leibniz's China adhered, these networks have manifold effects: aside from the image of China as the Other of Idealist philosophy and the cipherlike embodiment of pure literature in Goethe's "Chinese Matters," a fractured image of China emerges. Split along the lines of modern scholarly disciplines (e.g., botany, philology, literary hermeneutics), it uses objects and specialized language to signify China. Other images vanished because they were bound to literary genres that could not be mediated in the process of writing a national literary history or, for that matter, in the Western concept of world literature. Yet, looking past their master plots – which often have Goethe at their centre – indeed unearths the hitherto forgotten images and genres.

NOTES

1 Johann Wolfgang Goethe, "Chinesisches," *Über Kunst und Altertum*, 6/1 (1827), in *Werke* (= Frankfurter Ausgabe), vol. 22, edited by Anne Bohnenkamp (Frankfurt: Deutscher Klassiker Verlag, 1999), 370. See also Anne Bohnenkamp, "Kommentar," *Werke*, vol. 22, 870–964.

2 For a detailed account of Goethe's work with Thoms' text see Siegfried Behrsing, "Goethe's 'Chinesisches,'" *Wissenschaftliche Zeitschrift der Humboldt-Universität, Gesellschafts- und Sprachwissenschaft*, 19/3 (1970): 243–60, here 245.

3 On Goethe's notion of world literature, see Anne Bohnenkamp, "'Den Wechseltausch zu befördern': Goethes Entwurf einer Weltliteratur," in Goethe, *Werke*, Kunst und Altertum, 937–64.

4 Eric Hayot, Haun Saussy, and Steven Yao, "Sinographies: An Introduction," in *Sinographies: Writing China*, eds. Hayot et al. (Minneapolis: University of Minnesota Press, 2007), vii–xxi, here ix–x.

5 David Porter, *Ideographia: The Chinese Cipher in Early Modern Europe* (Stanford: Stanford University Press, 2001), 3, 135.

6 Robert Bernasconi emphatically underscored this point during the Pennsylvania State University conference. However, I also infer this claim in my reading of Bernasconi's take on Hegel's notion of world history. See Robert Bernasconi, "With What Must the Philosophy of World History Begin? On the Racial Bias of Hegel's Eurocentrism," *Nineteenth-Century Contexts*, 22/2 (2000): 171–202, here 177, and Birgit Tautz, *Reading and Seeing Ethnic Difference in the Enlightenment: From China to Africa* (New York: Palgrave, 2007), 16. On the exclusion of China from philosophy, see also chapter 2 in this collection: Franklin Perkins, "Leibniz on the Existence of Philosophy in China."

7 James Schmidt's review article "Mediation, Genealogy, and (the) Enlightenment/s" delineates this concept of Enlightenment vis-à-vis the competing attempt at describing Enlightenment as a mediating effort. See *Eighteenth Century Studies*, 45/1 (2011): 127–60.

8 Cf. Tautz, *Reading and Seeing*, 6–7,15–17. This label does not take into account the vast scholarship on narrative and narratology, which espouses a multitude of different understandings of narrative (also in differentiation from story and plot).

9 Adrian Hsia, "China in der deutschen Literatur der Aufklärung," in *China-Bilder in der europäischen Literatur* (Würzburg: Königshausen and Neumann, 2010) 99–102, here 100–1; Jonathan Israel, "China, Japan, and the West," in *Democratic Enlightenment: Revolution and Human Rights* (Oxford: Oxford University Press, 2011), 558–71.

10 Franklin Perkins, *Leibniz and China: A Commerce of Light* (Cambridge: Cambridge University Press, 2004), 12.

11 David Porter, "Sinicizing Early Modernity: The Imperatives of Historical Cosmopolitanism," *Eighteenth Century Studies*, 43/3 (2010): 299–306, here 301.

12 Ibid., 304.

13 Ibid., 303.

14 In order to delineate the significance of the shift towards instrumental amnesia, the following overview might be useful: For a long time, scholars have focused on Chinese remnants of material culture, detailing, for example, the social contexts in which Chinoiserie flourished as well as those that triggered its demise. Glamourized for their mystery, textual expressions of Chinoiserie depend, according to David Porter's *Ideographia*, on the formal beauty and aesthetic ideal that earlier generations saw in the written Chinese character. In other words, these new systems of representation stand for the signifier, by now an empty decorum or detail. They make a profound gesture of exteriorization and constitute, writes Porter, "an explicit rejection, in the aesthetic domain, of the very principle of substantiality that had been ascribed to China by those who had sought there a privileged site of linguistic or theological legitimacy" (135). Porter further points out that the rise of Chinoiserie went hand in hand with "the progressive delegitimization of Chinese imperial power" (135). See also Johannes Franz Hallinger, *Das Ende der Chinoiserie: Die Auflösung eines Phänomens der Kunst in der Zeit der Aufklärung* (Munich: Scaneg, 1996). Furthermore, scholars (such as Hsia and Israel) have pointed to the theological-philosophical roots of Sinophilia and discussed the Jesuit tradition up to and including Leibniz. Despite the attempts at historical differentiation and accuracy, most scholars have applied a narrative logic that assumes a gradual, teleological progress and a neat morphing of one image into another. In this process, the author's or philosopher's intention plays the crucial role in creating the image. Leibniz's China appears to have developed into Hegel's China or into Herder's China; however, how this happened – and which anonymous, discursive forces may have been at play – remains unclear.

15 The prime example of the encyclopedic genre, the French *Encyclopédie*, is very much connected to individual protagonists who formed the group of *encyclopédistes*, chiefly among them Diderot and D'Alembert.

16 Ulrich Johannes Schneider, "Der Aufbau der Wissenswelt: Eine phänotypische Beschreibung enzyklopädischer Literatur," in *Kulturen des Wissens im 18. Jahrhundert*, ed. Ulrich Johannes Schneider (Berlin: de Gruyter, 2008), 81–100, here 82.

17 Ibid., 84.

18 Jeff Loveland, "Encyclopedias and Genre, 1670–1750," *Journal of Eighteenth-Century Studies*, 36/2 (2013): 159–75, here 170.

19 "Vorrede über das Universal-Lexikon," 1–16, here 4, cited from http://
    www.zedler-lexikon.de/index.html?c=blaettern&seitenzahl=24&
    bandnummer=01&view=100&l=de (accessed 13 Oct. 2013).

20 Schneider, "Der Aufbau," 96.

21 Loveland, "Encyclopedias and Genre," 162–3.

22 "Sina, China, Tschina, ein Kaysertum," vol. 37, 1556–74, here 1556, cited
    from http://www.zedler-lexikon.de/ (accessed 18 Feb. 2012).

23 "So ist dieses unter dem Artickel Sinesische Mauer mit mehrern aus-
    geführt worden" (This is explained in the article Chinese Wall in several
    [ways]; ibid., 1557). "The Zedler" marks cross-references to other entries
    through bold print; the original contains syntactical ambiguity, i.e., it is
    unclear what "mit mehrern" refers to.

24 Hans-Jürgen Lüsebrink, "Enzyklopädismus und Kulturtransfer im
    Aufklärungszeitalter: Fallbeispiele und transkulturelle Perspektiven," in
    Epoche und Projekt: Perspektiven der Aufklärungsforschung, ed. Stefanie Stock-
    horst (Göttingen: Wallstein, 2013), 263–84, here 288.

25 Porter has described Leibniz's attitude as driven by the desire to impose
    linguistic unity upon a Europe ravaged by war. Despite these differences
    in our approaches, Porter has opened up the pathway towards a fresh
    look at China, one that has remained undervalued, in my opinion. Porter
    claimed that China's "celebrated status represented more than an aberra-
    tion in a discourse of colonization, exploitation, and subjection to a new
    imperial narrative of conceptualizing the world." Cf. *Ideographia*, 3.

26 For a model on incorporating, rhetorically, effective strategies of compari-
    son and contrast, see Leslie Chard, "The Urban Paradox: Two Ideas of the
    City in the *Encyclopédie*," *Studies on Voltaire and the Eighteenth Century*, 303
    (1992): 153–6.

27 Gu, Zhengxiang: "Zum China-Bild des Zedlerschen Lexikons: Bibliografie
    der in seinen China-Artikeln besprochenen oder als Quellen genannten
    Werke," in *In dem wilden und glücklichen Schwaben und in der Neuen Welt:
    Beiträge zur Goethezeit, Festschrift für Hartmut Fröschle*, ed. Reinhard Brey-
    meyer (Stuttgart: Heinz, 2004), 477–506.

28 Lüsebrink, "Enzyklopädismus und Kulturtransfer," 270, cf. 274.

29 Cf., most recently, Schneider's comprehensive study *Die Erfindung des
    allgemeinen Wissens* (Berlin: Akademie Verlag, 2013). But unlike in his ear-
    lier essay, here Schneider resorts to an assessment of China that is far less
    differentiated, even contradictory: "Der ausgestreckte Zeigefinger weist im
    Universal-Lexicon gewissermaßen nicht nur in die Ferne, sondern stigma-
    tisert das Andere" (In the Universal-Lexicon, the finger points not only in
    the distance, but becomes finger-pointing and stigmatizes the Other) (118).

30 The scholarship on the genre of encyclopedia is extensive, although often with particular focus on national encyclopedias or certain thematic articles. Another influential scholar, aside from Lüsebrink and Schneider, is Clorinda Donato. See, aside from numerous presentations on the subject matter, her "La Enciclopedia Metódica: Transfer and Transformation of Knowledge about Spain and the New World in the Spanish Translation of the Encyclopédie Méthodique," *Das Europa der Aufklärung und die außereuropäische koloniale Welt*, ed. Hans-Jürgen Lüsebrink (Göttingen: Wallstein, 2006), 74–113.

31 "Vorrede über das Universal-Lexikon," 1–16, here 1.

32 Ibid., 5.

33 The idea of comprehensive knowledge engages, in an ambiguous way, the idea of authorship: While source texts are identified, in part, by authors' name – and the fact that the encyclopedia author translates, copies, or paraphrases is not always acknowledged – the entry also capitalizes on anonymous, nameless authority (which precludes the challenge of invention, improvisation, etc.).

34 I develop the idea of the interrupting potential of small genres and local representation in loose reference to Koschorke, while setting myself apart from his universal theory of narrative. Cf. Albrecht Koschorke, *Wahrheit und Erfindung: Grundzüge einer allgemeinen Erzähltheorie* (Frankfurt: Fischer, 2012), esp. "V. Narrative und Institutionen," 287–328.

35 See Almut Spalding, *Elise Reimarus (1735–1805), The Muse of Hamburg: A Woman of the German Enlightenment* (Würzburg: Königshausen and Neumann, 2005), 144.

36 Elise Reimarus, "Der Thee," in Spalding, *Reimarus*, 340–1.

37 In Spalding, *Reimarus*, 341.

38 My interpretation follows the text in the following edition: Jens Baggesen, *Gedichte I &II* (Hamburg: Perthes, 1803), 99–103.

39 Ulrike Vedder, "Das Rätsel der Objekte: Zur literarischen Epistemologie von Dingen, Eine Einführung," *Zeitschrift für Germanistik*, 1 (2012): 7–16.

40 Ibid., 9 and 11.

41 Cf. also Daniel Fulda, "Sache und Sachen der Aufklärung: Versuch einer Antwort auf die Frage, wie sich Programm und Praxis der Aufklärung lesen lassen," in Stockhorst, *Epoche und Projekt*, 241–62, here: 252–3. Accordingly, the representation of things in Enlightenment narrative is tied (and confined) to small or peripheral genres.

42 The present argument makes only cursory use of the journals collected and digitized in the database Zeitschriften der Aufklärung. The full scope of the discourse on China and the emergence of small/local genres is the

subject of a project that uses textual and network analyses, along with statistical modelling, and is currently being developed with Jeremy Lewis as a co-author, with further assistance from Crystal Hall and Jen Jack Gieseking. See http://www.ub.uni-bielefeld.de/diglib/aufklaerung/suche.htm (accessed 7 July 2015).

43 *Mémoires concernant l'histoire, les sciences, les arts, les mœurs, les usages, & c. des Chinois: Par les Missionnaires de Pékin* (Paris: Nyon, 1776–1814). In *Hannoverisches Magazin*, subtitles make cursory reference to "the text that appeared in Paris in 1776."

44 K'ien-lung Kaiser von China, "Beispiel von der Toleranz des chinesischen Kaisers Kien-Long," *Historisch-politisches Magazin*, 4 (1788): 1390–2.

45 On the development of the anecdote as a historical and literary genre, see Sonja Hilzinger, "Anekdote," in *Kleine literarische Formen in Einzeldarstellungen* (Stuttgart: Reclam, 2002), 7–26.

46 Ibid., 11.

47 Koschorke, *Wahrheit und Erfindung*, 290–3.

48 Cf., among others, "Ein Paar Chinesische Anekdoten," *Hannoversches Magazin*, 12 (1774): 185–92.

49 Kai Hünemörder, "Strategien einer Schlüsselinstitution der Popularisierung agrarischen Wissens in Kurhannover: Die celler Landwirtschaftsgesellschaft (1764–1804)," in Schneider, *Kulturen des Wissens*, 339–45, here 341–2.

50 Cf. J.F. Schmid, "Chirurgische Versuche mit der Fieberrinde," *Hannoversches Magazin*, 13 (1775): 427–32. However, already in 1754, entries surface that locate the origins of quinine in Peru ("Peruvianische Fieberrinde"). The attribution to China is reaffirmed, in the journals, as late as 1790 (e.g., *Allgemeine Deutsche Bibliothek*, 93/1: 120–5) before being corrected in the encyclopedias of the nineteenth century.

51 Johann Samuel Ersch and Johann Gottfried Gruber, eds., *Allgemeine Encyklopädie der Wissenschaften und Künste*, vol. 16 (Leipzig: Brockhaus, 1834), 373; all subsequent citations are in the body of the text. Contrary to these observations, Lehner has claimed a delay in the cultural transfer of medicinal knowledge, asserting that the wisdom of Chinese medicine reached middle Europe with great delay. Accordingly, German and French encyclopedias refer to reports only in the early nineteenth century, when methods like acupuncture and moxibustion find greater popularity in France and Germany. The Brockhaus edition of 1827 claims that only in the 1820s were these methods sufficiently studied and recommended in France. Georg Lehner, "Le savoir de l'Europe sur la Chine: Transferts franco-allemands au miroir des encyclopédies (1750–1850),"

Revue germanique internationale, 7 (2008), put online 15 May 2011, http://
rgi.revues.org/390 (accessed 12 Feb. 2012). I also thank Franklin Perkins
for an important piece of information that I could not consider within the
scope of this essay, namely, that Leibniz shows interest in alternative medicine and seeks information from his Jesuit correspondents.

52 *Conversations-Lexikon,* 8th ed., vol. 2 (Leipzig, 1818), 604–15.

53 This formulation takes its inspiration from Clifford Siskin and William
Warner, *This Is Enlightenment* (Chicago: University of Chicago Press, 2010),
which characterizes Enlightenment, admittedly an overarching master
narrative, as "an event in the history of mediation" (1).

6 Eradicating the Orientalists: Goethe's *Chinesisch-deutsche Jahres- und Tageszeiten*

JOHN K. NOYES

One of Goethe's last cycles of poems, the *Chinesisch-deutsche Jahres- und Tageszeiten*, was written in 1827 and published in 1829. Readings of these poems have tended to focus on biographical connections, including Goethe's readings in Chinese literature, or they have insisted on the hermetic formality of the poems. In this chapter I explore the possibility of combining the biographical and formal analyses of the cycle. Biographical motifs and references in the poems are actualized formally in ways that anchor the movements of the mind in the sensory life of the body. This anchoring guarantees a fullness of life that stands in opposition to the tedious administrative tasks of the mandarin; and so the cycle moves the reader away from instrumental thought and action towards the aesthetic act. What this suggests is that the human condition is characterized by interrupting the flow of time through the power of reflection and aesthetic intervention. This, in turn, invokes the physicality of the reflecting eye, and its captivation by the passing of time. This leads to the recognition of a problem and a solution that Goethe came increasingly to associate with his readings of Chinese literature. His appreciation of the essential work of the aesthetic in securing the worth of human life causes him to remain suspicious of rationalist attempts to understand Chinese culture. Against the rationalism of the Orientalists, Goethe places the aesthetic work of poetic reflection. At the same time, his encounters with Chinese philosophy suggested that the struggle between rationalism and poetic reflection was not simply a pressing matter for contemporary German thought, but that it pointed to a more fundamental, transcultural problem in human life. In the following, I will argue that the theme of "Chinese" in this cycle, obscure as it is, marks the possibility of reconciling the forces of nature with the movement of the mind in aesthetic production. This is a concern that had occupied Goethe for a long time, and in the *Chinesisch-deutsche Jahres- und Tageszeiten* it attains a remarkable subtlety and maturity.

The cycle begins with a kind of joke, in which Goethe, who at the time had retreated to his garden house in Weimar, projects his lyrical voice as that of a mandarin:

> Sag, was könnt uns Mandarinen,
> Satt zu herrschen, müd zu dienen,
> Sag, was könnt uns übrigbleiben,
> Als in solchen Frühlingstagen
> Uns des Nordens zu entschlagen
> Und am Wasser und im Grünen
> Fröhlich trinken, geistig schreiben,
> Schal auf Schale, Zug in Zügen.

> (Tell us mandarins enquiring,
> Sated rulers, servants tiring,
> Tell, what's left us except yearning
> To be quit when spring's around us,
> Shaking off the North that bound us,
> And by ponds, on grass reclining,
> Gaily drink, write wit and learning,
> Cup on cup, brushed strokes entwining?)[1]

What remains, in these spring days, apart from ridding oneself of the north, sipping merrily from vessels among green leaves, and writing mindfully ("geistig schreiben")? If Goethe's connection to the Orient, or specifically to China, is given by his old complaint about how arduous it can be to carry administrative and executive responsibility in government, what has China to offer as a formal mitigation? What has changed since the days when the opposite of the North was, for Goethe, the land where the lemon trees bloom, Italy? And why does the poem drift from cultural and national specificity (mandarins) to the geographically indistinct? In this respect, the opening poem sets the stage for the entire cycle, since the remaining thirteen poems appear to have even less to do with China. In fact, at least one of them ("Dämmrung senkt sich von oben"), has more to do with Faust:

Dämmrung senkte sich von oben,
schon ist alle Nähe fern;
doch zuerst emporgehoben
holden Lichts der Abendstern!
Alles schwankt ins Ungewisse,
Nebel schleichen in die Höh';
schwarzvertiefte Finsternisse
widerspiegelnd ruht der See.

Nun im östlichen Bereiche
ahn' ich Mondenglanz und -Glut,
schlanker Weiden Haargezweige
scherzen auf der nächsten Flut.
Durch bewegter Schatten Spiele
zittert Lunas Zauberschein,
und durchs Auge schleicht die Kühle
sänftigend ins Herz hinein.

(Twilight down from far has drifted,
What was near's already far;
First, though, high above is lifted
Graced in light the evening star!
All on imprecision verges,
To the heights the mists slow snake;
Darkness into blackness merges
Mirrored in the resting lake.

Now I sense the moonlight presses
Ardent in the evening sky;
Slender willows' branching tresses
Jest upon the wave nearby.
Luna's quivering spell is glowing
Where the shadows play and dart,
Coolness through the eye is flowing
Soothingly into the heart.)

Wolfgang Schadewaldt showed in 1955 how, in this poem, Goethe repeats the song of the elves in the opening scene of *Faust II*.[2] And since this provides a clue to the question I will be posing here, let me repeat Katharina Mommsen's observation that this song helps solve one of the most pressing problems of *Faust II*, namely, how the healing forces of nature might overcome Faust's guilt:[3] the guilt of action that results from a life of contemplation far from experience, the perverse outcome when the a priori mind preys on nature. But what this has to do with China is a mystery.

Goethe's Chinese puzzle concerns how to situate the "Chinese" in the *Chinesisch-deutsche Jahres- und Tageszeiten*. Anke Bosse puts it well when she states that the mention of "Chinese" in the title has repeatedly initiated a "Sehzwang" (perspectival imperative) aimed, among other things, at identifying Chinese sources for the poems.[4] Woldemar von Biedermann already showed how this could be done in 1886;[5] and Hideo Fukuda lists a number of novels, novellas, and poems from the classical Confucian tradition that we know Goethe had read.[6] But the problem remains: as Bosse observes, there is nothing purely Chinese that can be identified in these poems.[7] And yet, she claims, the *Chinesisch-deutsche Jahres- und Tageszeiten* perfect "a 'west-easterly' culturally transcendent movement."[8] This tension between the evocative "Sehzwang" and the paucity of Chinese motifs has led to a general consensus in the scholarship that, as Andreas Anglet concludes, the Chinese quality in the *Chinesisch-deutsche Jahres- und Tageszeiten* is atmospheric and not mimetic or realistic.[9] The only way to read these poems then becomes formal, to read them as a cycle, as a "loosely connected sequence of lyrical texts." This involves a "detailed analysis of the individual poems," focused on "the grammatical and semantic features of the poetic language, the movement of figures of thought and speech, of images, motifs and introspection, as well as the characteristically playful quality in Goethe's late poetry."[10] Friedrich Burkhardt already pointed the way to this kind of analysis in his 1969 essay.[11] This can be overlaid, as has been shown, with the biographical readings, which bring them into connection with Goethe's love for Ulrike von Levetzow, or his troubled relationship with Charlotte von Stein.[12]

To read these poems in this way is, of course, correct and necessary. But it is only the first step towards understanding the place they assumed in Goethe's developing life problem, and why the Chinese suggested itself to him in the way it did. There is a leitmotif in the scholarship on Goethe and China that sees him gaining with his own advancing years in the understanding that the harmony of opposites, which he had come to see as his life quest, could be associated with the artistic works of the Far East. What exactly does this mean? In her introductory lecture to the 1982 Heidelberg Symposium on Goethe and China,

Katharina Mommsen introduced two points which are, in my opinion, crucial in understanding what Goethe expected from the Chinese in the *Chinesisch-deutsche Jahres- und Tageszeiten*: the influence of Herder and the controversies around idealist philosophy. It is true that the poem cycle was written almost twenty-five years after Herder's death, and Fichte had departed Jena even earlier. But by the time Goethe wrote the *Chinesisch-deutsche Jahres- und Tageszeiten* his views on China were firmly in place, and these early influences were decisive in setting the stage for the place that the motif of the Chinese was to assume in his subsequent writing.

A careful reading of the cycle will confirm that Goethe is using the theme "Chinese" to focus his ideas on the aesthetic as the place where forces of nature could be reconciled with the movement of the mind. As I will show, this is evident in the multilayered movement that gives the cycle its coherence. There is no surface-level narrative that unfolds over the course of the fourteen poems. What we have, instead, is an implied dialogue between rhetorical positions inhabited by speakers and addressees whose identities shift subtly throughout. They speak a series of observations that identify the passage of time, the changes that mark the times of the day and seasons of the year. Nature is seen to be caught in a relentless movement of time. The poet finds himself implicated in this process, but as an observer, he seems to stand outside it. In the course of the poems, it becomes increasingly clear that their enigma is given by the way the lyrical voice is both part of nature and apart from it.

The lyrical voice is initially situated firmly in dialogue with other mandarins, a positioning that appears to secure the Chinese reference in the title while at the same time making sly reference to Goethe's own position. This already begins to fade in the second poem, "Weiß wie Lilien," where it gives way to disembodied acts of perception and reflection. These continue until poem V, "Entwickle deiner Lüste Glanz," where a general, unspecified "du" becomes the addressee. Opposite this, the lyrical voice attaches to an "ich" in poem VI, "Der Guckuck wie die Nachtigal," whose comments identify closely with what we know about Goethe's own life. As I shall argue, it was important for Goethe not to allow his thoughts on nature and the mind to become overly abstract, but to remain tied to the life of the senses, and one way he did this was to make overt references to his own experience. The grounding of the lyrical voice in everyday life appears to solidify in poems VI and VII ("War schöner als der schönste Tag"), to the point where this voice can be clearly positioned in time and space, and can speak of its own thoughts and emotions. But in poems IX and X, "Nun weiß man erst, was Rosenknospe sei" and "Als Allerschönste bist du anerkannt," this solidity dissolves, allowing the return of the general reflecting voice that spoke earlier; but as it does, "du" reappears and becomes more specific, to the point where it can assume its most concrete manifestation in the entire cycle: the rose in poem X. Following this, something remarkable happens in poem XI, "Mich ängstigt das Verfängliche." The sudden use of direct speech splits the lyrical voice into an implied speaking self and an implied respondent self. This splitting underlines the earlier distinction that had only been implied, namely, that between the embodied voice and the reflexive voice. Thought begins to separate from speech, threatening to leave it behind. In the following poem (XII, "Hingesunken alten Träumen"), this split is repeated and overlaid with another one, this time between a voice that speaks a general idea (that the girls and wise ones cannot adequately praise the roses and the trees), and a "du" that is firmly situated in the world: it is sensual ("Buhlst mit Rosen"), it dreams and speaks, it is an aesthetic and a social being ("Kommen deshalb die Gesellen, / Sich zur Seite dir zu stellen, / Finden, dir und uns zu dienen, / Pinsel, Farbe, Wein im Grünen"). The abstraction of the self is enabled by removing thought from speech. But something important is lost in the process: "Begeisterung," the act of introspection that attaches mindfulness ("Geist") to stimulus and that enables the kind of writing identified in poem I as the cycle's telos ("geistig schreiben"). As Merideth Lee remarks, the poet's enthusiasm teaches him a new way of seeing, giving insight into the order of the physical world and therefore also into that which holds permanence, the world of eternal change.[13]

In the penultimate poem, the lyrical voice addresses a faceless group of intrusive agents, who must be avoided if this kind of authentic experience is to be possible. Finally, the split initiated in poem XI returns, where dialogue addresses the problem of the split self directly: the need to choose between the desire that negates presence ("Sehnsucht ins Ferne, Künftige"), and the affirmation of embodied life ("Beschäftige dich hier und heut im Tüchtigen"). Given the unfolding of the cycle, this final maxim that wants to cure longing with meaningful activity ("das Tüchtige") rings hollow – unless one understands activity in the sense in which it was introduced in the first poem, that is, the opposite of the instrumental discourses of administration and government that the poems seek to escape. This alternative activity is the one that is

practised in the poems themselves – the aesthetic resolution of embodiment and reflection. As a result, the entire cycle repeats the development in poem I from a dynamic of instrumentalism ("dienen" and
"herrschen") to one of expression and representation.

The challenge posed in the poems is to complete this development
in a manner that will not deny the lived experience of the writer. Thus,
the interweaving of rhetorical positions is given a certain biographical
stability by veiled references to Goethe's own life – the garden house on
the Ilm, the death of Charlotte von Stein in January 1827, memories of
meeting Christiane Vulpius in July 1788. The meeting with Christiane
appears explicitly in poem VII, with the lines

> War schöner als der schönste Tag,
> ...
> Im Garten war's, sie kam heran,
> Mir ihre Gunst zu zeigen;
> Das fühle' ich noch und denke dran
> Und bleib' ihr ganz zu eigen.

> (Than fairest day she was more fair,
> ...
> It was a garden, she drew near
> And so her favour rendered;
> I feel it still and mind it dear
> And stay to her surrendered.)

And thoughts of Charlotte von Stein are voiced in poem VI:

> Auch mir hat er [der Sommer] das leichte Laub
> An jenem Baum verdichtet,
> Durch das ich sonst zu schönstem Raub
> Den Liebesblick gerichtet;
> Verdeckt ist mir das bunte Dach,
> Die Gitter und die Pfosten;
> Wohin mein Auge spähend brach,
> Dort ewig bleibt mein Osten.

> (On my tree now the leaves' light weft
> Is densely concentrated
> Through which for love's most lovely theft

My eye once penetrated;
Now lattice, doors, and roof bright-crowned
Are covered altogether;
That place my searching eye once found,
Remains my East forever.)

These lines provide an oblique reference to the view Goethe enjoyed through the trees to Charlotte von Stein's house, as long as there were no leaves on the branches. While asking to be read with this biographical nuance, they move us beyond that, returning to the question of the Orient. But this Orient is not tied to the geography of Weimar. Charlotte's house lies to the northwest of Goethe's garden house, not the east. The task of vision is then to transcend geographical limitations and seek something that exceeds the view blocked by trees. With this, the general geographical movement from north to south, introduced in poem I, is shifting to a west-easterly movement. But at the same time, it is turning inward, where the eye's vision is at once its demise (the dual meaning of the verb "brechen" as breaking through and dying).

The dialectical movement between vision observing nature and vision turning inward accompanies the shift in rhetorical positions, and it unsettles the relentless rhythm of time marching onward through the days and through the seasons. Perhaps, the poems suggest, this is what it means to be human, to disturb time's progress with the power of reflection. Where times of the day and the year appear in the poem (and their appearance is scant indeed for a cycle that announces itself as a book of times and seasons), their appearance is more often than not implied, hinted at through signs that must be read and interpreted, apprehended as a potential for change in nature that has not yet been actualized, or as a marker of a past that is all but gone. It's true, time and the seasons are measured by the words: "Frühlingstagen" (I), "Abendsonne" (V), "Frühling," "Sommer" (VI), "Tag" (VII), "Dämmerung," "Abendstern," "Mondenglanz" (VIII), "Rosenzeit" (XI); but the general change in times and seasons is only implied by a hint of unseen stars (II), a promise of meadows yet to blossom (III), the rays of the sun shining on lovers beneath a blue sky (V), the cuckoo and the nightingale trying to delay the passing of spring (VI), the light of the moon announcing itself in the water's reflection (VIII), the rose marking the passing of summer (IX). As the cycle draws to a close, even the signs of change give way to meditations on change itself. The rose (introduced in poem IX) marks this process, and it is not by chance that it is the cycle's most overt addressee. In poem IX the sight of the rose deflects vision away from the present, the remains of actualization, to the knowledge of past potential: "Nun weiss man erst, was Rosenknospe sei, / jetzt da Rosenzeit vorbei" (Only now do we know the rosebud at last, / Now that the time for roses has passed). As the following poem goes on to explore, this amounts to vision and desire meeting in the anachronistic appearance of the last remaining blossom. The eye apprehends this blossom and realizes that what it is seeing goes beyond mere appearance: "Du bist es also, bist kein bloßer Schein." The experience of vision is also one of faith ("In dir trifft Schaun und Glauben überein"), inciting a desire to explore the foundations of this experience ("Doch Forschung strebt und ringt, ermüdend nie, / Nach dem Gesetz, dem Grund Warum und Wie").

It is interesting to note that, after all these years, Goethe is still uncertain about how he should read Kant's theory of beauty and the sublime. Goethe had no quarrel with Kant's notion that beauty allows the imagination to test its freedom from understanding and in doing so to remove itself from the grasp of instrumentality and interest. But how should the poet deal with situations like the one at hand, where beauty is coupled to the knowledge of its own destruction and the desire for its permanence? Goethe's answer (in poem X) challenges Kant's concept of beauty in two ways. First, the universality of judgments of beauty is given not by the fundamental universality of cognition, but it is an act of faith. Goethe underlines this with the words: "In dir trifft Schaun und Glauben überein" (In you belief agrees with vision clear). The confidence of this statement is undermined, however, by the wary hesitation with which the rose's beauty is spoken: the rose is *accepted* as the most beautiful object, it is *named* the queen of flowers, it stands unchallenged, banishes discord. Beauty is not judged by common cognitive principles, it is established by convention. It represents a principle that has yet to be determined, and to see it this way involves an act of faith. Here, Goethe is repeating Hamann's old criticism of Kant's metaphysics, and using it to question the Kantian confidence in rational processes when it comes to aesthetics. Reading this, one is reminded that in poem VI, where beauty reaches its full intensity, it aligns with desire ("Durch das ich sonst zu schönstem Raub Den Liebesblick gerichtet") and is associated directly with the Orient ("Wohin mein Auge spähend brach, Dort ewig bleibt mein Osten"). Just as beauty slips away from the rational mind and aligns itself with desire, it finds itself in the Orient. It is as if beauty itself proves that there is more to the East than can be spoken of by Orientalism's rational negation of the Orient's poetic potential. The refusal brings me to the second challenge to Kant: the beauty of the rose collapses his distinction between the beautiful and the sublime. The experience of beauty plunges the viewer into the kind of existential crisis Kant identifies with the sublime; and the observer responds accordingly, with a quest for the rational principle that can explain the limits of the imagination.

Because of the unsettling work of beauty, it has the power to bring about the shift in attitude that will preside over the rest of the poem: "Doch Forschung strebt und ringt, ermüdend nie, / nach dem Gesetz, dem Grund Warum und Wie" (Yet science strives and struggles, never tires, / For law and cause, for Why and How enquires). The recognition of this law brings with it the comfort that overcomes the melancholy of time passing, and it is named in the following poem: "Getrost! Das Unvergängliche, / es ist das ewige Gesetz, / wonach die Ros' und Lilie blüht" (Fear not! The indestructible / in the eternal law / is set by which the rose and lily be). But instead of closing the cycle with this observation, as he might well have done, Goethe takes the final three poems to develop the consequences that this realization of nature's law should have in everyday life. In poem XII we find the poet noting the inability of intellectual and erotic interactions to do justice to nature: "Buhlst mit Rosen, sprichst mit Bäumen, / statt der Mädchen, statt der Weisen; / können das nicht löblich preisen" (Trees you talk to, fondle roses, / Girls and sages you're excluding; / that won't do, forever brooding). It is in the community of artists that nature's law can be appreciated. There remains only to acknowledge that art itself involves a dialectic of communication and withdrawal (poem XIII), and then the cycle can end with the resolution offered in poem XIV, to pursue quotidian (aesthetic) activity.

By 1827 the general ground on which Goethe is unfolding this lyric experiment had long been familiar territory to him. If we are to do justice to the idea of the Orient in these poems, we need to remember that the question of other literatures always led him to the same conviction: it may be true that China is in many respects a very different culture than Goethe's Weimar, but when he looks at these differences, he still sees the fundamental principles that unite the two. Mommsen is right in observing Herder's role in opening Goethe's eyes to this essential human unity via the folk songs of other cultures. But it's also important to understand how Herder passed on to Goethe the more fundamental problem of conceptualizing what it is that allows one culture to understand the songs of another while recognizing their difference. When he and Goethe were friends in Strassbourg, Herder had already been labouring over this problem for six or seven years, and the way he had come to think about it was to understand the experience of Being ("das Sein") as the founding, shared experience of human life. And he saw this as nature's force at work in human life. But individual cultures express this experience in different ways, depending on their own specific experiences of time and space, that is, their history and geography. It was poetry, Herder thought (following Hamann), that best expresses nature's force from the point of view of a culture's history and geography. This spoke powerfully to Goethe's poetic sensibility, and when he finally began to show real interest in the culture of the Orient in the second decade of the nineteenth century, it appeared to him as something to be accessed intuitively, through poetic sensibility.

The matter is not that simple, however. Oriental motifs can find their way into lyric poetry because of a shared experiential core in human life that transcends cultures. This is what Goethe had experimented with in the *West-östlicher Divan*. But how is this experiential core to be accessed? Aesthetic sensibility is grounded in culture, and it cannot necessarily rely on unreflected responses to transcend that grounding. These responses are just as likely to shy away from cultural difference. Walter Veit speaks of Goethe's "marked dislike for the Orient" based on a perceived "threat to his aesthetic sensibility."[14] So, does this mean that the Orient's foreignness can best be accessed by a better rational understanding of the Orient? Goethe also experimented with this extensively in his years of "orientalisieren," but here he continued to be suspicious of a priori judgments about distant cultures, since the rational figures of thought that have been developed within a culture are unreliable in accessing the ideas of another culture.

Again, Goethe developed this suspicion of rationalist appropriations of distant cultures during the initial phase of his long and troubled friendship with Herder, and he developed it specifically with respect to the Orient. After reading Herder's *Älteste Urkunde des Menschengeschlechts* in 1774, Goethe wrote to the diplomat and poet Gottlob Friedrich Schönborn: "He has descended into the depths of his sensibilities and has there stirred up all the lofty, holy force of simple nature; and now he directs these, in dawning, lightning-flashing, morning-land-smiling, Orphic song, from their beginnings onward, out into the wide world. But not before he has eradicated in fire and brimstone and storm-floods the evil spawn of the new spirits, the Deists and Atheists,

Philologists, Critics (*Textverbesserer*) and Orientalists. In particular, Michaelis is killed by scorpions."[15] Goethe felt Herder needed to eradicate these voices in order to allow a different kind of voice to emerge. So, is this lightning flash of Orphic song powerful enough to overcome an inherent and marked dislike for the Orient? Can it show us what Enlightenment science cannot? In the Orient, Goethe was glimpsing a problem in his understanding of scholarship itself, of how it relates to artistic production, of how cultural creation and cultural critique interact. As he experimented with different ways to understand the Orient, it became clearer that the real problem did not really have to do with the Orient itself, nor its specific differences from Goethe's own culture. The problem he was facing had to do more with the aesthetic problem of representing cultural difference and common humanity.

This turn to the aesthetic came to be associated with China at the end of the decade when Goethe had been studying Kant's third critique and had been seeking a way of reconciling the problem of the will with the force of nature, a decade which he later called an "extremely happy period in my life."[16] Kant, too, had prepared his thinking on aesthetics with a decisive stance on the Orient. John Zammito makes this point in his commentary on Kant's response to Herder's *Älteste Urkunde des Menschengeschlechts*. Zammito shows how Kant dismisses Herder's defence of the poetic and intuitive way of being in the world that he associated with the Orient. For Kant, Herder's defence of the poetic was nothing less than the incoherent ravings ("Schwärmerei") of the kind he had attacked in his writings on Swedenborg. In the *Älteste Urkunde des Menschengeschlechts*, Herder emphasized "the vividness and immediacy of poetic imagery of the Hebrews in the Old Testament as a ground for their greater validity than rational arguments could provide."[17] Kant's response was: "Would to God we could be spared this Oriental wisdom; nothing can be learned from it; the world has received no instruction from them but a kind of mechanical artifice, astronomy and numbers. Once we had Occidental education from the Greeks then we were able to lend some rationality to the Oriental scriptures, but they would never have made themselves understood on their own."[18] By the time Kant writes the *Critique of Judgement*, the Orient is no longer really on his mind; but he has preserved the problem of how to reconcile poetic responses to the world with the rational ground on which moral consensus is built.

Goethe saw this as a revaluation of the place poetic thought holds in the common human experience of being in the world. But the Orient and China had all but disappeared as a focus of this process. Most commentators agree that what Goethe got out of his reading of the *Critique of Judgement* was humanity's knowledge of its own limitations in the face of what Kant called a "large family of creatures" whose relationship was one of "thoroughly coherent kinship."[19] There was, as Angus Nicholls observes, "an aspect of the external world, embodied in Kant's essentially unknowable things in themselves, that would always exceed the internally generated ideas of the striving subject."[20]

Although the Orient seems irrelevant in these considerations, we can see how important it continues to be by the way it re-emerges in Goethe's turn to the Orient in the second decade of the nineteenth century. Here it continues to serves as a focus of what Robert Richards calls his Kantian problem: how to think of the intersection of mental and natural processes.[21] This can be seen in the way he began to speak about his Orientalism in 1815 when he was working on the *West-östlicher Divan*. Writing to Zelter in April 1815, Goethe speaks of the dangers of projecting one's own reading interest onto the Orient: "I find orientalizing (*das Orientalisieren*) very dangerous, since, before you know it, the crudest poem leaves your hands and rises up into the air, filled with rational and spiritual gas."[22] Goethe wrote this at a time when he was beginning to make a serious effort to engage with contemporary Orientalism.[23] In this, he relied, for example, on the Orientalists Heinrich Friedrich von Diez, Heinrich Eberhard Gottlob Paulus, Julius Heinrich Klaproth, and Sergej Graf Semenowitsch von Ouvaroff. And he also began to regard himself as a student of Orientalism. In a letter to Diez, he writes: "The broad field of Oriental studies provides me with very pleasant prospects. Unfortunately, however, I'm lacking in knowledge of the languages, hardly able to think about them since my youth. For that reason, I can hardly do justice to the mediation provided by Your Excellency. Studying your introduction to the Book of Kabus and then the work itself is to find oneself in the presence of the spirit and mind of these remarkable peoples. The writings of Ahmet Efendi cast the brightest light on more recent ideas and contemporary conditions."[24] A couple of weeks later he writes to Ouvaroff: "A particular turn of events has caused me, through my studies, to come closer to the Orient, though admittedly my ignorance of the languages is an obstacle. However, I have taken the opportunity to consider your suggestions regarding an Orientalist Society, and have used this to my advantage, a matter that is cause for me to express my thankful admiration to you."[25] And a month later, again to Diez: "The lessons I have learned from this are priceless, and so I have been able to regard your Excellency's works as the foundation for my own knowledge of the Orient, in that exactitude and certainty are the delightful hallmarks of your works."[26]

These and other statements may give the impression that Goethe felt he was on the way to becoming an Orientalist. However, he understood that this was not the path he wanted to take when it came to incorporating the world view of the Orient into his own. Instead, poetic imagination has to be harnessed, transcending the gap between Weimar and the Orient. Goethe saw this transportation as moving in two directions. First, it was a transplantation of Oriental form to his own environment. This was a difficult task, and he realized that to bring Oriental form to Weimar without a facile repetition of the Rococo fashion for chinoiserie, he would have to balance Orientalist research with the poetic spirit driving it and, to a certain extent, working against it. A week after the letter to Zelter, he writes to Willemer that "although such embellishments are not foreign to the Orient, it cost some effort to transplant them to Weimar."[27] But increasingly, we find in Goethe's notes a sense that the effort of transplanting form to Weimar can be augmented with the pleasure of transporting himself to the Orient, at least in his studies.

This dual understanding of transportation places the Orient in a dual perspective in Goethe's works. Todd Kontje insightfully observes that Goethe's Orient is "at once ancient and modern, rooted and uprooted, essential and virtual."[28] He "makes easy reference to the Orient as a world of presence, voice, and origin, but seems at the same time aware that the source is always already erased, deferred, bracketed, or, to put it more positively, that the Orient can always be appropriated for an Occidental masquerade."[29] Kontje is right that Goethe chose not to pursue "grand narratives of cultural evolution or linguistic development that might provide an organic link between East and West, a continuous uninterrupted flow."[30]

However we choose to read Goethe's repeated references to imaginary journeys to the Orient, it makes sense to place them in the context of Herder's early ideas on cultural exchange between different language groups. Herder began outlining these in the decade leading up to his initial meeting with Goethe, and by the time the two made friends it had become central to his ideas on culture that there are forces of the imagination moving individuals to transcend their own linguistic and cultural boundaries. The clearest early statement of this is to be found in *Über den Fleiß in mehreren gelehrten Sprachen* (On Diligence in the Learning of Several Foreign Languages; 1764). On the surface, this essay argues the not particularly surprising position that the mother tongue will always have priority over acquired languages, since "nature imposes upon us an obligation only to our mother tongue."[31] The growing child's early experiences of pleasure in the mother tongue "impressed themselves upon us first and somehow shaped themselves together with the finest fissures of our sensibility."[32] Why, then, would a person ever choose to learn a foreign language? In asking this question, Herder is introducing a theme that will remain of central importance in his anthropology, the distinction between the forces that work on the individual to perpetuate the specific culture into which he or she is born, and those that work to ensure communication between cultures. On the face of it, the diversity of languages may look like an "indispensable evil," but seen from the perspective of humanity, it is "almost a genuine good."[33] True progress is only possible through the sharing of insights and achievements across linguistic barriers, and since Herder dismisses the possibility of a universal language enforced by authority, just as he dismisses translation as a solution, the only path to progress is the learning of foreign languages. Learning foreign languages is, therefore, an exercise in the internalization of diverse world views that have grown organically as possible manifestations of the growth of humanity. To learn foreign languages is to "encompass the spirit of each people in my soul!"[34]

As his interest in the Orient grew, Goethe came increasingly to explore the idea that poetic form can accomplish what Herder ascribed to the learning of foreign languages: it can transcend the limitations of culture to give access to the shared nature of humanity. This implies the same fundamental idea that led Herder to his comments about learning foreign languages – that there is an underlying force, a process of entelechy that aligns an individual's development not only with the development of his or her culture, but also with the ideal progress of humanity. That this can be shown to be the case is the unspoken wager presiding over the *Wilhelm Meister* project.

Already at the end of the decade that began with the reading of the *Critique of Judgment*, China reappeared in a surprising way, suggesting a change in the way Goethe was to think about aesthetics. For Goethe the task of aesthetics is to present both the force of nature (which, as Herder had insisted, is culturally mediated from the very start) and the limits of its conceptualization (itself culturally mediated – again, as Herder had insisted). In the late 1790s Goethe began to see that it was not only German idealism that was struggling with this problem; the problem of the will and how it relates to nature was not only culturally located in his own time and place, it was a shared problem that transcends cultures. Goethe saw evidence of this in an extract from Erasmus Francisci's *Neu-polirter Geschicht- Kunst- und Sitten-Spiegel ausländischer Völcker* (The Newly Polished Mirror of the Tales, Art and Manners of Foreign Peoples) published in 1670,[35] which Goethe enclosed in a letter to Schiller on 6 January 1798.[36] Francisci recounts a conversation between the Jesuit missionary Matteo Ricci (1552–1610) and a seventy-year-old Buddhist monk, who had made a name for himself as an outspoken opponent of Confucianism. When Ricci asks the standard proselytizing opener about who made heaven and earth, the monk replies: "I will not deny that such a sovereign of heaven and earth can be found, but I don't believe that he has any particular majesty, strength, or divine power. Consider, too ... that I and every other person is his equal and must not yield to him in any matter." When asked if he, too, could bring heaven and earth into being, the monk responds in the affirmative. When Goethe read this he must have heard his own voice from the time when he wrote "Prometheus" (about 1772). Ricci then challenges the monk to prove his creative power by bringing into being a metal hearth ("Glut-Pfanne") like the one before him. The monk raises his voice in protest, claiming that he has been unfairly challenged.

Francisci takes pleasure in showing how the clever Jesuit outsmarted the arrogant heathen – the "Götzen-Pfaff," as he calls him. But Goethe saw something else in this exchange, something important enough that Wolfgang Bauer can read this letter as a turning point in Goethe's views on China.[37] Previously, Bauer claims, Goethe had regarded China with twofold suspicion – it was strange enough and far enough away that it was dangerous for Europeans to speculate on what the Chinese thought system might look like (this could be called the Herderian suspicion); and the Rococo appropriations of and enthusiasm for chinoiserie could be read as proof of how such speculation can go wrong. Also, Goethe felt that the individual's creativity is stifled in Chinese thought. It was only two years previously that he had sent Johann Heinrich Meyer the well-known poem about the Chinaman in Rome, "Der Chinese in Rom."[38] But if this letter to Schiller was a turning point, what exactly did Goethe take from Francisci's anecdote? Bauer emphasizes Goethe's discovery that China is not the place of neo-Confucianism with its extreme conservatism and (in Bauer's words) "rigid, self-congratulatory morality."[39] China was also home to Buddhist and Daoist thought, testing the limits of idealism in manners very similar to what Goethe saw around him in Weimar and Jena. Mommsen picks up on Goethe's comments about how the Buddhist monk speaks like a "creative idealist" (schaffender Idealist), that is, a Fichtean, while Ricci reveals himself a complete Reinholdian.[40] Schiller wanted Goethe to publish this insight in the *Horen*; but Goethe (tactful as always) did not want to open this can of worms. The conflict between Fichte and the Reinholdians was about to reach crisis point, and Fichte was soon to depart from Jena. But not before Reinhold himself began to see that his *Elementarphilosophie* would have to concede to Fichte the dominance of the will. If the force of nature presented humans with an a priori material principle, then the priority of the independent will becomes problematic. As Friedrich Beiser notes, Fichte will simply take the next logical step in Reinhold's *Elementarphilosophie*, and ground philosophy not in representation but in the will.[41] We know that Goethe was not prepared to take this step – if from nothing else, then from his biting satire of a Fichtean in the Baccalaureus in *Faust II*, who speaks like the Buddhist monk.[42] Goethe couldn't see the world as (in Schiller's words) "nothing more than a ball which the self has thrown, and which it catches again in the act of reflection."[43]

Goethe saw more in this letter, however, than the dispute between Fichte and the Reinholdians, and what he saw will return us to the *Chinesisch-deutsche Jahres- und Tageszeiten*. When he sends Schiller the copy from Francisci three days later, he writes: "I would have liked the Chinese monk even more if he had grasped the hearth and handed it to his interlocutor with the words: 'Yes, I create it. There, take it and use it.'"[44] He then changes the topic to Schelling. Goethe is intrigued by Schelling's *Philosophy of Nature* (1797) with its distinction between unconscious and conscious creative production, but he is still not convinced about the way the transcendental idealist tries (dogmatically, Goethe thought) to elevate himself above the forces of nature: "I gladly admit that it is not nature that we know, but instead that it is assimilated by us according to specific forms and capacities of our minds. Of course, there may well be very many stages in perception (*Anschauen*) between the child's appetite for the apple on the tree and its fall, which, so they say, inspired Newton's theory; but it would be desirable for these to be presented clearly once and for all while at the same time explaining what is considered to be the highest of these stages. Of course, the transcendental idealist considers himself to be at the very top."[45]

Goethe expressed his mistrust of transcendental idealism with the same gesture he uses repeatedly in the *Chinesisch-deutsche Jahres- und Tageszeiten*: against the self-appointed primacy of the transcendental mind, Goethe presents the materiality of the world of things. And, although he is decidedly not prepared to be co-opted by Herder's campaign against Kantian metaphysics,[46] he still holds on to Herder's insistence that the representation of nature has a history embedded in everyday life. He continues to Schiller: "But there is one thing I don't like about [the transcendental idealist], that he has a quarrel with the modes of representation (*Vorstellungsarten*). In fact, it is not possible to have a quarrel with a mode of representation. Who would talk a given person out of the external purposiveness of nature (*Zweckmäßigkeit der Natur nach außen*), since experience itself seems to confirm this doctrine every single day?"[47] No matter how sophisticated the arguments of the idealists, experience continues to resist the idea that nature lies inert and inaccessible until it is enlivened or conjured by the mind.

There was something else Goethe read in these pages from Francisci, and my guess is that it reminded him of how Schelling's position had been prefigured in Herder's objections to Jacobi in the "Spinoza-Streit" of the previous decade. A few pages past the "Glut-Pfanne" anecdote, Francisci writes:

Es ist aber zu mercken, daß die Sinische Götzen-Secte unter andren diesen schändlichen Irrthum lehre; GOtt [*sic*] und alle übrige Dinge seye von einerley Substanz: welcher Irr-Satz allgemach auch in die Schulen der Gelehrten eingeschlieche; und darauf ausgelauffen scheinet, daß GOtt [*sic*] die Seele der gantzen Welt und gleichsam ein Verstand oder Geist dieses so grossen Körpers sey.

(It should be noted that, among other things, the Sino-Heathen-Sect preaches this disgraceful misconception: that God and all other things are of one and the same substance, which false doctrine has gradually also crept in to the schools of the learned; it appears to point to God being the soul of the entire world and at the same time the understanding or mind of this so huge body).[48]

Not only did Chinese thought confront Fichtean idealism, it proposed Spinoza's substance and what would soon be Schelling's "Weltseele." But in Francisci's retelling, the stance of the Buddhist monk still did not offer any real philosophical models for how to deal with the substantial matter of the object. Hence Goethe's comment to Schiller about the "Glut-Pfanne":

In the same way, the idealist can resist things in themselves as much as he wants, he will still bump into things outside of himself before he knows what has happened, and, so it seems to me, they will get in his way at the first encounter, just like what happened to the Chinese monk with the hearth. I am always under the impression that, while the one school of thought will never be able to reach the mind from outside of it, the other will scarcely be able to find its way to bodies from the inside outwards, and that, as a result, one is always well advised to remain in a philosophical state of nature,[49] and to make the best possible use of one's undivided existence until the philosophers will one day agree on how they are to reunite that which they have separated.[50]

This state of waiting opened up opportunities for poetry, since it defined the position between objective experience and a priori thought in terms of aesthetics. In his correspondence with Schiller, it was at this moment not poetry that was uppermost in Goethe's mind, but the "relationships and effects of visible differences in nature."[51] Nevertheless, the challenges Goethe sees in scientific method are aesthetic, and understanding them gives us insight into what he tried later to achieve in the *Chinesisch-deutsche Jahres- und Tageszeiten*. This is clear in a short piece to which Trunz gives the title "Erfahrung und Wissenschaft," and which Goethe attached to the letter of 17 January.[52] Here Goethe outlines a dynamic process whereby the aesthetics of observation can achieve some measure of scientific validity, a degree of universality. This is a dialectical process, beginning with the apprehension of empirical phenomena, which are raised through experimentation to the status of scientific phenomena. This process (Herder or the pre-critical Kant would have called it "analytic method") is in itself by definition incomplete, since scientific knowledge cannot encompass all that is given. What emerges is the idea of pure phenomena. This "can never be isolated, but reveals itself instead in a constant series of appearances. In order to represent it, the human mind determines that which is empirically unstable (*das empirisch Wankende*), excludes the contingent, sets aside the impure, develops that which is muddled, and even discovers the unknown."[53] That Goethe himself understood this process of scientific discovery as the same one which is at work in poetic production is clear in the closing lines of the "Prologue in Heaven," which he was conceptualizing (possibly even writing) at this time:

Doch ihr, die echten Göttersöhne,
Erfreut euch der lebendig reichen Schöne!
Das Werdende, das ewig wirkt und lebt,

Umfass' euch mit der Liebe holden Schranken,
Und was in schwankender Erscheinung schwebt,
Befestiget mit dauernden Gedanken.

(But you the genuine sons of light,
Enjoy the living beauty bright!
Becoming, that works and lives forever,
Embrace you in love's limits dear,
And all that may as Appearance waver,
Fix firmly with everlasting Idea!)[54]

To reside in a philosophical state of nature, to represent the wavering, unstable phenomena of life, is to understand the dilemma of the Orientalists, to see that Orientalist knowledge will always bump up against the Orient like the Chinese bumps against the materiality of the "Glut-Pfanne," just like thought bumps up against the materiality of nature. This act of bumping is preserved in aesthetic activity, and one way to do this is shown in the *Chinesisch-deutsche Jahres- und Tageszeiten*. Eradicating the Orientalists meant finding a way to hold their knowledge in reserve, to comprehend the foreignness of what is geographically and culturally remote, while at the same time presenting its familiarity. Performing this encounter in poetry meant finding a way to speak about shared limits in understanding.

NOTES

1 All English translations of the cycle are cited from Johann Wolfgang von Goethe, *Selected Poems*, translated by John Whaley (London: Dent, 1998), 153–9.

2 Wolfgang Schadewaldt, "Zur Entstehung der Elfenszene im zweiten Teil des Faust," *Deutsche Vierteljahrsschrift für Literaturwissenschaft und Geistesgeschichte*, 29 (1955): 227–36.

3 Katharina Mommsen, "Goethe und China in ihren Wechselbeziehungen," in *Goethe und China – China und Goethe: Bericht des Heidelberger Symposiums*, eds. Günther Debon and Adrian Hsia, 15–33 (Bern: Peter Lang), 18.

4 Anke Bosse, "Chinesisch-Deutsche Jahres- und Tageszeiten," *Gedichte von Johann Wolfgang von Goethe*, 255–80 (Stuttgart: Reclam, 1998), 259.

5 Woldemar von Biedermann, "Chinesisch-Deutsche Jahres- und Tageszeiten," *Goetheforschungen*, 2: 426–46.

6 Hideo Fukuda, "Über Goethe's Letzten Gedichtszyklus 'Chinesisch-Deutsche Jahres- und Tageszeitungen,'" *Goethe Jahrbuch*, 106 (1968): 194–6). See in particular and esp. Christine Wagner-Dittmar, "Goethe und die chinesische Literatur," in *Studien zu Goethes Alterswerken*, ed. Erich Trunz, 122–8 (Frankfurt: Athenaeum).

7 Bosse,"Chinesisch-Deutsche Jahres- und Tageszeiten," 260.

8 Ibid., 259.

9 Andreas Anglet, "Die lyrische Bewegung in Goethes Chinesisch Deutsche Jahreszeiten," *Goethe Jahrbuch*, 113 (1996). Anglet claims that there has been consensus on this since the 1970s.

10 Ibid., 180.

11 Friedrich Burkhardt, "Goethes Chinesisch-Deutsche Jahres- und Tageszeiten: Eine Ergänzung zur Entdeckung des Biographischen Hintergrundes durch Wolfgang Prisendanz," *Jahrbuch der Deutschen Schillergesellschaft*, 13 (1969).

12 Hans Sachse, *Goethes "Chinesisch-deutsche Jahres- und Tageszeiten": Ein verschlüsseltes Gedenkblatt* (Hamburg: Goethe-Gesellschaft, 1971). The biographical reading is troubled by Walter Benjamin's claim that some of the poems in the cycle were co-authored by Marianne von Willemer; see Walter Benjamin, "Goethe" [1928], in *Gesammelte Schriften*, vol. 2, *1927–1934*, edited by Michael W. Jennings, Howard Eiland, and Gary Smith, 161–93 (Cambridge: Belknap, 1999), 192.

13 Meredith Lee, "Goethes Chinesisch-Deutsche Jahres- und Tageszeiten," in *Goethe und China – China und Goethe: Bericht des Heidelberger Symposiums*, eds. Günther Debon and Adrian Hsia, 37–50 (Bern, 1985), 45.

14 Walter Veit, "Goethe's Fantasies about the Orient," *Eighteenth-Century Life*, 26/3 (2002): 164.

15 Johann Wolfgang von Goethe, *Goethes Werke*, 143 vols. (Munich). *Weimarer oder Sophienausgabe*: Werke. Edited im Auftrage der Großherzogin Sophie von Sachsen. Abtlg. I–IV. 133 Bde. in 143 Tln. (Weimar: H. Böhlau, 1887–1919). Repr. [Tb.-Ausg.] (Munich: Deutscher Taschenbuch Verlag 1987). -Erg. durch: 3 Nachtrags-Bde. zu Abt. IV, Briefe. Edited by Paul Raabe (Munich: Deutscher Taschenbuch Verlag, 1990). Known as *Weimarer Ausgabe*; cited here as *WA*. Unless otherwise noted, all translations from the *Weimarer Ausgabe* are my own. Goethe to Schönborn, 8 June 1774, *WA* IV/2, 173.

16 Goethe, *WA* XI/11, 50.

17 John H. Zammito, *The Genesis of Kant's Critique of Judgment* (Chicago: University of Chicago Press, 1992), 39.

18 Immanuel Kant, *Reflection* (789), as cited in Zammito, *Genesis*, 39.

19 Immanuel Kant, *Critique of Judgment* [1790], translated by Werner S. Pluhar (Indianapolis: Hackett, 1987), 304–5.

20 Angus Nicholls, *Goethe's Concept of the Daemonic: After the Ancients* (Rochester: Camden House, 2006), 184.

21 Robert Richards, "Nature Is the Poetry of Mind, or How Schelling Solved Goethe's Kantian Problems," in *The Kantian Legacy in Nineteenth-Century Science*, eds. Michael Friedman and Alfred Nordmann (Cambridge, MA: MIT Press, 2006).

22 Goethe to Zeltner, 17 April 1815, *WA* IV/25, 269.

23 This has been well documented by Wagner-Dittmar, "Goethe und die chinesische Literatur."

24 Goethe to Dietz, 15 Nov. 1815, *WA* IV/26, 152–3.

25 Goethe to Ouvaroff, 2 Dec. 1815, *WA* IV/26, 171.

26 Goethe to Dietz, 1 Feb. 1816, *WA* IV/26, 246.

27 Goethe to Willemer, 26 Apr. 1815, *WA* IV/26, 285.

28 Todd Kontje, *German Orientalisms* (Ann Arbor: University of Michigan Press, 2004), 124.

29 Ibid.

30 Ibid. This choice is not in contrast to Herder, as Kontje thinks, it is one of the alternatives Herder contemplated when considering the status of his own cross-cultural studies.

31 Johann Gottfried Herder, *Selected Early Works, 1764–1767: Addresses, Essays, and Drafts; Fragments on Recent German Literature*, edited by Ernest A. Menze and Karl Menges, translated by Ernest A. Menze and Michael Palma (University Park: Pennsylvania State University Press 1992), 30.

32 Johann Gottfried Herder, *Über den Fleiß in mehreren gelehrten Sprachen* (1764, 32).

33 Ibid., 31.

34 Ibid., 32.

35 Erasmus Francisci, *Neu-polirter Geschicht- Kunst- und Sitten-Spiegel ausländischer Völcker* (Nürnberg: Endter, 1670), vol. 1, 41–4.

36 Goethe to Schiller, 6 Jan. 1798.

37 Wolfgang Bauer, "Goethe und China: Verständnis und Misverständnis," in *Goethe und die Tradition*, ed. Hans Reis (Frankfurt: Athenaeum, 1972).

38 Goethe, *WA* I/2, 132.

39 Bauer, "Goethe und China," 182.

40 Goethe to Schiller, 3 Jan. 1798, *WA* IV/13, 4.

41 Friedrich Beiser, *The Fate of Reason: German Philosophy from Kant to Fichte* (Cambridge, MA: Harvard University Press, 1993), 265.

42 Düntzer reads Goethe's Baccelaureus as "ein Idealist derbsten Schlages" (an idealist of the most vulgar kind) and gives a detailed account of Goethe's satire on Fichte (1857, 516–22).

43 Schiller to Goethe, 28 Oct. 1794.

44 Goethe, *WA* IV/13, 9.

45 Goethe, *WA* IV/13, 10.

46 Nicholas Boyle, *Goethe: The Poet and the Age*, vol. 2, *Revolution and Renunciation, 1790–1803* (Oxford: Oxford University Press), 594.

47 Goethe, *WA* IV/13, 10).

48 Fancisci, *Neu-polirter ... ausländischer Völcker*, 45.

49 Schelling, *Ideas*, xvi.

50 Goethe to Schiller, 6 Jan. 1798, *WA* IV/13, 11.

51 Goethe to Schiller, 17 Jan. 1798, *WA* IV/13, 28.

52 Johann Wolfgang von Goethe, *Werke*, critical text with commentary by Erich Trunz et al. (Hamburg: C. Wegner, 1961–4), 14 vols. Known as *Hamburger Ausgabe*; cited here as *HA*. Unless otherwise noted, all translations from the *Hamburger Ausgabe* are my own. *HA* 13, 23–5.

53 Ibid., 25.

54 Johann Wolfgang von Goethe, *Faust, Parts I & II*, translated by A.S. Kline, http://www.iowagrandmaster.org/Books%20in%20pdf/Faust.pdf (accessed 10 July 2015).

7 China on Parade: Hegel's Manipulation of His Sources and His Change of Mind

ROBERT BERNASCONI

Hegel's first extensive encounter with China seems to have been in 1822–23, when he lectured for the first time on the philosophy of world history. Just before Christmas of that year he wrote to Edouard-Casimir Duboc, a hat manufacturer who had taken an interest in his philosophy, and in an attempt to excuse himself for not responding to Duboc's letters Hegel offered this account of the research he was doing for his lectures on world history: "I am still, to begin with, occupied with the Indian and Chinese sphere, absorbed in quarto and octavo volumes. Yet, it is a very interesting and pleasant occupation to have the peoples of the world pass in review before me."[1] That Hegel, who would lecture on the philosophy of history four more times before his death in 1831, should have enjoyed this self-imposed task of reading studies of China written by Europeans is no surprise. There was a long tradition of philosophers studying travellers' reports and drawing conclusions on their basis, and Hegel seems to have been especially assiduous in doing so. Nevertheless, however pleasant this occupation was to him, it was never entirely innocent because in the process he, like his predecessors, played a role in shaping stereotypes that persisted for a long time.

I have previously shown how Hegel distorted the reports he read on Africa, and I will here show that the same was true for his treatment of China.[2] It is in observing the way Hegel departs from his sources that one can most readily find evidence about his intent, because there one sees his own contributions. I shall investigate what lay behind his choice of sources and his use and abuse of them. In his treatment of what he called "Africa proper," Hegel indulged in a vicious and scurrilous attack on Africans as savages that went far beyond what his sources allowed and that amounts to clear evidence of anti-black racism. It is tempting to conclude that Hegel's treatment of the Chinese, because it is less vicious than his treatment of Africans or Native Americans, was driven only by the desire to make his picture of China conform with the larger philosophical aims of his philosophy of history, even if those larger aims had a Eurocentric and even Germanocentric component.[3] This view might be sustainable if one confined oneself to the first version of his lectures on the philosophy of history, those of 1822–23.[4] However, after examining Hegel's use of his sources on China, I will argue that on the evidence that is now available to us, in his lectures on the philosophy of history after 1823 he presented a portrait of the Chinese that in its calumnies went beyond what was necessary for him to sustain his philosophical position.[5]

Taken as a whole, the lectures on the philosophy of world history served Hegel's students in Berlin and subsequent generations both as a ladder to the absolute standpoint from which alone the System of Science could be accessed and as a vindication of the absolute standpoint, much as the *Phenomenology of Spirit* was supposed to do when it was written.[6] When Hegel wrote to Duboc of the peoples of the world passing before him in review, he was drawing a remarkable parallel between the perspective of a sovereign on his troops as they present themselves to him for inspection and the perspective of the philosopher of history as Hegel understood the role. Kant's proposal that universal history should be written from a cosmopolitan perspective is a clear forerunner of Hegel's philosophy of world history, even though it is somewhat tendentious to think of Hegel in terms of cosmopolitanism and there is nothing in Kant that parallels Hegel's thesis about the annulment of time.[7] The annulment of time, announced in the chapter on absolute knowing in the *Phenomenology of Spirit*, and reiterated in the introduction to the lectures on the philosophy of world history, means that the narrative of history gives way to an account of spirit where the self empties itself out, sinks into the substance, and becomes a content for a subject that recognizes itself in that otherness.[8] In the 1822 introduction to the lectures on the philosophy of world history, Hegel articulated the change of perspective that enabled him to see the peoples of the world pass before him as follows: "For spirit is eternally present ... and for it there is no past."[9]

Part of the fascination of China for Hegel was that it represented for him a kind of eternal present. He characterized it as stationary, unchanging, whereas Hegel's philosophy is fundamentally about movement, the movement of the dialectic, and to read Hegel is to be caught up in this sense of movement. But there is no passage from China to else-where. It is only one isolated moment of the dialectic, and it is only when the moments come together that there is a living advance ("Fort-gang").[10] That is why the Chinese Empire has a place in the historical series only in itself and for us. The same is true for India.[11]

The peoples who passed before Hegel for review came into existence and then departed. By placing China outside of history, he placed it beyond the judgment of history as the world tribunal.[12] But then where is the justice in the fact that, unlike those peoples Hegel celebrates later in his lecture course, China continues to exist? It was perhaps because history in its progressive march had apparently not passed a nega-tive judgment on the Chinese, as it had on other peoples, that Hegel believed it necessary to make clear that they were not immune from judgment and that they did not in their radical alterity and incommen-surability represent a viable alternative to Christianized Europe, which would have opened the door to a kind of historical relativism. China, after all, did not belong to the past; still less did it belong to Europe's past, as the Greeks or Romans did. But although China is always the same, that did not mean it was "eternally present" in Hegel's terms. It was, no doubt, for the same reason that Hegel himself looked forward to the time when China would be subjected to Europeans.[13]

Hegel's position on China's status as unhistorical was not new, but it was extreme. Herder, for example, presented an image of the Chi-nese Empire as "an embalmed mummy," but he also saw "a slow pro-gress" that encouraged him to look for the obstacles that prevented its further advance.[14] Hegel saw only stasis. Whereas Africa, with the strange exception of Egypt that I have discussed elsewhere, was unam-biguously outside history, China is nevertheless placed outside what he called "history proper."[15] More precisely, the Chinese Empire was understood as "unhistorical" (ungeschichtlich).[16] This is because, on Hegel's view, in China "every change is excluded, and the fixedness of a character which recurs perpetually, takes the place of what we should call the historical."[17] This enabled him to set out the basic terms of his account of peoples before having to address historical change that, on his account, comes through the encounter and mixing of peoples.[18] As Karl Hegel, the philosopher's son, explained in his preface to the 1840 edition of the lectures, "In proceeding to treat of China and India, he [Hegel] wished, as he said himself, only to show by example how phi-losophy ought to comprehend the character of a nation; and this could be done more easily in the case of the stationary nations of the East, than in that of the peoples which have a *bona fide* history and a historical development of character."[19] We can therefore say that Hegel included China and India in his lectures on the philosophy of world history less because he thought them integral to the subject matter of history proper and more because he thought their treatment would prove a useful pedagogical tool.

Hegel still had to deal with a fact that had challenged Europeans long before him, that the Chinese have a continuous, well-ordered, and well-attested record of their history going back at least five thousand years. He conceded that the Chinese wrote history books and, as he suggested in the *Aesthetics*, were perhaps unique among Orientals in doing so.[20] But, for Hegel, history proper begins with continuous history, and this begins only when the Caucasian race enters the picture in place of the Mongols.[21] In order to support his claim that the history of China is not yet history proper, Hegel exaggerated the familiar trope that the character of the Chinese Empire had remained unchanged throughout that time, and disconnected from other peoples. So the Chinese state is said to be the product of an internal undisturbed process of cultivation, whereas European states are the product of an "ongoing linkage of traditions."[22]

China is static, because the Chinese are excluded from spirit. Deprived of movement, they also lack the moment of subjectivity. "The universal Will displays its activity (*betätigt*) immediately through that of the individual" who does not know himself as differentiated from the substance.[23] This takes place in China in the figure of the emperor: "the substance is immediately a subject, the emperor."[24] This was Hegel's understanding of what Europeans meant when they described Chinese society as patriarchal. Indeed, already in 1818 Hegel characterized China in terms of a patriarchal relationship that permeated the whole society from the emperor down.[25] However, in the lectures on world history, he also used the phrase "familial principle," most likely because the family had been such an important category in the *Philosophy of Right*, and he wanted to draw the parallel.[26] One should always remember that Hegel's lectures on world history belong to the account of objective spirit at the culmination of the philosophy of right, and they were intended to show the historical realization of the institutions that shape the categories that had already been explained abstractly. There are other indications of how Hegel's treatment of China was governed by the categories developed in the *Philosophy of Right*. Hegel's *Philosophy of Right* can be read – and in my opinion should be read – as being about determining the conditions of freedom, and the argument is that freedom can only be accomplished in the state: "The idea of the state in modern times has the distinctive characteristic that the state is the actualization of freedom ... in accordance with its [the concept of the will's] universality and divinity."[27] From their very first publication it was recognized that Hegel's lectures on the philosophy of history were a history of the appearance of freedom.[28]

Herder's portrait of China was not so very different from Hegel's in its main outlines, and the chief difference between Herder and Hegel is the setting in which they placed their accounts, that is, their different conceptions of the philosophy of history.[29] Both of them promoted the idea that the duties of the subject to the state are founded on the duties a son owes to his father; they agreed that there is no hereditary nobility and that merit alone ennobles; and they characterized Chinese laws as founded in morals.[30] This measure of agreement is easily explained. Although Hegel lectured on China for the first time almost forty years after Herder published his treatment of China in the third volume of his *Ideen* in 1787, both thinkers relied largely on the same sources. In particular, they both drew heavily on the *Mémoires concernant l'histoire, les sciences, les arts, les moeurs, les usages, etc. des chinois*, prepared by the missionaries to Beijing, and Joseph de Mailla's *Histoire générale de la Chine*, which included the first edition of Jean-Baptiste Grosier's *Description générale de la Chine*.[31] In 1818 Grosier's description of China was expanded from the equivalent of two volumes to seven. It appears that Hegel used both the German translation made from the 1785 edition and the 1818 edition.[32] Karl Heinz Ilting and the other editors of Hegel's 1822–23 lectures meticulously identified some of Hegel's sources for his account of China, and thereby confirmed just how much time he must have spent with those quarto and octavo volumes.

Nevertheless, there are two additional and important sources not recognized by the new edition of Hegel's lectures on world history. Once they are recognized one gains valuable insights into Hegel's use and abuse of his sources. The first of them is Sir George Staunton's account of his visit to China, published in 1797 under the title *An Authentic Account of an Embassy from the King of Great Britain to the Emperor of China*, and translated into German the following year. The proof that Hegel read it emerges in the context of his account, the initial part of which was taken from Grosier and the *Memoires*, that every five years "each mandarin must submit a written confession of the errors of which he knows himself guilty."[33] However, Hegel was intrigued by the further suggestion that in China mandarins were held responsible also for things that they did not know about: "In office, the mandarin is responsible (*verantwortlich*) for all that takes place."[34] Hegel's source for this claim was almost certainly Staunton's description that "the rigorous maxims of the Chinese government render the mandarines [*sic*] responsible for whatever evil it is supposed possible for them to have prevented."[35]

Later in the book Staunton returned to this peculiar idea of responsibility in China and referred to the magistrate: "He lies under the hardship, also, of being frequently responsible for events which he seldom can control. Upon the general principle that it is his duty to watch over the morals of the people, he is in many cases considered as a criminal for not preventing crimes which he had not been able to prevent."[36] Staunton seems to have been concerned only to observe the injustice of such a system, but Hegel had a more profound purpose: he wanted to show the radical alterity of the Chinese. First, he insisted that this notion of responsibility was widespread in China and was not limited to mandarins. He referred to the responsibility of parents for the misbehaviour of their children.[37] This enabled him to show how this concept of responsibility extended in China beyond the patriarchal system of government to include also the family. In addition, he showed that the Chinese lacked a clear understanding of accountability. "Accountability (*Die Imputation*) for crime is not a consideration in China. The suicide who wishes to revenge himself on another will plunge that entire family into ruin; so he takes his own life because by doing that he plunges into ruin the other as well as the other's family too. What the Chinese person gains from such a revenge is that a penalty cannot be imposed on him and his family together, nor can there be confiscation of his goods."[38] Hegel seems to have been one of the first to see clearly the difference between accountability for what one has done and the more general notion of responsibility according to which one is called to respond to a situation that one may not have brought about. This notion of responsibility was relatively new and Hegel, who probably learned it from Benjamin Constant, was sensitive to it.[39] However, more important to Hegel than the excessive idea of responsibility among the Chinese was that they lacked a clear notion of accountability. He saw this as connected with the deficiency of the Chinese understanding of morality that he sought to associate with a lack of interiority. Responsibility, by contrast, did not depend on a notion of inwardness and so, for Hegel, was a less advanced concept.

One reason it is significant for our understanding of Hegel to recognize Staunton as one of his direct sources is because it enables us see that elsewhere Hegel contradicted this source and, so far as I can tell, without the support of other sources. In 1822–23 Hegel referred to the Chinese religion as a state religion.[40] This is also emphasized in the published editions: "religion is in China essentially state-religion."[41] And yet Hegel would have read in Sir George Staunton's book the clearest denial of it: "There is in China no state religion. None is paid, preferred, or encouraged by it."[42] Indeed, Herder, too, was clear that there was no compulsory religion in China and that, in fact, there was tolerance of other sects.[43] It might seem that Hegel was drawing instead on Jean-Baptiste Grosier's account of China, but we should read carefully what he wrote there. In all editions of Grosier's book we read of the Tribunal of Ceremonies, described as one of the supreme courts of the empire, where the ancient doctrine of the Tien is presented as the established and prevailing religion. "We will allow, that the mandarines [sic] themselves, who form this tribunal, may sometimes, in secret, and in their houses, give themselves up to superstitious practices; but this personal attachment to particular acts of worship has no influence over their public conduct: when they sit on their benches, they know no other religion but that of the state."[44] And yet before one tries to use this passage to support Hegel's insistence that religion in China is essentially state religion, one should recall the case that he was trying to make against the Chinese. He was denying interiority and thus subjectivity to them. "Personal attachment to individual acts of worship" of the kind Grosier affirmed in this passage is precisely what Hegel wanted to deny. My suggestion that Hegel was thereby making a point specific to his treatment of the Chinese in the context of his philosophy of history is supported by the fact that, although Hegel treated the religion of China extensively in the *Lectures on Philosophy of Religion*, and especially in 1827, the phrase "state religion" so prominently promoted in the lectures on history is not highlighted there. In the three sets of lectures on religion – 1824, 1827, and 1831 – the phrase "state religion" appears only once apart from the titles added by the editors.[45]

Hegel insisted that Chinese religion is not what Europeans could call religion.[46] No more is Chinese philosophy philosophy.[47] The same is true of science and art. Hegel's explanation of China's radical alterity is that "everything which belongs to Spirit ... is alien to it."[48] Hegel's philosophy is a philosophy of spirit, and China is allegedly marked by a complete absence of spirit. When Hegel tried to explain why Europeans could not imitate the external and perfectly natural skillfulness

("Geschichklichkeit") of the Chinese successfully, he suggested that this was because the Europeans have spirit, whereas the Chinese do not.[49]

Hegel chose to present the Chinese in such a way that they appeared to lack spirit, even if to make the case as strong as possible, he had to distort his sources. It seems that he forced the issue in order to make more plausible his claim that the actualization of spirit took place in the course of history proper, a history from which China and India were excluded.[50] However, Hegel also chose to present the Chinese as savage, and his decision to do so seems to have been gratuitous, much like his decision to exaggerate grossly the reports he had read about Africa. The major difference in the case of the calumnies he directed against the Chinese was that he had some support in the travel literature for his claims. The problem in this case is that even though, as I will show, he must have known that these claims were contested, he did not present them as such. Nevertheless, Hegel's decision to present the Chinese as utterly degraded was taken only after his initial set of lectures on the philosophy of history in 1822–23. In 1822–23 China filled Hegel with astonishment and wonder. He called it "a wondrously unique Empire" because he saw it as self-sustained, having developed without external contacts and because he judged its government to be "well-regulated to the highest degree, that is most just, most benevolent, most wise."[51] This characterization and the astonishment of Europeans it attracted was included in the posthumously prepared editions, but in a distinctly downgraded version. In these later editions China was simply "thoroughly organized."[52] Although the 1822 lectures contained serious criticisms of the deficiencies of the Chinese state, such as the fact that whole families might be punished for a crime committed by only one of its members, it was only subsequently that Hegel saw the need to sensationalize the shortcomings of the Chinese character.[53] Indeed, it is only in the versions published by the so-called Friends of Hegel in their complete edition of his works that Hegel's criticisms come to be directed primarily against the character of the Chinese people rather than their ethics and laws.[54] Even what looked like equality among the Chinese was dismissed as evidence not of an inner humanity, but of an inferior self-perception.[55] They were equally degraded.[56]

Hegel's early admiration for China had dissipated by the time he delivered the judgment reported in the published versions of the lectures that "it appears nothing terrible to them to sell themselves as slaves, and to eat the bitter bread of slavery."[57] Hegel here failed to acknowledge Grosier's observation that whereas slavery was authorized in China, the Chinese had "greatly moderated its severity."[58] Instead, the lectures published by the Friends of Hegel continued the calumnies: "Suicide, the result of revenge, and the exposure of children, as a common, even daily occurrence, shows the little respect in which they hold themselves individually, and humanity in general."[59] I have already mentioned the evidence for his account of how the Chinese committed suicide from a spirit of revenge, but the claim that the exposure of children was a common almost daily occurrence shows him again selecting his sources. This issue of infanticide had become a controversial one in discussions of China, not least because of the accusations levelled in 1804 by John Barrow in his *Travels in China*. Grosier had mentioned the charge in passing in the original edition of his book, commenting that it had been exaggerated in Europe.[60] However, by 1819 Grosier devoted a whole chapter to the crimes of suicide and infanticide in China, in large part to answer the case made by Barrow. Whether or not Hegel read Barrow's book, which, like Staunton's, was translated into German in the same year as its first English publication, has not yet been established.[61] But Grosier, whom we know Hegel did read, was clear that Barrow's charges were a libel.[62]

It would seem then that the calumnies Hegel introduced against the Chinese after 1823 were gratuitous in the sense that, unlike the positioning of China outside history, they were not necessary on philosophical grounds. In arguing that the Chinese withheld respect from themselves individually and from humanity in general, Hegel seemingly issued a judgment on behalf of humanity in favour of humanity. But his manner of doing so, in effect, made the Chinese less human. That is, he undermined the basis on which he passed judgment on them and an examination of the way he distorted his sources in order to establish his case amplifies his own moral failure. Hegel says he found reading about China a "very interesting and pleasant occupation," but reading what Hegel made of this reading, while interesting, is, especially when read in the context of his sources, anything but pleasant.

NOTES

1 "Es ist mir aber ein sehr interessantes und vergnügliches Geschäfte, die Völker der Welt Revue passieren zu haben." Hegel to Duboc, 22 Dec. 1822, in *Briefe von und an Hegel*, vol. 2, edited by Johannes Hoffmeister (Hamburg: Felix Meiner, 1953), 367; translated by Clark Butler and Christiane Seiler as *Hegel: The Letters* (Bloomington: Indiana University Press, 1984), 494.

2 On Hegel's treatment of Africa, see Robert Bernasconi, "Hegel at the Court of the Ashanti," in *Hegel after Derrida*, ed. Stuart Barnett (London: Routledge, 1998), 41–63.

3 On Hegel's account of Native Americans, see Sûrya Parekh, "Hegel's New World: History, Freedom, and Race," in *Hegel and History*, ed. Will Dudley (Albany: SUNY Press, 2009), 111–31.

4 For an old and one-sided (materialist), but still valuable, critique of Hegel on China, see K.A. Wittfogel, "Hegel über China," *Unter dem Banner des Marxismus*, 5 (1931): 346–62.

5 The 1822–23 lecture course is available as G.W.F. Hegel, *Vorlesungen über die Philosophie der Weltgeschichte*, Vorlesungen 12, edited by K.H. Ilting, K. Brehmer, and Hoo Nam Seelmann (Hamburg: Felix Meiner), 1996; translated by R.F. Brown and C. Hodgson as *Lectures on the Philosophy of World History* (Oxford: Oxford University Press, 2011). I will focus initially on this edition not only because it is the most reliable, but also because it is the version that contains the most sustained discussion of China. Until the publication of this edition in 1996, it would have been impossible to recognize that Hegel changed his portrayal of China radically after 1823 and, as far as I am aware, I am the first to notice this. Furthermore, this edition is to date the only integral text of the lectures we possess insofar as the other editions – Edouard Gans's 1837 text, Karl Hegel's 1840 revision which was translated into English in 1852 and is still in print, and Lasson's larger 1919 edition – were all amalgams of texts drawn from the five different occasions on which Hegel lectured on the topic. The exception is the recent publication of Heimann's notes from Hegel's late lecture course in the winter semester 1830–31: see Georg Wilhelm Friedrich Hegel, *Die Philosophie der Geschichte*, edited by Klaus Vieweg (Munich: Wilhelm Fink, 2005). Although I have consulted this text and occasionally refer to it, I have largely left it to one side as we await the full publication of Karl Hegel's notes from the same course, which apparently will soon be available. It should be noted that Heimann's text was used by Gans in preparing his edition. On the different versions, see Peter C. Hodgson, *Shapes of Freedom* (Oxford: Oxford University Press, 2012), 1–6. The extent to which the lecture courses published under Hegel's name accurately report what he actually said will no doubt always be in question.

6 See Robert Bernasconi, "'We Philosophers': Barbaros médeis eisitó," in *Endings: Questions of Memory in Hegel and Heidegger*, eds. Rebecca Comay and John McCumber (Evanston: Northwestern University Press, 1999), 77–96.

7 Hegel, of course was no cosmopolitan, but neither was Kant in the modern sense. His cosmopolitanism was explicitly Eurocentric in intent. See

Immanuel Kant, "Idee zu einer allgemeinen Geschichte in weltbürger-licher Absicht," in *Werke*, 8th Akademie ed. (Berlin: de Gruyter, 1912–), 30; translated by Allen W. Wood as "Idea for a Universal History with a Cosmopolitan Aim," in *Anthropology, History, and Education*, eds. Gunter Zoller and Robert B. Louden (Cambridge: Cambridge University Press, 2007), 119.

8 G.W.F. Hegel, *Phänomenologie des Geistes*, edited by W. Bonsiepen and R. Heede, *Gesammelte Werke* 9 (Hamburg: Felix Meiner, 1980), 429–34; trans-lated by A.V. Miller as *Phenomenology of Spirit* (Oxford: Oxford University Press, 1978), 487. For more on this, see Robert Bernasconi, "'The Ruling Categories of the World': The Trinity in Hegel's Philosophy of History and the Rise and Fall of Peoples," in *A Companion to Hegel*, eds. Stephen Houl-gate and Michael Baur (Oxford: Wiley-Blackwell, 2011), 315–31.

9 Hegel, *Vorlesungen* 12, ed. Ilting et al., 15; trans. Brown and Hodgson, *Lectures*, 140.

10 G.W.F. Hegel, *Vorlesungen über die Philosophie der Weltgeschichte*, part 2, edited by Georg Lasson (Hamburg: Felix Meiner, 1988), 275. Until 1996 the Lasson edition, which originally appeared in 1919, was the best available, but it inexplicably tended to be ignored in the English-speaking world. Lasson's edition already showed that Hegel may have read and at the very least knew details of the visits to China by Earl Macartney and Lord Amherst (316 and 308). For a comparison between the treatment of China in the Lasson edition and earlier versions, see Kurt Leese, *Die Geschichts-philosophie Hegels auf Grund der neu erschlossenen Quellen untersucht und dargestellt* (Berlin: Furche, 1922), 153–8.

11 G.W.F. Hegel, *Vorlesungen über die Philosophie der Geschichte*, in *Werke*, vol. 9 (Berlin: Duncker and Humblot, 1840), edited by Karl Hegel, 212; translated by J. Sibree as *The Philosophy of History* (New York: Willey, 1900), 173. I will also refer, where applicable, to the earlier edition edited by Edward Gans, as it is interesting to see the level of continuity across the editions: *Vor-lesungen über die Philosophie der Geschichte*, in *Werke*, vol. 9 (Berlin: Duncker und Humblot, 1837), 176. The importance of this lecture course for Hegel's contemporaries is reflected in the fact that it was newly re-edited by the "Friends of Hegel" less than three years after they published a first version.

12 G.W.F. Hegel, *Grundlinien der Philosophie des Rechts*, edited by Eduard Gans, *Werke* 8 (Berlin: Duncker und Humblot, 1833), 430; translated by H.B. Nisbet as *Elements of the Philosophy of Right* (Cambridge: Cambridge University Press, 1991), 371.

13 Hegel, *Vorlesungen* 9 (1837), 147; *Vorlesungen* 9 (1840), 174; trans. Sibree, *Philosophy of History*, 142–3.

14 Johann Gottfried Herder, *Ideen zur Philosophie der Geschichte der Menschheit*, vol. 3 (Riga: Johann Friedrich Hartknoch, 1787), 17 and 9; translated by T. Churchill as *Outlines of a Philosophy of the History of Man* (London: J. Johnson, 1800), 296 and 292. On the image of China as static, see Anthony Pagden, "The Immobility of China: Orientalism and Occidentalism in the Enlightenment" in *The Anthropology of Enlightenment*, eds. Larry Wolff and Marco Cipolloni (Stanford: Stanford University Press, 2007), 56–64.

15 The phrase "history proper" is associated by Hegel with the Caucasians. See Robert Bernasconi, "With What Must the Philosophy of World History Begin? On the Racial Basis of Hegel's Eurocentrism," in *Nineteenth-Century Contexts*, 22 (2000): 171–201. On the Egyptians, see my "The Return of Africa: Hegel and the Question of the Racial Identity of the Egyptians," in *Identity and Difference: Studies in Hegel's Logic, Philosophy of Spirit and Politics*, ed. Phil Grier (Albany: SUNY Press, 2007), 201–16.

16 Hegel, *Vorlesungen* 12, ed. Ilting et al., 122–3; trans. Brown and Hodgson, *Lectures*, 213–14.

17 Hegel, *Vorlesungen* 9, ed. Gans (1837) 113; *Vorlesungen* 9, ed. Karl Hegel (1840), 141; trans. Sibree, *Philosophy of History*, 116.

18 Hegel, *Vorlesungen* 9 (1840), 141; trans. Sibree, *Philosophy of History*, 115. This passage is not found in the 1937 edition. On Hegel's account of a stagnant China, see Zhijian Tao, *Drawing the Dragon: Western European Reinvention of China* (Bern: Peter Lang, 2009), 95–9.

19 Karl Hegel, "Vorrede zur zweiten Auflage," in Hegel, *Vorlesungen* 9 (1840), xxi; trans. Sibree, *Philosophy of History*, xi.

20 G.W.F. Hegel, *Vorlesungen über die Aesthetik*, edited by H.G. Hotho, *Werke* 10.3 (Berlin: Duncker and Humblot, 1838), 257; translated by T.M. Knox as *Aesthetics*, vol. 2 (Oxford: Oxford University Press, 1975), 987.

21 Hegel, *Vorlesungen* 9 (1837), 176; *Vorlesungen* 9 (1840), 211; trans. Sibree, 173. In 1822–23 when he makes the same point he seems to be using the term "Mongol" not as a racial designation, following Blumenbach, but as a narrower term for a people distinguished from the Chinese and the Indians. Hegel, *Vorlesungen* 12, ed. Ilting et al., 234; trans. Brown and Hodgson, *Lectures*, 304.

22 Hegel, *Vorlesungen* 12, ed. Ilting et al., 132; trans. Brown and Hodgson, *Lectures*, 223.

23 Hegel, *Vorlesungen* 9 (1837), 118; *Vorlesungen* 9 (1840), 147; trans. Sibree, *Philosophy of History*, 120.

24 Hegel, *Vorlesungen* 9 (1837), 119; *Vorlesungen* 9 (1840), 147; trans, Sibree, *Philosophy of History*, 120.

25 G.W.F. Hegel, *Vorlesungen über Naturrecht und Staatswissenschaft*, Vorlesungen 1 (Hamburg: Felix Meiner, 1983), 259, translated by J. Michael

Stewart and Peter C. Hodgson as *Lectures on Natural Right and Political Science* (Berkeley: University of California Press, 1995), 309.

26 Another or complementary explanation was that he adopted this language from Peter Feddersen Stuhr (Pseud: Feodor Eggo), *Der Untergang der Naturstaaten dargestellt in Briefen über Niebuhr's Römische Geschichte* (Berlin: Salfeld, 1812), 20–4. Hegel knew this book and cited it in his discussion of the Oriental World in *Grundlinien der Philosophie des Rechts* (Berlin: Nicolai, 1821), 351–2; trans. Nisbet, *Elements of the Philosophy of Right*, 378.

27 Hegel, *Grundlinien der Philosophie des Rechts* (1833), 322; trans. Nisbet, *Elements of the Philosophy of Right*, 282. On the importance of freedom for understanding Hegel's account of China, see Lydia L. Moland, *Hegel on Political Identity: Patriotism, Nationalism, Cosmopolitanism* (Evanston: Northwestern University Press, 2011), 106–7.

28 Karl Rosenkranz, Review of Hegel "Vorlesungen über die Geschichte der Philosophie," ed. E. Gans, *Hallische und deutsche Jahrbücher für Wissenschaft und Kunst*, 18 (20 Jan. 1838): 139.

29 Sonia Sikka has recently argued that what drove Herder's negative response to China was his positive attitude to religion. Herder used his account of China to respond to Voltaire's championing of Chinese religion as, in effect, superior to Christianity. Sonia Sikka, *Herder on Humanity and Cultural Difference* (Cambridge: Cambridge University Press, 2011), 112.

30 Herder, *Ideen*, vol. 3, 7–8; trans. Churchill, *Outlines*, 291.

31 Jean Joseph Marie Amiot, *Mémoires concernant l'histoire, les sciences, les arts, les moeurs, les usages, etc. des chinois* (Paris: Gay and Gide, 1797), 15 vols. Joseph-Anne-Marie de Moyriac de Mailla, *Histoire générale de la Chine* (Paris: Clouseie, 1777–83), 12 vols., was expanded in 1785 to include Jean Baptiste Gabriel Alexandre Grosier, *Description générale de la Chine* (Paris: Moutard, 1785).

32 Grosier's work was translated into German by G.S. Schneitler as *Allgemeine Beschreibung des Chinesischen Reichs nach seinem Gegenwärtigen Zustande*, 2 vols. (Frankfurt and Leipzig: Fleischer, 1789). It was also translated into English as *A General Description of China*, 2 vols. (London: G.G.J. and J. Robinson, 1788). The third and final edition was *De la Chine ou description générale de cet Empire* (Paris: Pillet and Arthus Bertrand, 1818). On the editions used by Hegel, see *Vorlesungen* 12, ed. Ilting et al., 540 and 548.

33 Hegel, *Vorlesungen* 12, ed. Ilting et al., 137; trans. Brown and Hodgson, *Lectures*, 228.

34 Hegel, *Vorlesungen* 12, ed. Ilting et al., 137; trans. Brown and Hodgson, *Lectures*, 228. Hegel was still making this point in 1831: see Hegel, *Die Philosophie der Geschichte*, ed. Vieweg, 83.

35 Sir George Staunton, *An Authentic Account of an Embassy from the King of Great Britain to the Emperor of China*, vol. 2 (London: G. Nicol, 1798), 216; translated as *Des Grafen Macartney Gesandtschaftsreise nach China*, vol. 2 (Berlin, 1798), 85. It is possible that Hegel read Staunton in the French translation from 1798 by Jean-Henri Castera that was recently reprinted and which was more faithful to the original than the German version; see *Voyage dans l'intérieur de la Chine et en Tartarie fait dans les anneés 1792, 1793 et 1794* (Geneva: Olizane, 2005), 516. R.F. Merkel earlier identified Staunton as one of Hegel's sources on the basis of another passage; see "Herder und Hegel über China," *Sinica*, XVII (1942): 15 note d.

36 Staunton, *An Authentic Account*, vol. 2, 299; *Voyage dans l'intérieur*, 571. This passage is missing from the German translation. Also missing from the German translation is a passage that supports Hegel's view that the Chinese have a servile consciousness. Staunton wrote: "The political, moral, and historical works of the Chinese contain no abstract ideas of liberty, which might lead them to the assertion of independence," in *An Authentic Account*, vol. 2, 298; trans. *Voyage dans l'intérieur*, 570.

37 Hegel, *Vorlesungen* 12, ed. Ilting et al., 134; trans. Brown and Hodgson, *Lectures*, 225.

38 Hegel, *Vorlesungen* 12, ed. Ilting et al., 150; trans. Brown and Hodgson, *Lectures*, 237. Translation modified. Compare Amiot, *Mémoires concernant l'histoire*, vol. 4, 289–90, and 439, and vol. 7, 37, with Grosier, *De la Chine*, vol. 5 (1819), 73–5.

39 On the novelty of this idea of responsibility at this time and its place in Hegel's philosophy, see Robert Bernasconi, "Before Whom and for What? Accountability and the Invention of Ministerial, Hyperbolic, and Infinite Responsibility," in *Difficulties of Ethical Life*, eds. Shannon Sullivan and Dennis J. Schmidt (New York: Fordham University Press, 2008), 132–6.

40 Hegel, *Vorlesungen* 12, ed., Ilting et al., 157; trans. Brown and Hodgson, *Lectures*, 244.

41 Hegel, *Vorlesungen* 9 (1987), 131; *Vorlesungen* 9 (1840), 160; trans. Sibree, *Philosophy of History*, 131. See also ed. Vieweg, *Die Philosophie der Geschichte*, 83.

42 Staunton, *An Authentic Account*, vol. 2, 101. Compare the German translation: "Keine Religion ist herrschend in China: Die Regierung beschüsst keine, und zieht keine vor," in *Des Grafen Macartney*, vol. 2, 42. The French translation reads: "Il n'y a point en Chine de religion dominante. Les prêtres d'aucun culte ne sont payés, préférés, ni encouragés par l'Etat," in *Voyage dans l'intérieur*, 436.

43 Herder, *Ideen*, vol. 3, 7–8; trans. Churchill, *Outline*, 291.

44 Jean-Baptiste Grosier, *Description générale de la China*, in *Histoire générale de la Chine*, vol. 13 (Paris: Moutard, 1785), 562; translated as *Allgemeine Beschreibung des Chinesichen Reichs*, vol. 2 (Frankfurt: Johann Georg Fleischer, 1789), 154; translated as *A General Description of China*, vol. 2 (London: G.G.J. and Robinson, 1788), 191. Jean-Baptiste Grosier, *De la Chine ou description générale de cet Empire*, vol. 4 (Paris: Pillet and Bertrand Ainé, 1819), 394.

45 G.W.F. Hegel, *Vorlesungen über die Philosophie der Religion*, part 2, edited by W. Jaeschke, Vorlesungen 4a (Hamburg: Felix Meiner, 1985), 618; translated by Peter Hodgson as *Lectures on the Philosophy of Religion*, vol. 2 (Berkeley: University of California Press, 1987), 729.

46 Hegel, *Vorlesungen* 9 (1837), 131; *Vorlesungen* 9 (1840), 161; trans. Sibree, *Philosophy of History*, 131.

47 G.W.F. Hegel, *Vorlesungen über die Geschichte der Philosophie*, part 1, Vorlesungen 6, edited by Pierre Garniron and Walter Jeschke (Hamburg: Felix Meiner, 1994), 268–9, 369–74, and 347; translated by Robert F. Brown and J.M. Stewart as *Lectures on the History of Philosophy 1825–6*, vol. 1 (Oxford: Oxford University Press, 2009), 91, 106–10, and 285. On the context of Hegel's denial of Chinese philosophy, see *Africa, Asia, and the History of Philosophy* (Albany: SUNY Press), 2013. For a discussion of Hegel's detailed treatment of Chinese philosophy, see, Eun-Jeung Lee, *"Anti-Europa": Die Geschichte der Rezeption des Konfuzianismus und der Konfuzianischen Gesellschaft seit der frühen Aufklärung* (Münster: LIT, 2003), 274–320.

48 Hegel, *Vorlesungen* 9 (1837), 138; *Vorlesungen* 9 (1840), 168–9; trans. Sibree, *Philosophy of History*, 138.

49 Hegel, *Vorlesungen* 9 (1837), 138; *Vorlesungen* 9 (1840) 168; trans. Sibree, *Philosophy of History*, 138.

50 Hegel, *Vorlesungen* 11, ed. Ilting et al., 151–4; trans. Brown and Hodgson, *Lectures*, 86–8.

51 Hegel, *Vorlesungen* 12, ed. Ilting et al., 121–2; trans. Brown and Hodgson, *Lectures*, 212–3.

52 Hegel, *Vorlesungen* 9 (1837), 116; *Vorlesungen* 9 (1840), 144; trans. Sibree, *Philosophy of History*, 118. It should be noted that in 1831 Hegel comments not on the astonishment that Europeans have for China but only on the attention (*"Aufmerksamkeit"*) they have given to it. However, I do not build too much on that as we await publication of Karl Hegel's notes. Hegel, *Die Philosophie der Geschichte*, ed. Vieweg, 77.

53 Hegel, *Vorlesungen* 12 ed. Ilting et al., 147, trans. Brown and Hodgson, *Lectures*, 235.

54 Hegel, *Vorlesungen* 9 (1837), 138; *Vorlesungen* 9 (1840), 168; trans. Sibree, *Philosophy of History*, 138. The term *Charakter* does not appear in the Heimann manuscript at this point.

55 Hegel, *Vorlesungen* 9 (1837), 139; *Vorlesungen* 9 (1840), 169; trans. Sibree, *Philosophy of History*, 138. Hegel would have found in Grosier an account of "the general character of he Chinese" that describes them as "sweet, affable, polite to the point of scruple" and so on; see *Description générale de la Chine* (1785), 688–90.

56 Hegel, *Die Philosophie der Geschichte*, ed. Vorwieg, 86.

57 Hegel, *Vorlesungen* 9 (1837), 138–9; *Vorlesungen* 9 (1840), 169; trans. Sibree, *Philosophy of History*, 138. The 1822–23 version was more matter of fact. He had established the principle that "it is not permissible for a person to be a slave." And then he simply states a little later: "In China there is slavery. People sell themselves, and parents can sell their children." *Vorlesungen* 12, ed. Ilting et al., 143 and 145; trans. Brown and Hodgson, *Lectures*, 233 and 235. See Grosier, *Memoires*, 2.410 and 7.16.

58 Grosier, *Description générale*, 518; trans. *Allgemeine Beschreibung*, 100; trans. *A General Description*, vol. 2, 126–7.

59 Hegel, *Vorlesungen* 9 (1837), 139; *Vorlesungen* 9 (1840), 169; trans. Sibree, *Philosophy of History*, 138. In 1830–31 Hegel used the term "frequent" (*häufig*); see *Die Philosophie der Geschichte*, ed. Vieweg, 86.

60 Grosier, *Description générale*, 516–17; trans. *Allgemeine Beschreibung*, 98–9; trans. *A General Description*, vol. 2, 124–5.

61 On infanticide, see John Barrow, *Travels in China* (London: T. Cadell and W. Davies, 1804), 166–75; translated by Johann Christian Hüttner as *Reise durch China*, vol. 1 (Weimar, 1804), 204–13. To be sure, the numbers proposed by Barrow far exceeded "a daily occurrence."

62 Grosier, *De la Chine*, vol. 5 (1819), 73–89. At very least Hegel should have echoed the comments of an anonymous reviewer of Clarke Abel's *Narrative of a Journey in the Interior of China and of a Voyage to and from that Country in the Years 1816 and 1817* (London: Longman, Hurst, Rees, Orne, and Brown, 1818), 233–5. Commenting on the fact that Abel found little evidence of infanticide, the reviewer remarked: "That the practice exists, admits not of a shadow of doubt; to what extent it exists is not likely ever to be known," in *The Quarterly Review*, 21 (1819): 77. It is to Hegel's discredit that he did not echo this more cautious judgment.

8   Neo-Romantic Modernism and Daoism: Martin Buber on the "Teaching" as Fulfilment

JEFFREY S. LIBRETT

To fulfil means ... to raise something received through the tradition from the conditioned up to the unconditioned (Erfüllen bedeutet ... ein Überliefertes aus dem Bedingten ins Unbedingte heben).

Martin Buber, "Die Lehre vom Tao"[1]

Martin Buber's approach to Chinese culture is inextricably intertwined with his ongoing reinterpretation of Jewish culture and his attempt to protect that culture against both modern anti-Semitism specifically and the logic of the Christian supercessionist narrative (as constituted by Paul) more generally. Because he is not just a neo-Romantic modernist but a philosophically and religiously educated Jew who possesses significant understanding of the fundamental structures of European anti-Semitism, his critique of European models of progressive rationality is focused, among other things, on the critique of Christian "typological" thinking.[2] The implications of this "typology" for European Orientalism as well as anti-Semitism are profound, as Buber knows, because modern Western notions of the superiority of the Occident over the Orient are modelled on pre-modern Christian notions of the abrogation of Judaism by Christianity. Accordingly, Buber's defence of Jewish culture is embedded within a larger defence of "Oriental" culture, of which his considerations on Chinese culture form an integral part.[3] More narrowly, Buber's reading of Daoism – "The Teaching of the Dao" (Die Lehre vom Dao"), first published in 1910 as an afterword to his anthology of selections from Zhuangzi's writings – belongs within his emphatic general interpretation of the "Oriental" world as a unity that includes the ancient Hebrew origins of Judaism up through the very earliest Christianity, but from which he would exclude Pauline

Christianity. Buber articulates this more general understanding of the "Oriental" world also in an essay entitled "The Spirit of the Orient and Judaism" ("Der Geist des Orients und das Judentum"), which he writes a few years after the essay on Daoism. And he will go on to develop his critique of Pauline "pistis" much more fully some forty years later in an extraordinary essay entitled "Two Types of Faith" ("Zwei Glaubens-weisen").[4] Here, I will focus on the Daoism essay, and I will limit myself to an analysis of Buber's reception of Daoism, without considering the many questions that would arise in any attempt to determine the degree of adequacy or inadequacy of this reception with respect to the Daoist tradition as such.

Before exploring the essay, however, it is important to note that Buber's approach to Chinese culture by way of Daoism is not just peculiar to his own work or to modernist Jewish cultural historiography. Rather, it is one instance of a much wider phenomenon in the history of East-West cultural interactions and influences. The German-Austrian culture of the early twentieth century, especially in a number of its other neo-Romantic modernist authors (such as the broadly divergent œuvres of C.G. Jung, Martin Heidegger, and Hermann Hesse), evinced in its approach to China a tendency to privilege Daoist traditions over Confucianist ones. This represented a striking new development.[5] As we have seen in several of the contributions to this volume, the first broad, modern European Sinophile movement flourished in the seventeenth and eighteenth centuries and had a decidedly Confucian tendency, receiving strong support from Leibniz and Wolff. The first Romantic generations reacted against this Enlightenment-style Sinophilia principally through the Indomania propagated by Herder, Forster, the Schlegel brothers, Humboldt, and many others. Some one hundred years later, the (neo-Romantic) modernists, especially when they were not inclined to follow the Aryanist direction, in several important cases "discovered" anew the Daoist alternative to Confucianism.[6]

This turn can be understood, in part, in terms of the widespread questioning of both traditional and also rationalist ethical values in German-Austrian (especially urban) modernist environments from the late nineteenth century on. Such questioning rendered increasingly implausible the reliance on conventional canons of social relations and pragmatic rationality with which Confucianism is commonly associated in the West. The crumbling of both traditionalist and rationalist certitudes was attended, furthermore, by increasingly pervasive anxieties about the fragmentation of experience, the acceleration of modern life, and the vanity and ultimate irrationality of ostensibly rational progress. Daoism, it seems, promised to some modernists in this situation a restoration of wholeness that did not rely on an investment in substantial social values, reason, or the productivity ethos of industrial capitalism. While some of the neo-Romantic modernists tended to scapegoat Judaism for modern fragmentation, Buber upheld Judaism along with other Eastern traditions, including Daoism, as an "Oriental" force for unity.

The sense in which the Daoist tradition represents a conscious alternative to the Confucian one is revealed in Buber's address before the China Institute of Frankfurt am Main in 1928. Here, like other late neo-Romantic modernists, he expresses a concern about the modern Occidental industrial-technological principle of "disintegration" (121).[7] He explicitly argues first of all that the Western Enlightenment's appropriation of Confucianism was untrue to its "living Chinese reality" (122). Second, he claims that the West is currently in no position to "receive" the Confucian tradition because the West lacks both the Chinese "ancestor cult" – an "organic relation between the dead and the living" (123) – and the Chinese faith in the "original man" (124), a "trust in the original being of the human substance" (124).[8] The "warranting of the institutional principle" (124) that Confucianism provides is thus not available to the Western sensibility in the twentieth century.

Instead, Buber suggests here – some eighteen years after writing the first and major essay on Daoism, "Die Lehre vom Tao," to which we will turn in a moment – that the twentieth-century West can perhaps learn from the Daoist teaching of "non-action" because the West has begun to learn that "success," as the application of instrumental reason to the ends of power, "is of no consequence" (124). Buber feels that the West can learn from Daoism that "genuine effecting is not interfering, not giving vent to power, but remaining within one's self" (125). Thus, Buber argues for the appropriateness of Daoism to a specifically modernist Occidental sensibility, at the far end of the nineteenth-century adventures of positivism and imperialism. While it is not possible to reconstruct further here the broader turn towards Daoism in the reception of Chinese culture within the anti-rationalist stream of the twentieth-century German-language intelligentsia, the present reading of Buber tries to retrace one of its tributaries.

In the early essay on Daoism, Buber develops the theory that all great Oriental cultural formations constitute "teachings" (Lehren) and that such teachings are neither incomplete "doctrines" in need of Occidental fulfilment nor simply "doctrines" about how to live the fulfilled life. Indeed, they are not "doctrines" at all, but ways of living that have already been fulfilled by being lived out as the fulfilling life. In examining Buber's notion of these teachings, and of the Daoist teaching in particular, I attempt to clarify here both its strategic sense and the conceptual difficulties it poses for Buber in his attempt to do justice in Western philosophical terms to a tradition that remains indeterminably Other. In order to begin to understand the sense of this notion of "teachings" and the importance of the stress that Buber lays upon "fulfillment" (Erfüllung) a word/concept that recurs with emphatic frequency throughout this text, we have to sketch briefly first how Paul employs this notion and how his employment of it ramifies, as I have suggested above, for both anti-Jewish and Orientalist discourse, which in various ways Buber also attempts to criticize in these texts.

Very briefly: in Paul's writings and the traditions he founds, the Jewish religion relates to Christianity (and Jews relate to Christians) as the dead letter of the law relates to the living spirit of faith and mercy, the law prefiguring or anticipating its fulfilment or realization as faith. In my first book, *The Rhetoric of Cultural Dialogue: Jews and Germans from Moses Mendelssohn to Richard Wagner and Beyond*, I trace the importance of this structure for modern relations between Jewish and Christian Germans in literature and philosophy from the eighteenth century to the twentieth. In my recent book, *Orientalism and the Figure of the Jew*, I show how this structure – the basis of medieval "typology" or "figural interpretation" – is applied in the same period, as a structuring device, to Oriental-Occidental relations. In the present essay, I want to suggest that Buber is responding through his Daoism text to *both* of these manifestations of Pauline supercessionist logic, albeit more explicitly to the Orientalist one. On Buber's account, the Oriental "teachings," including the Jewish law or *halachah* (a word whose verbal root, "to go" or "to walk," gives it for Buber an affinity with the "way," i.e., *Dao*), *begin* as "fulfilments" and require no (Hegelian or other) developmental narrative. Accordingly, Buber also polemicizes against "dialectics" at various points in this essay, although his polemical remarks do not suffice to liberate him entirely from the gravitational field of Hegelianism, as I shall suggest below.[9]

Against this background, we can now almost begin to move towards an understanding of the manner in which the notion of "Lehren" as "fulfilments" in the Daoism essay is designed to resist Pauline logic. Another preliminary step, however, is necessary at this point, namely, to adumbrate further Buber's notion of "Lehren." As I indicated above, Buber's starting point is that the Orient constitutes a unity, and that the most essential phenomenon in terms of which this unity can be grasped is that of the "teaching" (Lehre). Each of the great Oriental civilizations, he writes (stressing Daoism, Indian Buddhism, and the Jewish–Early Christian teaching of the Kingdom of God), has created a "teaching" in Buber's very specific sense. This "teaching" represents, moreover, not only what unifies all of the Oriental civilizations with one another, but also what makes each one unified within itself.[10] For the "teaching" unifies the two other "fundamental powers" (Grundmächte) of the "directive" (weisender) spirit in such a culture.[11] These two "fundamental powers" are "science," which concerns itself with the "is" of "being" (Sein); and "law," which concerns itself with the "ought" of obligation (Sollen). Although these two instances, science and law – which Buber also characterizes as "belief" (Glauben) and "action" (Handeln) or "knowledge" (Kunde) and "commandment" (Gebot) (1025 passim) – "belong always to each other" (1024), they are increasingly separated in the West, whereas in the East, they are forever united, and precisely in the "teaching." Before considering directly the position of the "teaching" in relation to the Pauline problematic of fulfilment, it is important to consider it briefly in relation to the German Idealist tradition from Kant to Hegel, because Buber is evoking echoes of that tradition in his definition of the "teaching," echoes that provide us with important modern philosophical figures of "fulfilment" itself. I will mention two of these echoes.

First, given that in a Kantian philosophical framework the two opposed tendencies of "science" and "law" appear as the epistemology of the theoretical understanding and the ethics of practical reason, evidently Buber's notion of the "teaching" fits roughly into the space that Kantian and post-Kantian traditions tend to determine as the (organicist) *aesthetic*. For Kant mobilizes the aesthetic (the reflexive judgment) to synthesize (disjunctively) the faculties of understanding and reason that determine the forms and fortunes of epistemic and ethical claims, respectively. It will suit this conceptual determination, then, when at the end of his essay Buber speaks of Zhuangzi as both philosopher and poet. This makes sense, of course, also because Zhuangzi's text necessarily appears to a Western reader, in its intriguingly "parabolic" or at least highly "figural" dimension, as an aesthetic or literary text. Nonetheless, it is important for the notion of the "teaching" that Buber invokes these Kantian philosophical categories at the outset, pointing us to the *aesthetic* as interplay and "Mittelglied" between the faculties of "is" and "ought." In short, it is in this (Kantian) aesthetic space of the synthesis of the epistemic with the ethical that the "teaching" is situated. This echo remains problematic, however, since Buber evidently does not want to be proposing Daoism as an aesthetic experience, as an illusion, or as a literary fiction.[12]

Second, rather than being concerned with either *truth* (as associated with possibility, or what *should* be) or *reality* (conceived as what *is* the case), the "teaching" concerns "the one thing necessary" (das Eine, das not tut) (1024), or "the necessary, which is realized in the true life" (das Notwendige, das verwirklicht wird im wahrhaften Leben) (1024). In this modal language of the "necessary," the Kantian echoes of the aesthetic are supplemented by echoes of the Hegelian philosophy of history, in accordance with which the rational is real and the real rational.[13] However, Buber explicitly rejects the Hegelian tendency to think in terms of "the dialectical opposition between inner and outer" (1025) here, and he thus attempts to silence these echoes, because he wants to conceive of the unity of the "teaching" not as a developmentally achieved unification of the disparate, but as an originally fulfilled unity of the same. On the other hand, Buber speaks of the "teaching" as a "totality" (Ganzheit) in which "all oppositions to totality are sublated into the one" (sind alle Gegensätze der Ganzheit in dem Einen aufgehoben) (1025). Evidently, it is not so easy for Buber to get rid of the binary conceptualities that seem to structure Western thinking and languages, and possibly *all* thinking and *all* languages altogether. (Indeed, this is perhaps the most important philosophical-anthropological question here: the question of the potential universality of binary thinking.) Thus, he both includes in the originary unity a sort of mini-narrative of development *and* opposes the originary unity of the "teaching" to what comes regressively after. "The teaching develops itself (*bildet sich*) independently of science and law, until it finds in a central human life its pure fulfilment. Only in its downfall, which begins soon after this fulfilment, does the teaching mix itself up with the elements of science and law" (1025). The separate existence of science and law appear as products of the later disintegration of the original unity of the "teaching." And even religion as such appears as a "product of contamination" (1025) in which knowledge, ethical precepts, and "teaching" intermingle as a mixed plurality of principles in an experience that has lost touch with the fundamental unity of things. The reversal of the order of development – from a progression towards fulfilment in the in-and-for-itself to a regression from such fulfilment towards the separation of in-and-for-itself into mutually distant object and subject ("Sein" and "Sollen") – will not enable Buber to escape entirely from the dialectical tensions and aesthetic implications that haunt his notion of the Oriental "teaching," although I do not mean to imply that his project is therefore nonsensical. To consider now the relation between Buber's notion of "teaching" and the logic of Pauline supercession will take us one step closer to confronting Buber's attempt to arrange this escape.

How, then, does Buber's initial determination of the "teaching" relate to the traditional Pauline construction of the Jewish-Christian relationship? Since Judaism always appears in Paul's construction as the principle of "law," while Christianity appears as its opposite, that is, as associated with "faith" and "doctrine," the Oriental teachings here function as the originary unity that falls asunder in the Christian account of the passage from prefigural Jewish law to its realization in Christian faith. In order to grasp Buber's gesture more clearly, however, we should situate it briefly within the tradition of the Jewish-German philosophy of religion. For it is useful to recall here that, in Moses Mendelssohn's response to the Pauline tradition, which Mendelssohn spelled out in *Jerusalem, or on Religious Power and Judaism*, the great Jewish-German Enlightener posited that Judaism was a revealed law, rather than a religion per se. Against Moses Maimonides, Mendelssohn argued that Judaism distinguished itself from Christianity in not embracing any "Lehre" (here in the sense of articles of faith or fixed doctrine), as did Christianity. In this way Judaism proved itself for Mendelssohn more profoundly compatible with rationality than was Christianity, even in the latter's rationalist Protestant forms. In contrast to this strategy, Buber refuses the law-faith opposition, either as an outer-inner opposition (1025) or as a form-content opposition (1028), both of which oppositions he associates with "dialectics" in a pejorative sense. Instead, he posits the "teaching" as what precedes the disintegration of the unity of the necessary into these two separate aspects. In pursuing this strategy, Buber can at once embrace the anti-dogmatic tradition that Mendelssohn also supported, questioning with him the Maimonidean notion of specific dogmas in Judaism, and at the same time refuse to allow Judaism to be reduced to the formality or externality of a mere legalism, a texture of empty ceremonial prescriptions.[14]

Against this background of his Enlightenment predecessor, we can now see more clearly Buber's strategy in constructing the "teaching" as an originary fulfilment that unifies law with faith. But how can he prevent this unity from having either an aesthetic-illusory or a dialectically synthetic status? Buber will struggle with this question throughout his essay "The Teaching of the Dao." In order to illustrate how he does so, I will consider in the remainder of this essay two examples. The first is a more rhetorically gestural instance. The second is a more conceptual one. While these two levels – as Buber rightly argues – cannot be held entirely apart, they also continually separate from each other in our thinking.

First example: One task to which Buber's notion of the unity of the "teaching" commits him is the fusion of language as a medium of thought ("Wissenschaft") with language as a medium of action ("Gesetz" or "Gebot"), or in more contemporary terms, the fusion of constative with performative and of literal with figural usages of language.[15] (Note that the Pauline Christian opposition between the letter and spirit, which the Oriental teachings are supposed to precede, is also an opposition between the letter as figural and the spirit as literal, as well as one between the letter as performative – and manipulative – action through language, and the spirit as constative element, the pure – and non-violent – saying of what is the case.) Given the pressure on him to show the unity that precedes the Pauline dialectics, Buber is pushed to go beyond distinctions of the "understanding" (as in "Verstand"). Thus, when attempting to clarify the necessity of the realization of the necessary in a true life, and to argue specifically that its unity is not an abstract one, but rather "the most lively" (die allerlebendigste), Buber writes that it is not the unity of either reality (the world) or possibility (spirit), but rather:

> It is the unity of this human life and of this human soul, which fulfils itself within itself, the unity of your life and your soul, you who are seized by the teaching. The true life is the unified life.

> Sie ist die Einheit dieses Menschenlebens und dieser Menschenseele, die sich in sich selber erfüllt, deines Lebens und deiner Seele Einheit, du von der Lehre Ergriffener. Das wahrhafte Leben ist das geeinte Leben. (1026)

Striking here is the performative dimension of the address to the reader, which suddenly erupts from within the use of the third person, although it is introduced subtly by the introduction of the repeated demonstrative adjective ("this"), as Buber turns from an I-It to an I-Thou grammatical modality *avant la lettre*. But this performative address, further, hovers between an actual performance and a mere quotation of the logic and attitude of a teaching properly so-called. Yet, since to quote the others is only different from speaking oneself when the world is not yet a unified place, the conflation of quotation, on the one hand, and speaking as a separate ego, on the other, functions here like a performance of the denial of the divided life, an active assertion of the unity that it is talking about. The reader is identified by the writer with the exemplary subject, and with the writer himself through the mediation of the address itself (along with the demonstrative adjectives). By addressing the reader thus, Buber performs what he constatively claims, except that the reader may not be "seized" (ergriffen) by the "teaching," and the address can easily appear to be an aesthetic experience (possibly even a failed one), subjective, and hence divided from its own, only potential, objective realization.

Second example: how does one envision the concrete fulfilment of an abstract possibility that has not yet appeared as such, a fulfilment that *gives rise to* a possibility of fulfilment (i.e., to an abstract pattern of a possible life), where this possibility nonetheless remains immediately in touch with the original fulfilment itself? That is, how does one present and retain both reality and potentiality in their unity, while separating them at the same time? In the case of the teaching, Buber tries to understand this – as we saw in the passage cited above about the "central human life" – in terms of the realization of the teaching in an exemplary life (e.g., the life of Laozi or the Buddha or Jesus). This exemplary life then functions as a model for subsequent lives lived, in terms of the teaching, through identification with the exemplary individual. Buber's problem then becomes: how can we retain in a mere *representation* of the exemplary life the fusion of possibility (or idea) and reality (or being) that occurs as the necessity of/in that life? How can we understand such a mode of representation, which is, in fact, tasked with being precisely *more* or *less* than a representation? This is the burden of Buber's account of Zhuangzi, whom he reads as the exemplary disciple, as opposed to Paul's "violent" and therefore failed attempt to serve as the disciple of Jesus. I shall indicate here only the general outlines of Buber's construct – brilliant, but also fragile and, indeed, broken.

The passage from "teaching" to "religion," or from the unity of possibility and reality in necessity, on the one hand, to the separation of each of these modalities from the others, on the other hand, is mediated according to Buber by two steps, "Gleichnis" (or what we can translate as "parable") and "Mythen" (myths). In parables, it is only the *words* of the "central man" that are retained, while in myths, it is his *life*. But even more important than the content represented at these two levels in the passage from "teaching" to "religion" is the representational mode involved. Buber tells us, "In parable," "the absolute is placed into the world of things; in myth, the things are placed into the world of the absolute" (Das Gleichnis ist die Einstellung des Absoluten in die Welt der Dinge. Der Mythus ist die Einstellung der Dinge in die Welt des Absoluten) (1027). But from our contemporary vantage point, it is possible to discern that this opposition between the parabolic and the mythical modes of representation is analogous to, and indeed a version of, the traditional Romantic and post-Romantic opposition between allegory and symbol. Accordingly, as with this traditional opposition between allegory and symbol, on the far side of deconstruction the question of principle that poses itself here is this: how can we ever really have one without the other? How can we have a passage from abstraction to concretion without having, conversely, a passage from concretion to abstraction? Or in slightly different, semiological terms: how can we have an insertion of the signified into the signifier without having an insertion of the signifier into the signified?[16] The inseparability of these two representational modes – or, more fundamentally, these two *aspects* of representation – does not imply, however, their fusion into an absolute unity. What I am suggesting, rather, is that Buber's two steps in the disintegrative passage from the unity of the "teaching" to the disunity of "religion" are *inseparable* from one another, even as they comprise two opposite tendencies within a dialectical movement. And, in turn, this movement cannot be entirely separated from either "teaching" or "religion," because it continually and constitutively mediates their inter-relationship. This suggestion is perhaps already contained and acknowledged in Buber's remark that "in the parable of the master rests already germinating the intoxication of all rites and the delusion of all dogmas" (im Gleichnis des Meisters ruht schon keimend aller Riten Rausch und aller Dogmen Wahn) (1022). It cuts against the grain of Buber's entire analysis of Zhuangzi, however, where he makes a sustained effort to portray Zhuangzi as the creator of Laozi's "Gleichnis" but at the same time as preventing himself from entering the disintegrating ground of "Mythos." Let us retrace this argument before concluding.

Buber argues that while language already implies some dimension of "parable" (Gleichnis), Laozi's teaching is "the most non-parabolic" (die gleichnisloseste) (1032). It remains, Buber posits, on the border between silence and speech, at the level of the "image" – "imagistic, but non-parabolic" (bildhaft, aber gleichnislos) (1034). Zhuangzi, in contrast, wrote down the teaching of Laozi in a parabolically poetic mode ("ihr Gleichnis dichtete") (1035), such that its fundamentally extralinguistic character, its fundamental silence – for "naked unity is silent" (nackte Einheit ist stumm) (1032) – was never really broken. In this sense, according to Buber, Zhuangzi contrasts radically with Paul:

> While ... that other apostle who did not know his master while still alive, Paul, dissected his teaching of the unity of the true life and perverted it into an eternal opposition between spirit and nature – which one cannot sublate, but only yield to, Zhuangzi was in truth the messenger of his teaching: its messenger to the things of the world.

> Während ... jener andere Apostel, der seinen Meister nicht leiblich kannte, Paulus, dessen Lehre von der Einheit des wahrhaften Lebens zersetzte und in einen ewigen Gegensatz von Geist und Natur – den man nicht aufheben, dem man nur entweichen könne – verkehrte, war Tschuang-tse in Wahrheit ein Sendbote seiner Lehre: ihr Sendbote zu den Dingen der Welt. (1035)

Despite the fact that one can certainly distinguish Zhuangzi from Paul in various ways, it seems problematic – phantasmic or fictional, idealizing or ideological – for Buber to claim that Zhuangzi is able to bring Laozi's pure silence to speech, that is, to enable Laozi to be communicatively iterated, and at the same time to repeat Laozi's silence such that nothing of the unity is lost that depends on the condition of absolute silence and cannot maintain itself in the medium of language. It is on this stumbling block, the abyss of the border between language and its outside, that Buber's in many respects both powerful and admirable attempt to articulate the Daoist teaching as the exemplary Oriental teaching comes to grief. For in his own definitional formulations silence is to speech as the absolute is to the world of things. And religion arises as the conflation of the absolute with things. So, if the barrier between teaching and parable breaks down (because in parable silence has to speak and speech has to reach back into the silence it expresses), then this implies that in parable things are already entering into the domain of the absolute, and therefore that myth is already present in the teaching, accomplishing the passage to religion there implicitly from the outset. When silence speaks, things contaminate the absolute.

Finally, in a sense, Buber himself can be shown to be aware of this failure and ultimately, in giving up the prospect of "success," to capitulate to and account for the failure. For at the end of his afterword he develops a number of comparisons – interpretations – the failure of which he then grants. First, he construes Zhuangzi as a "poet of the idea, like Plato," thereby establishing an analogy between the Socrates-Plato pair and the Laozi-Zhuangzi relationship. And then, beyond this, he compares Zhuangzi to a number of poetic writers in the West. Above all, he goes on to acknowledge that all of these comparisons are merely "a passage to an approach in which one no longer tries to situate Zhuangzi" (nur Durchgang ... zu einer Aufnahme, in der man Tschuang-tse nicht mehr einzureihen versucht) but "rather receives him in his entire essentiality without comparison or categorization, him, that is: his work, the parable" (sondern ihn in seiner ganzen Wesenhaftigkeit ohne Vergleich und Zuordnung empfängt, ihn, das ist sein Werk, das Gleichnis) (1051). Thus, while clinging to the last to the language of parable, Buber ends with a kind of enthusiastic admission of failure. This admission, however, constitutes a radical resistance to the hermeneutic logic of Pauline supercessionism. Buber proposes precisely the opposite: not that we can understand the Other better than he or she can have understood himself or herself, but rather that we must translate ourselves into the idiom of the Other in order to receive him or her as he or she is.[17] Even the aesthetic and poetic analogy, similitude, "Vergleich" or "Gleichnis" would not be quite applicable to Zhuangzi, due to the partial and autonomous status of the aesthetic discourse in Western modernity. Nor presumably would the Hegelian language of a unity of truth and reality quite do as a conceptualization of the teaching of the Dao, although it might have to suffice provisionally as a distant approximation. In this sense, Buber's characterization of the "teaching" of the Dao itself, in its acknowledged inadequacy to what it is trying to approach, emulates the kind of speech it attributes to Zhuangzi: speech that is in some measure self-cancelling, or speech that gives silence the floor.[18]

Where does one go from here, in the analysis of this theme of the Jewish-Chinese connections in Buber's work? Buber's interest in Chinese parabolic narrative structures as disruptions of hermeneutics is connected to his investment in Jewish culture not only through the "substantial" motif of the "teaching," but also through the "formal" motif of short narrative structures that resist one-dimensional readings. Buber's editions of Chinese texts obviously communicate with his lifelong interest in Hasidic tales. In the Hasidic texts, too, the representation of exemplary lives beyond any strictly theoretical teachings or morals is at stake. There, too, what engages Buber is the resistance to a totalizing reading on the level of pneumatological meaning in a Pauline vein.[19] In both cases, a certain "Oriental" mode of representations that exceeds or undermines the Pauline split between matter (or letter) and spirit is what Buber envisions, in his attempt to resist anti-Semitism and Orientalism at once. More detailed rhetorical and cultural-historical analysis of the correspondences and divergences between these various narratives and their representational modes in Buber's œuvre remains to be done.

NOTES

1 Martin Buber, "Die Lehre vom Tao," *Werke*, vol. 1, *Schriften zur Philosophie* (Munich: Kösel, 1962), 1021–52, here 1031. Translations are my own; subsequent citations given in parentheses in the text.

2 See Erich Auerbach, "Figura," *Scenes from the Drama of European Literature* (Minneapolis: University of Minnesota Press, 1984), 11–78.

3 For an insightful analysis of the more specific traditional associations made between Chinese and Jewish culture, see Jay Geller, *The Other Jewish Question: Identifying the Jew and Making Sense of Modernity* (New York: Fordham University Press, 2011).

4 My discussion of "The Spirit of the Orient and Judaism" is in chapter 7 of my *Orientalism and the Figure of the Jew* (New York: Fordham University Press, 2015). In the "Spirit" essay, Buber proposes Judaism as the ancient Eastern cultural formation that is best positioned to establish a mediation between East and West both because it arose late, as the last of the great Eastern cultures, and because it entered into the constitution of the West by providing the foundations of Christianity. For some aspects of the context in which Buber writes "Two Types of Faith," see Maurice Friedman, *Martin Buber's Life and Work: The Later Years, 1945–65* (New York: E.P. Dutton, 1983), 83–101. For a useful summary of the argument and stakes of "Two Types of Faith," as well as its relationship to Buber's critical responses to Kierkegaard, see Malcolm L. Diamond, *Martin Buber: Jewish Existentialist* (New York: Oxford University Press, 1960), 173–206.

5 For Jung on Daoism, see *The Secret of the Golden Flower: A Chinese Book of Life*, translated and explained by Richard Wilhelm, foreword and commentary by C.G. Jung (New York: Harcourt, Brace, and World, 1962), translated

by Cary F. Baynes. On Heidegger's relationship with Daoism, see the essays by Otto Pöggeler, Joan Stambaugh, Paul Shih-yi Hsiao, Graham Parkes, and Hwa Yol Jung, in *Heidegger and Asian Thought*, ed. Graham Parkes (Honolulu: University of Hawaii Press, 1987), and Reinhard May, *Ex oriente lux: Heideggers Werk unter ostasiatischem Einfluß* (Stuttgart: Steiner, 1989), who shows how Heidegger, in fact, made significant use of Buber's edition of Zhuangzi. On Hesse's extensive engagement with Chinese thought and culture, see Adrian Hsia, *Hermann Hesse und China: Darstellung, Materialien und Interpretation* (Frankfurt: Suhrkamp, 1974).

6 According to Arthur F. Wright, "The Study of Chinese Civilization," in *Discovering China: European Interpretations in the Enlightenment*, eds. Julia Ching and Willard G. Oxtoby (Rochester: University of Rochester Press, 1992), Henri Maspero (who died in Buchenwald in 1945) published the first systematic Western study of the history of Daoism posthumously in 1950. See Henri Maspero, *Le Taoïsme et les religions chinoises* (Paris: Gallimard, 1971), translated by Frank A. Kierman, Jr, as *Taoism and Chinese Religion* (Amherst: University of Massachusetts Press, 1981).

7 "China and Us," in Martin Buber, *Pointing the Way: Collected Essays*, translated by Maurice Friedman (New York: Harper and Brothers, 1957), 121–5. For a useful overview of Buber's writings, speeches, and lectures on Daoism, see Irene Eber, "Martin Buber and Taoism," *Monumenta Serica*, 42 (1994): 445–64. Eber traces Buber's involvement with Daoism from the two early volumes of translations, the *Reden und Gleichnisse des Tschuang Tse* (Leipzig: Insel, 1910) and *Chinesische Geister- und Liebesgeschichten* (Frankfurt: Rütten and Loening, 1911), through the private lectures on the *Dao-Te-Ching* in Ascona in 1924, to the lecture at the China Institute in 1928, to the later notes and published translations of selections from the *Dao-Te-Ching* in Jerusalem in the early 1940s, and the revision of the *Zhuangzi* translations in the 1950s. Concerning the 1928 lecture at the China Institute, she notes that Buber's emphasis on the potential importance of Daoism, rather than Confucianism, for the contemporary West, constituted a critique of Richard Wilhelm's arguments in favour of Confucianism. On Buber's communication with Richard Wilhelm, Hermann Hesse, and C.G. Jung concerning the importance of Daoism, 448–9. See also Irene Eber, "Martin Buber and Chinese Thought," in *Wege und Kreuzungen der Chinakunde an der Johann Wolfgang Goethe-Universität Frankfurt am Main*, eds. Georg Ebertshäuser and Dorothea Wippermann (Frankfurt: IKO, Verlag für Interkulturelle Kommunikation, 2007), 23–50. In addition to sketching in the philological and institutional backgrounds, Eber indicates that the early period of Buber's work on Daoist sources, in the years of the translations,

coincides roughly with a period of intense involvement with Hasidism, especially the writing of the *Legend of the Baal Shem Tov*. But other than musing upon the question of whether or not the Dao can be understood as a personal deity, as well as quoting Buber to the effect that this was his "mystical period," she has little to say about how the Jewish and Chinese motifs are related, and how Buber's interest in Chinese philosophy actually relates to his interest in Judaism. I try to sketch this in here, in relation to the problem of Pauline typology.

8 Note that in the foreword to the *Chinesische Geister- und Liebesgeschichten* (Frankfurt: Literarische Anstalt Lütten und König, 1916), by Pu Songling, which he published originally in 1911, Buber speaks of the easy rapport between the dead and the living in these stories, in which ghosts and demons are "beings of our own world, merely arising from a deeper, darker region" (ix), and where "nothing interferes with the plenitude of life, and everything living carries the seed of the ghostly" (ix). Here, the translations are from Martin Buber, *Chinese Tales*, translated by Alex Page, introduction by Irene Eber (Amherst, NY: Humanity Books, 1991). The easy commerce between dead and living is suggestive of the commerce between "dead letter" and "living spirit" in Jewish thought, perhaps especially in aggadah, the storytelling aspect of Talmudic discourse.

9 Reading these polemical remarks, we can imagine how excited Buber must have been to read Franz Rosenzweig's *The Star of Redemption* when it came out in 1921.

10 Maurice Friedman, "Martin Buber and Asia," *Philosophy East and West*, 26/4 (1976): 411–26, argues that from *I and Thou* on, Buber moved beyond the monistic emphasis still present in "The Teaching of the Dao." Friedman stresses, as does Eber, Buber's interest in *wu wei*, (non-)action. The importance of this notion for Buber's anti-Pauline reformulation of the "teaching" as informing action – the entire realm of "works" – is one of the aspects of Buber's interest in Daoism that I would emphasize. Without regard for the Jewish-Christian problematic, Friedman does demonstrate the important affinities between the notion of *wu wei* and the *kavanah*, or mindset, in which Jewish rituals should be accomplished, according to Buber's book on the Baal Shem.

11 Buber makes a distinction between "directive" (weisender) and "forming" (gestaltender) spirit here, although he leaves the latter undeveloped.

12 Without making any reference to the Kantian problematic, R.J. Zwi Werblowsky, "Buber and the East Asian (Chinese) Religions," in *Martin Buber: A Contemporary Perspective*, ed. Paul Mendes-Flohr (Jerusalem: Israel Academy of Sciences and Humanities, 2002), 166–73, points out

the aestheticizing and neo-Romantic tendencies in Buber's early fascination with Daoist thought. Steven Shankman, "'These Three Come Forth
Together, but Are Differently Named': Laozi, Zhuangzi, Plato," in *Early
China/Ancient Greece: Thinking through Comparisons* (Albany: SUNY Press,
2002), 75–92, eds. Steven Shankman and Stephen W. Durrant, argues that
Zhuangzi's writings emphasize a balance between "intentionalist" and
"participationist" aspects of consciousness. Note that the notion of going
beyond "intentional" consciousness is one Buber inherits, among other
things, from early German Romanticism (e.g., in Friedrich Schlegel, or later
in Joseph, Freiherr von Eichendorff), where it was supported by the Kantian definition of aesthetic experience as "purposiveness without purpose."

13 Let us not omit to recall here, in passing, Hegel's own "anxiety of influence" with respect to certain "Oriental" cultural formations, especially the
ancient Indian culture, but also ancient China as an "origin" of history,
which Hegel both wants to, and must not, acknowledge. I discuss this
anxiety in chapter 5 of *Orientalism and the Figure of the Jew*.

14 In "Two Types of Faith" (a book-length essay published in 1950), Buber
places in question much more explicitly Paul's attempt to reduce Judaism to the faithless law of works. Buber accomplishes this by arguing
that Judaism and Christianity exemplify two different types of faith: the
former, *emunah* in the Hebraic form, is a matter of trusting someone, and
it is based on contact; the latter, *pistis* in its Pauline version, is a matter
of acknowledging a thing to be true, and it is based on acceptance. (Note
that Mendelssohn also defined *emunah* as "trust" (Vertrauen). In this, the
Enlightener and the neo-Romantic coincide.) The Pauline idea of faith is,
for Buber, of Greek provenance. By pursuing the explication of these two
types of faith through exegetical discussions of both "Old" and "New"
Testament texts, Buber not only undermines the law/faith opposition
as the model for the Jewish/Christian relation, but argues at length that
Jesus' teachings are essentially in accord with the Prophetic and Pharisaic
unfoldings of the notion of faith as trust, and at odds with the Pauline
mobilization of Hellenic faith as *doctrinal* faith *that* X or Y is the case. Along
with this notion of Judaism as faith qua trust goes a reinterpretation of
Torah not as "law" but as "direction of the heart" (Richtung des Herzens)
(692), in which the actions of "works" are predicated on "the intention to
surrender one's self" (die Intention der Selbsthingabe) (692), as it were, in
meditative exercises of simultaneous and equal inwardness and outward-
ness – "Inwendigkeit" and "Auswendigkeit" (697). This approach to
Torah situates the "fulfilment" (Erfüllung) (690 passim) of the command-
ments as enactment "in conformity with the full capacities of the person

and in the complete intention of faith" (690). Since this law is a matter of teaching qua direction, it is strikingly appropriate that Buber here repeatedly speaks of "the teaching of Jesus" (die Lehre Jesu) (692 passim) in accordance with the concept of "teaching" (Lehre) that he had unfolded many years earlier in the Daoism essay. Likewise, the position of the Rabbis is here a "Lehre," and by giving a "direction" (Richtung) to the human heart, which is by nature without direction ("richtungslos") (696), this "teaching" also creates a pathway.

15 See the last books of Paul de Man, e.g., *Aesthetic Ideology*, ed. Andrzej Warminski (Minneapolis: University of Minnesota Press, 1996), for pointed analyses of the complex interplay of constative and performative dimensions at crucial moments in modern literary and philosophical texts.

16 Another way of putting this questioning of the distinction between parable and myth would be to ask whether the representation of the *words* of a particular individual and the representation of her or his *life* can be absolutely separated.

17 Of course, where there is "opposition," we are not far from Hegelian dialectics.

18 Cf. the extended discussion of the hermeneutical questions raised by Buber's engagement with Zhuangzi in Jonathan R. Herman, *I and Dao: Martin Buber's Encounter with Chuang Tzu* (Albany: SUNY Press, 1996). See Emmanuel Levinas, "Martin Buber's Thought and Contemporary Judaism," in *Outside the Subject*, translated by Michael B. Smith (Stanford: Stanford University Press, 1994), 4–19, for a critical, but also appreciative, reading of the limits of Buber's capacity to formulate the relation of openness to the other.

19 Buber began working on the Hasidic tales in the early twentieth century, but continued this work through and after the Second World War, when he published *Tales of the Hasidim: Early Masters* (New York: Schocken Books, 1947), and *Tales of the Hasidim: The Later Masters* (New York: Schocken Books, 1948). In the preface to the first of these volumes, Buber discusses, e.g., "legend, this late form of the myth" (vi), and differentiates formally the "two genera of legend" as "the legendary short story" (viii), i.e., "the recital of a destiny which is represented in a single incident" (ix), and "the legendary anecdote" (viii), i.e., "the recital of a single incident which illumines an entire destiny" (ix), describing also "hybrid" (ix) forms of these two.

Contributors

Robert Bernasconi is Edwin Erle Sparks Professor of Philosophy and African American Studies at Penn State University and the outgoing President of the Hegel Society of America. In addition to his publications on German and French philosophy, including two books on Heidegger and and one on Sartre, he is co-editor of the journal *Critical Philosophy of Race.*

Bettina Brandt is on the faculty of the German Department at Pennsylvania State University. She has published on women and the avantgarde (Emine Sevgi Özdamar, Yoko Tawada, Herta Müller, Elfriede Jelinek, Meret Oppenheim) as well as on literary multilingualism and translation studies. She is co-editor of *Herta Müller: Politics and Aesthetics* (2013) and the editor and Dutch translator of Yoko Tawada's *De Berghollander* (2010.) In 2016–17, Brandt will be a Fellow at the Netherlands Institute for Advanced Studies in the Humanities and Social Sciences (NIAS).

Michael C. Carhart is an associate professor of History at Old Dominion University. He is the author of *The Science of Culture in Enlightenment Germany* (2007). As Fellow of FRIAS (The Freiburg Institute of Advanced Studies) and of the American Council of Learned Societies Carhart has been working on his newest research project entitled "The Caucasians: Central Asia in the European Imagination."

Walter Demel is a professor of Early Modern History at the *Universität der Bundeswehr* in Munich, Germany. Publications directly related to early modern German imaginations of China include: *Als Fremde in*

China: Das Reich der Mitte im Spiegel frühneuzeitlicher europäischer Berichte (1992) (As Strangers in China: Reflections on the Middle Kingdom in Early Modern European Accounts) and, most recently, an edited collection of essays entitled *Race and Racism in Modern East Asia: Western and Eastern Constructions* (2013).

Jeffrey S. Librett is a professor of German and head of the Department of German and Scandinavian at the University of Oregon. He is the author of *The Rhetoric of Cultural Dialogue: Jews and Germans from Moses Mendelssohn to Richard Wagner and Beyond* (2000) and *Orientalism and the Figure of the Jew* (2015), as well as numerous essays on literature, philosophy, psychoanalysis, and theory from the eighteenth century to the present.

Carl Niekerk is a professor of German, with affiliate appointments in French, Comparative and World Literature, and Jewish Studies, at the University of Illinois / Urbana-Champaign. He is currently the editor of the *German Quarterly* and a co-editor of the *Lessing Yearbook*. His publications on early anthropology include *Zwischen Naturgeschichte und Anthropologie: Lichtenberg im Kontext der Spätaufklärung* (2005), "Translating the Pacific: Georg Forster's 'A Voyage round the World' / 'Reise um die Welt' (1777-1780)" (*Travel Narratives in Translation, 1750–1830: Nationalism, Ideology, Gender*, ed. by Alison E. Martin and Susan Pickford, 2012), and "Romanticism and Other Cultures" (*The Cambridge Companion to German Romanticism*, ed. Nicholas Saul, 2009).

John Noyes has been a professor of German at the University of Toronto since 2001. Before that, he was a professor of German and Theory of Literature at the University of Cape Town. He has written on the cultural history of colonialism, postcolonial theory, and the history of sexuality. His most recent book is *Herder: Aesthetics against Imperialism* (2015).

Franklin Perkins is a professor of Philosophy at DePaul University and former director of DePaul's Chinese Studies Program. He is the author of *Leibniz and China: A Commerce of Light* (2004), *Leibniz: A Guide for the Perplexed* (2007), and *Heaven and Earth are not Humane: The Problem of Evil in Classical Chinese Philosophy* (2014), and he was co-editor of *Chinese Philosophy in Early Excavated Bamboo Texts* (*Journal of Chinese Philosophy Supplement* 2010) (with Chung-ying Cheng), and *Chinese Metaphysics and Its Problems* (2015) (with Chenyang Li).

Daniel Leonhard Purdy is a professor of German at the Pennsylvania State University. Author of *The Tyranny of Elegance: Consumer Cosmopolitanism in the Era of Goethe* (1998) and *On the Ruins of Babel: Architectural Metaphor in German Thought* (2011) as well as an edited anthology entitled *The Rise of Fashion* (2004), Purdy is President of the North American Goethe Society.

Birgit Tautz is an associate professor of German at Bowdoin College, Maine, USA. A specialist in eighteenth and nineteenth century German literature, culture, and philosophy, she is the author of edited *Reading and Seeing Ethnic Differences in the Enlightenment: From China to Africa* (2007) and editor of *Colors 1800/1900/2000: Signs of Ethnic Difference* (2004). Her articles have appeared in *DVjS*, *German Quarterly*, *Zeitschrift für Germanistik*, and *PEGS*, among others. Her book "Translating the World: Remaking Late Eighteenth-Century Literature between Hamburg and Weimar" is forthcoming.

Index

GERMAN AND EUROPEAN STUDIES
General Editor: Jennifer L. Jenkins